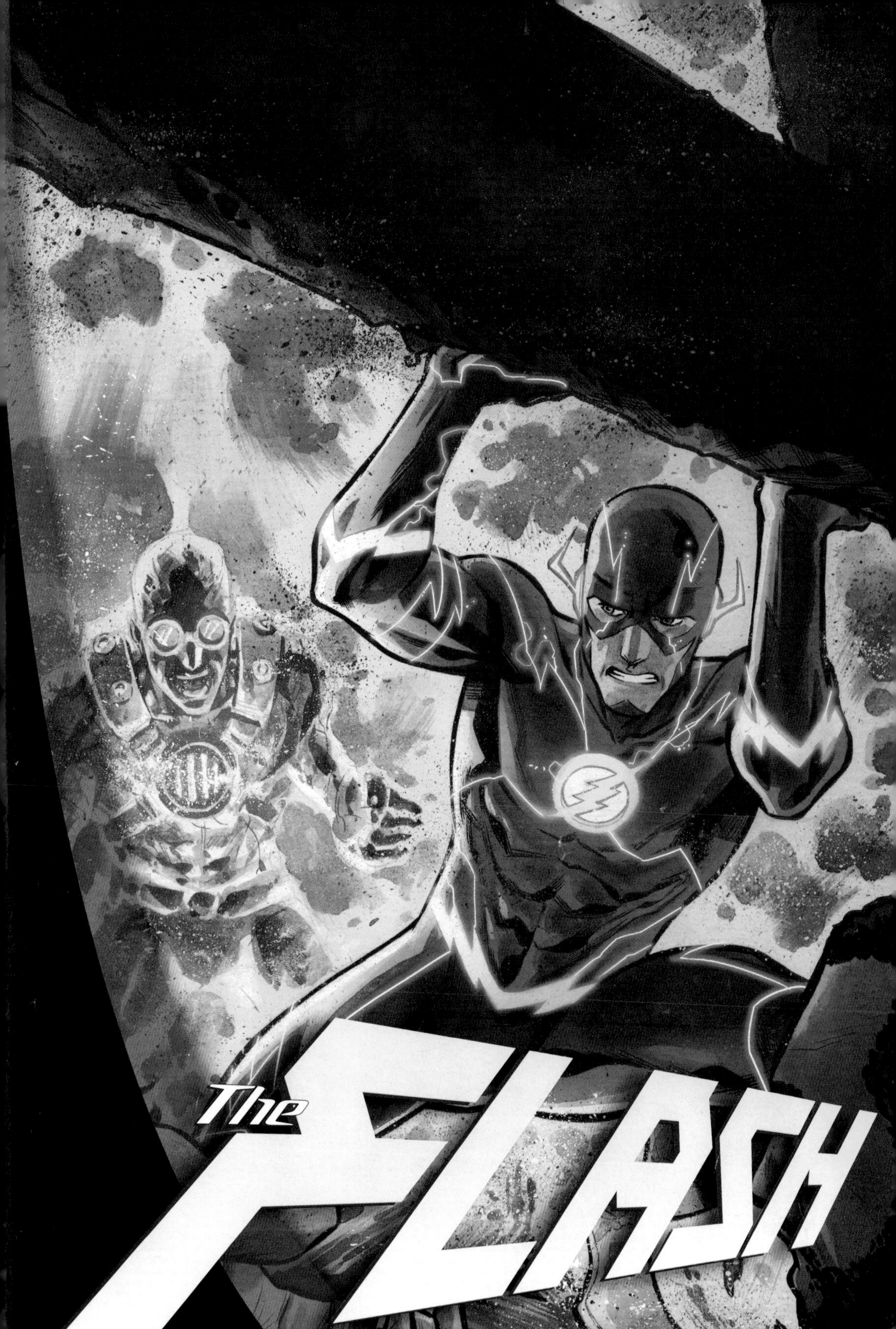
The
FLASH

VOLUME 2 **ROGUES REVOLUTION**

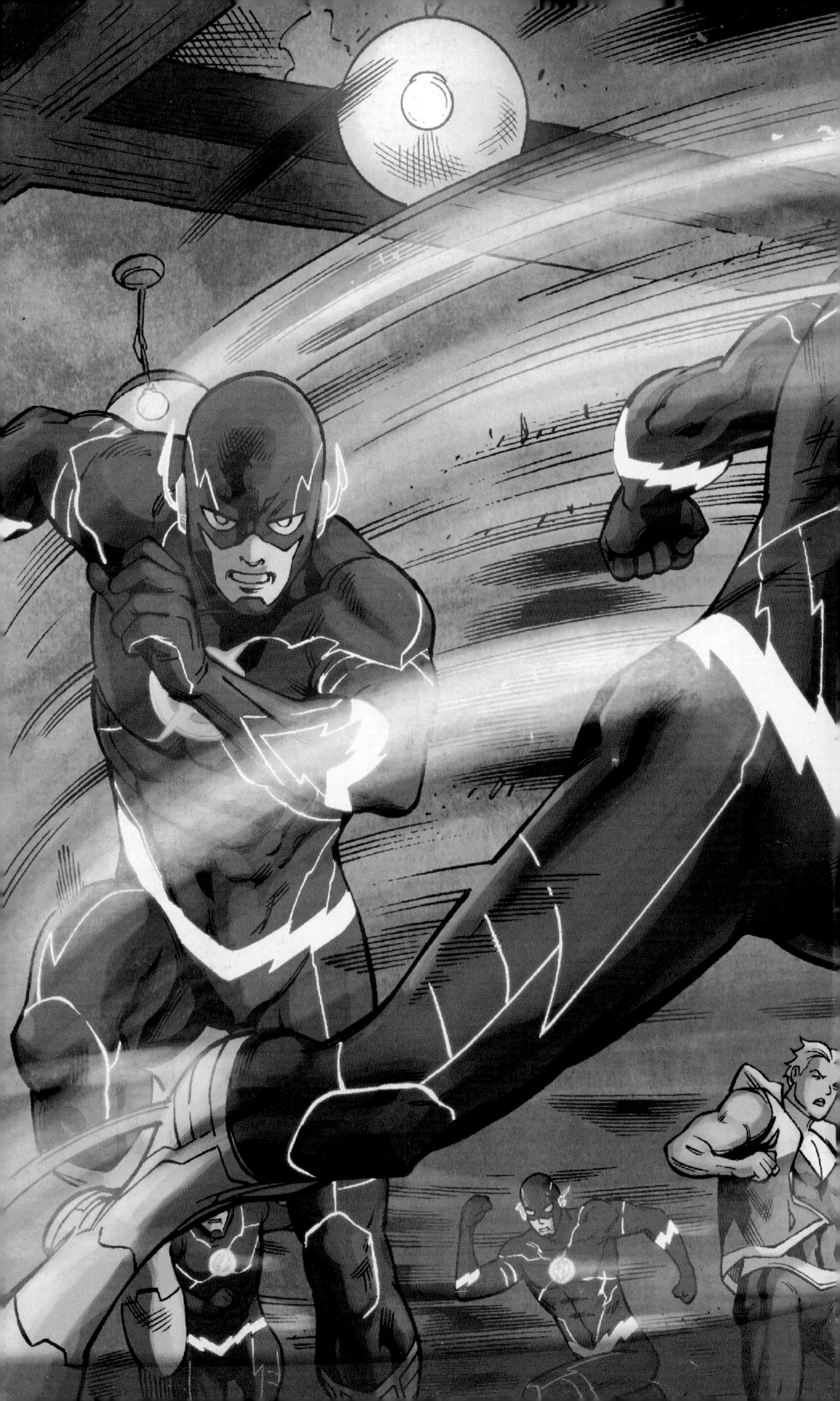

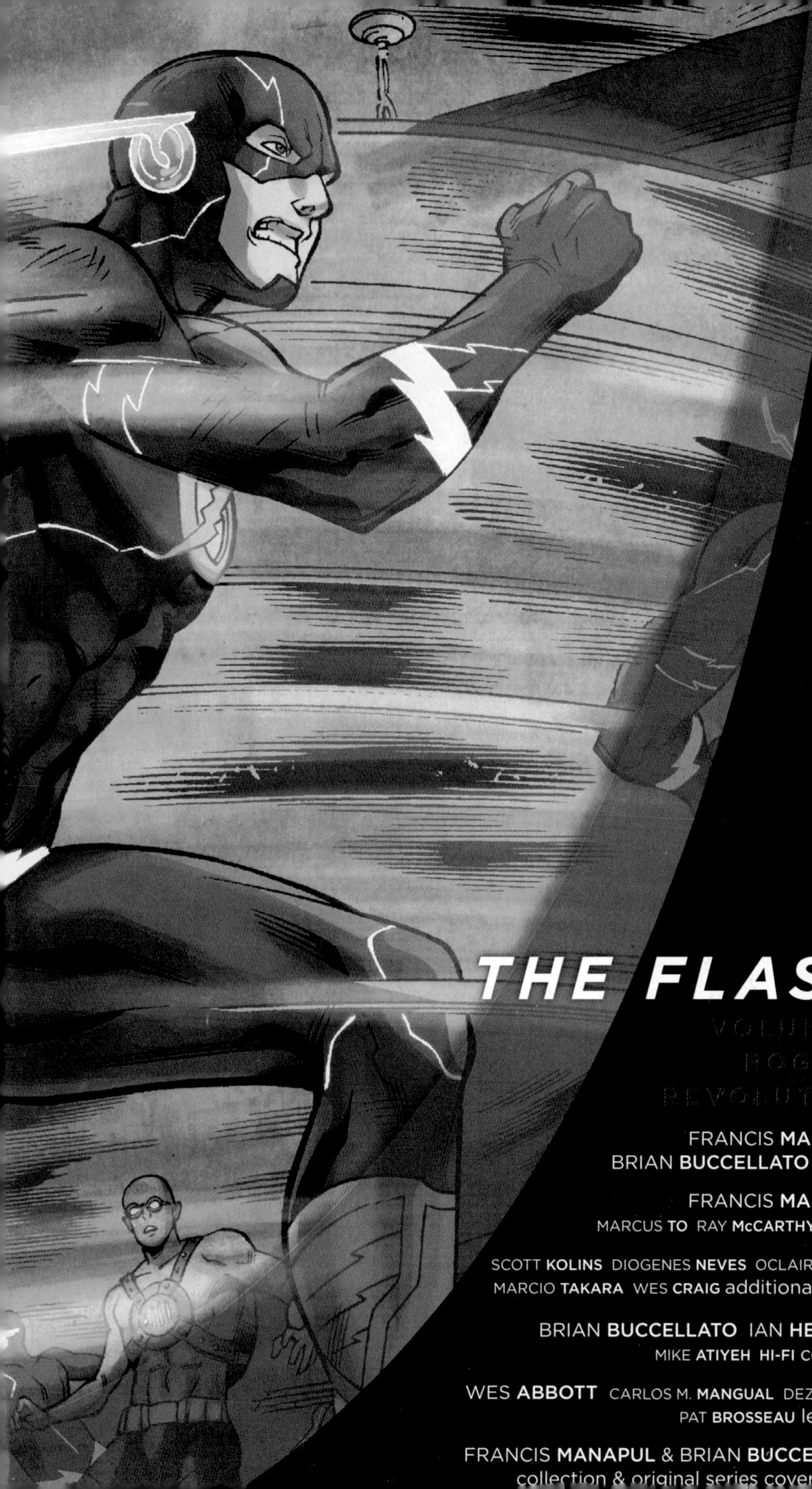

THE FLASH

VOLUME 2 ROGUES REVOLUTION

FRANCIS **MANAPUL**
BRIAN **BUCCELLATO** writers

FRANCIS **MANAPUL**
MARCUS **TO** RAY **McCARTHY** artists

SCOTT **KOLINS** DIOGENES **NEVES** OCLAIR **ALBERT**
MARCIO **TAKARA** WES **CRAIG** additional artists

BRIAN **BUCCELLATO** IAN **HERRING**
MIKE **ATIYEH** **HI-FI** colorists

WES **ABBOTT** CARLOS M. **MANGUAL** DEZI **SIENTY**
PAT **BROSSEAU** letterers

FRANCIS **MANAPUL** & BRIAN **BUCCELLATO**
collection & original series cover artists

MATT IDELSON BRIAN CUNNINGHAM Editors – Original Series CHRIS CONROY Associate Editor – Original Series
DARREN SHAN Assistant Editor – Original Series PETER HAMBOUSSI Editor ROBIN WILDMAN Assistant Editor
ROBBIN BROSTERMAN Design Director – Books ROBBIE BIEDERMAN Publication Design

BOB HARRAS Senior VP – Editor-in-Chief, DC Comics

DIANE NELSON President DAN DIDIO and JIM LEE Co-Publishers
GEOFF JOHNS Chief Creative Officer
JOHN ROOD Executive VP – Sales, Marketing and Business Development
AMY GENKINS Senior VP – Business and Legal Affairs NAIRI GARDINER Senior VP – Finance
JEFF BOISON VP – Publishing Planning MARK CHIARELLO VP – Art Direction and Design
JOHN CUNNINGHAM VP – Marketing TERRI CUNNINGHAM VP – Editorial Administration
ALISON GILL Senior VP – Manufacturing and Operations HANK KANALZ Senior VP – Vertigo & Integrated Publishing
JAY KOGAN VP – Business and Legal Affairs, Publishing JACK MAHAN VP – Business Affairs, Talent
NICK NAPOLITANO VP – Manufacturing Administration SUE POHJA VP – Book Sales
COURTNEY SIMMONS Senior VP – Publicity BOB WAYNE Senior VP – Sales

THE FLASH VOLUME 2: ROGUES REVOLUTION

Published by DC Comics. Compilation Copyright © 2013 DC Comics. All Rights Reserved.

Originally published in single magazine form in THE FLASH 9-12, 0, THE FLASH ANNUAL 1 Copyright © 2012, 2013 DC Comics.
All Rights Reserved. All characters, their distinctive likenesses and related elements featured in this publication
are trademarks of DC Comics. The stories, characters and incidents featured in this publication are entirely fictional.
DC Comics does not read or accept unsolicited ideas, stories or artwork.

DC Comics, 1700 Broadway, New York, NY 10019
A Warner Bros. Entertainment Company.
Printed by RR Donnelley, Salem, VA, USA. 7/12/13. First Printing.

HC ISBN: 978-1-4012-4031-8
SC ISBN: 978-1-4012-4273-2

Library of Congress Cataloging-in-Publication Data

Manapul, Francis.
The Flash. Volume 2, Rogues Revolution / Francis Manapul, Brian Buccellato.
pages cm
"Originally published in single magazine form in The Flash 9-12, The Flash Annual 1."
ISBN 978-1-4012-4031-8
1. Graphic novels. I. Buccellato, Brian. II. Title. III. Title: Rogues Revolution.
PN6728.F53M37 2013
741.5'973—dc23
2013010703

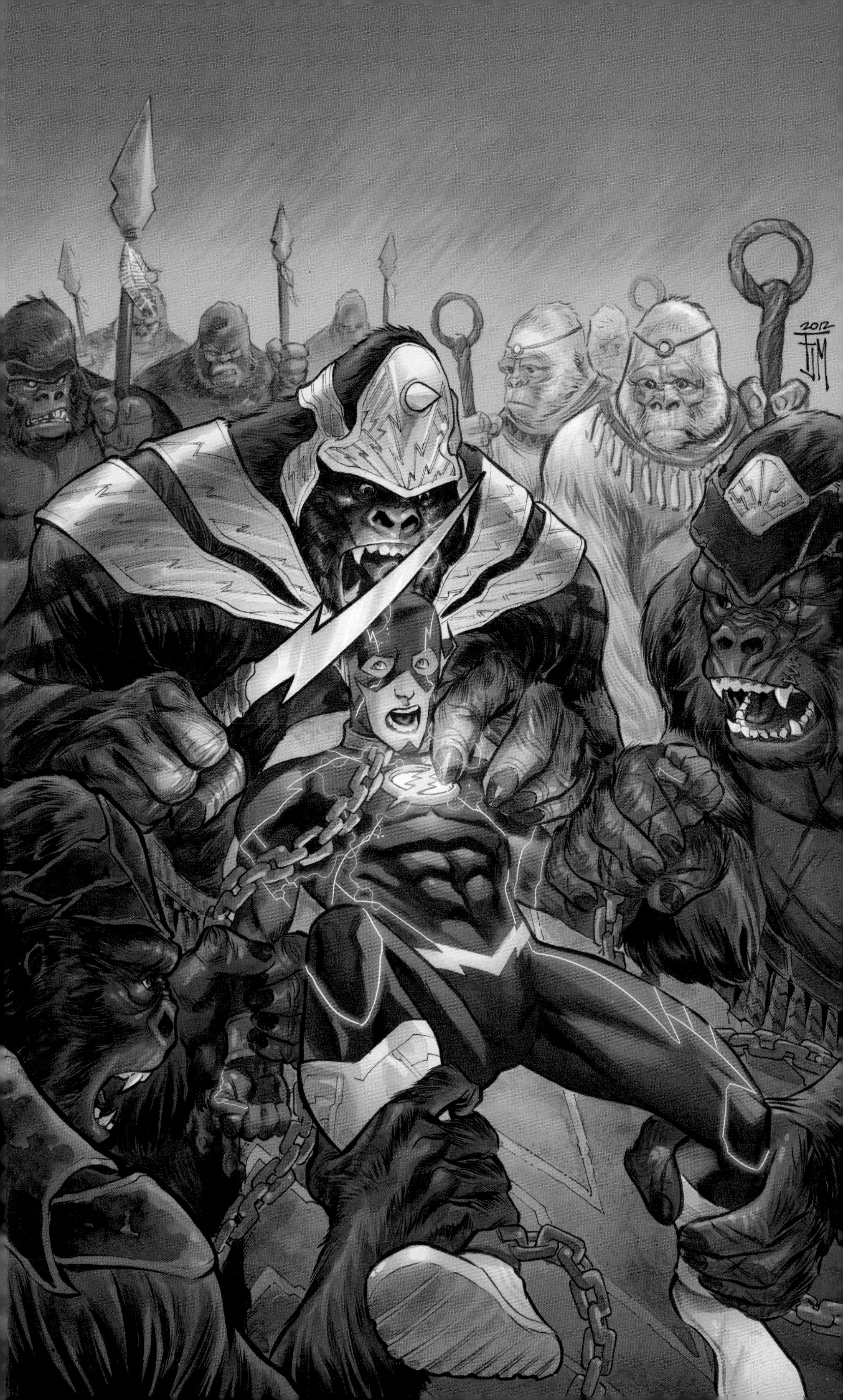
2012

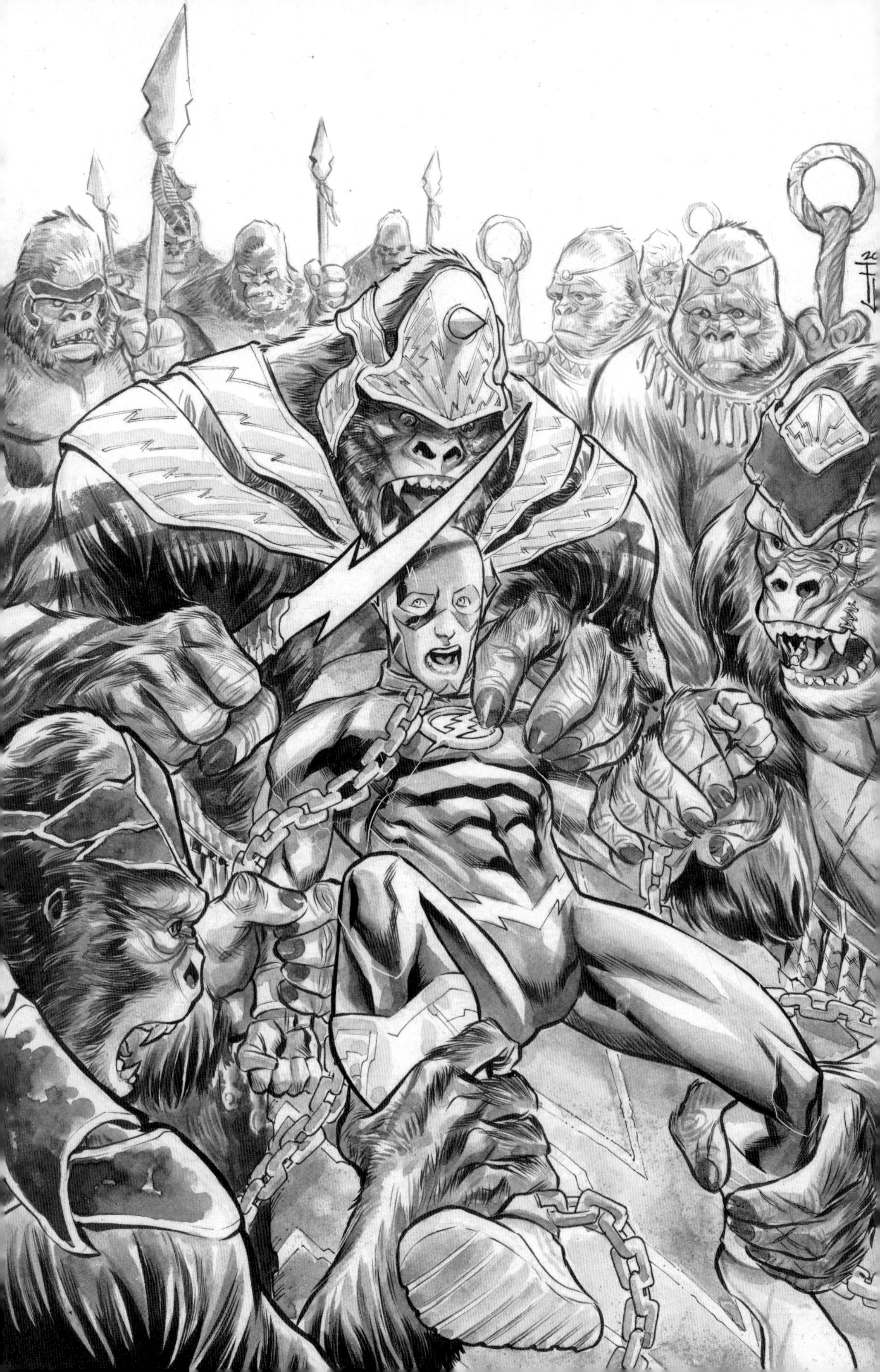

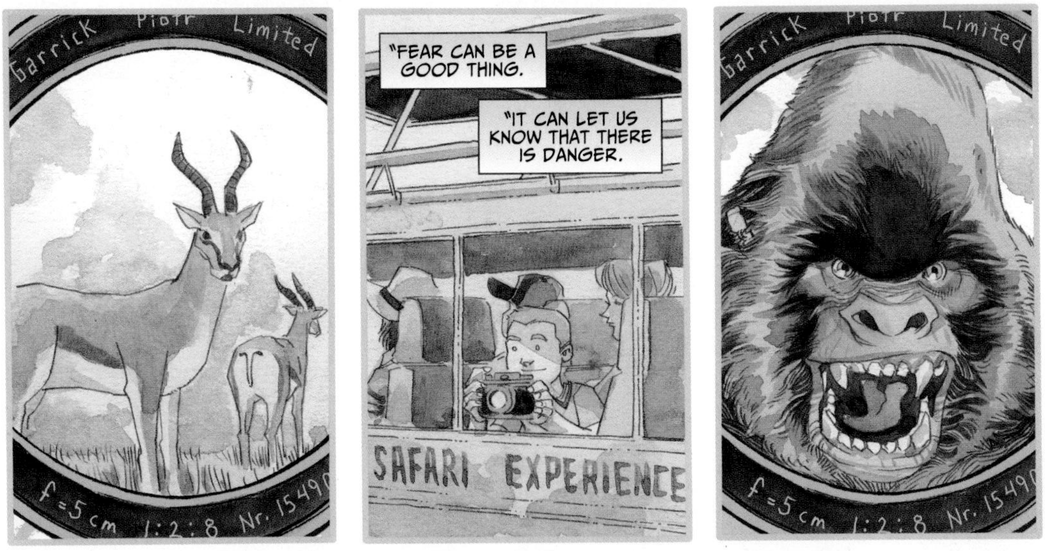
Garrick Piotr Limited
f=5cm 1:2:8 Nr. 15490
"FEAR CAN BE A GOOD THING.
"IT CAN LET US KNOW THAT THERE IS DANGER.
SAFARI EXPERIENCE
Garrick Piotr Limited
f=5cm 1:2:8 Nr. 15490

DC COMICS

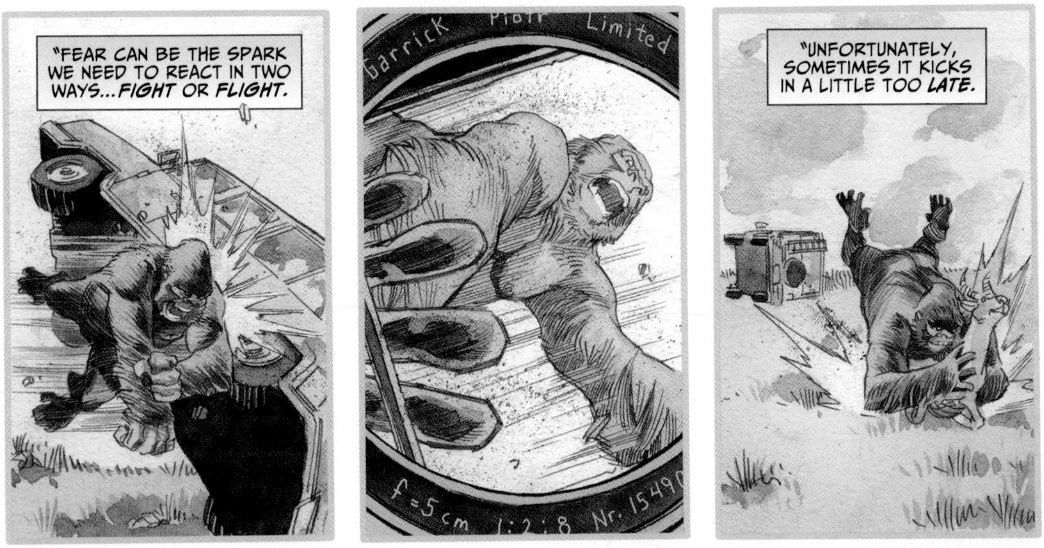
"FEAR CAN BE THE SPARK WE NEED TO REACT IN TWO WAYS...*FIGHT* OR *FLIGHT*.
Garrick Piotr Limited
f=5cm 1:2:8 Nr. 15490
"UNFORTUNATELY, SOMETIMES IT KICKS IN A LITTLE TOO *LATE*.

PROUDLY PRESENTS

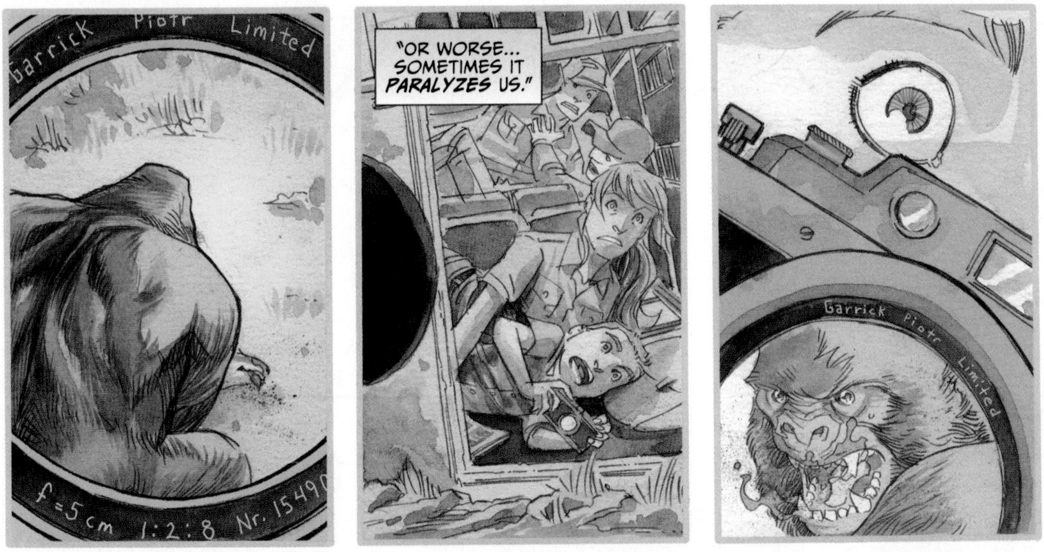
Garrick Piotr Limited
f=5cm 1:2:8 Nr. 15490
"OR WORSE... SOMETIMES IT *PARALYZES* US."
Garrick Piotr Limited

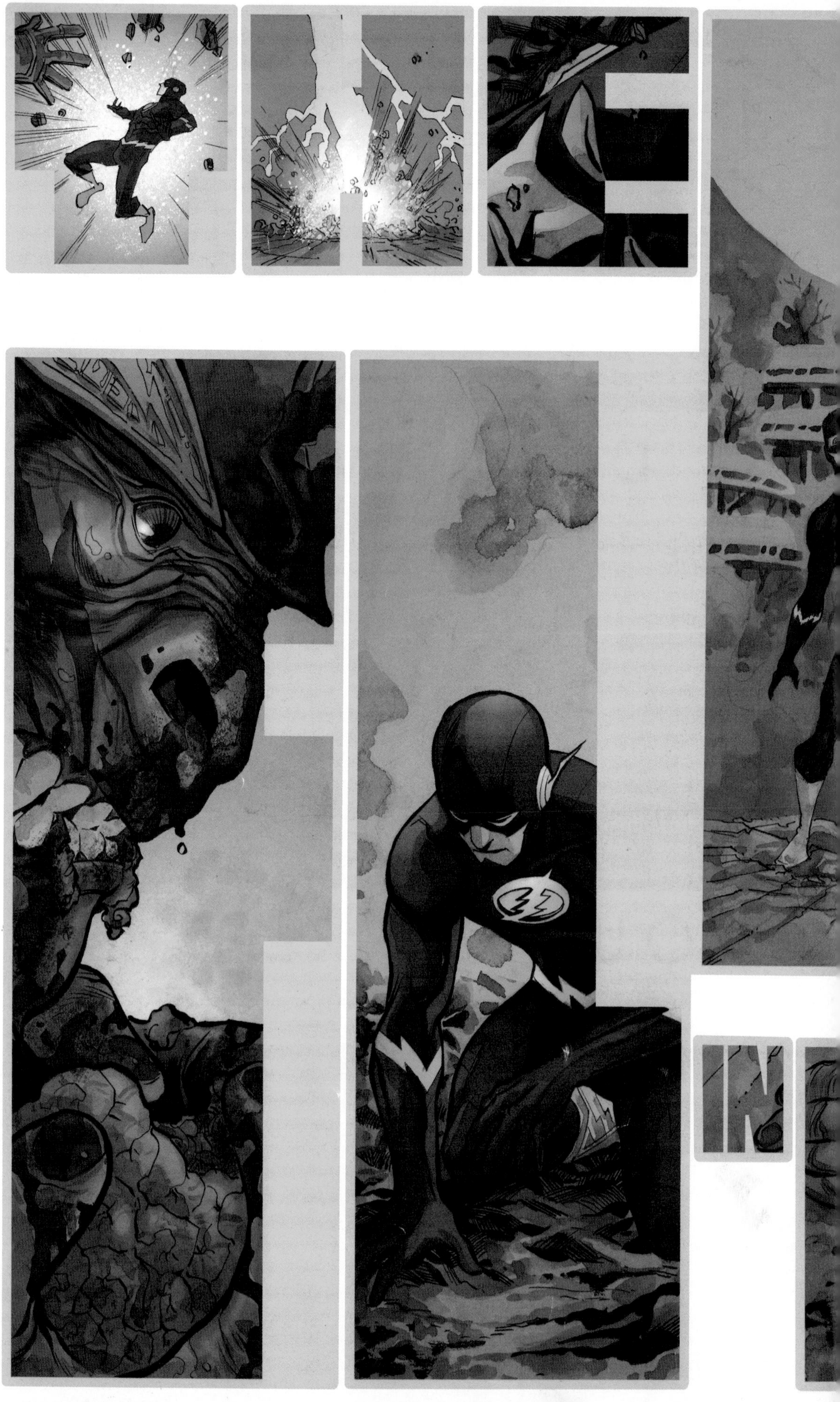

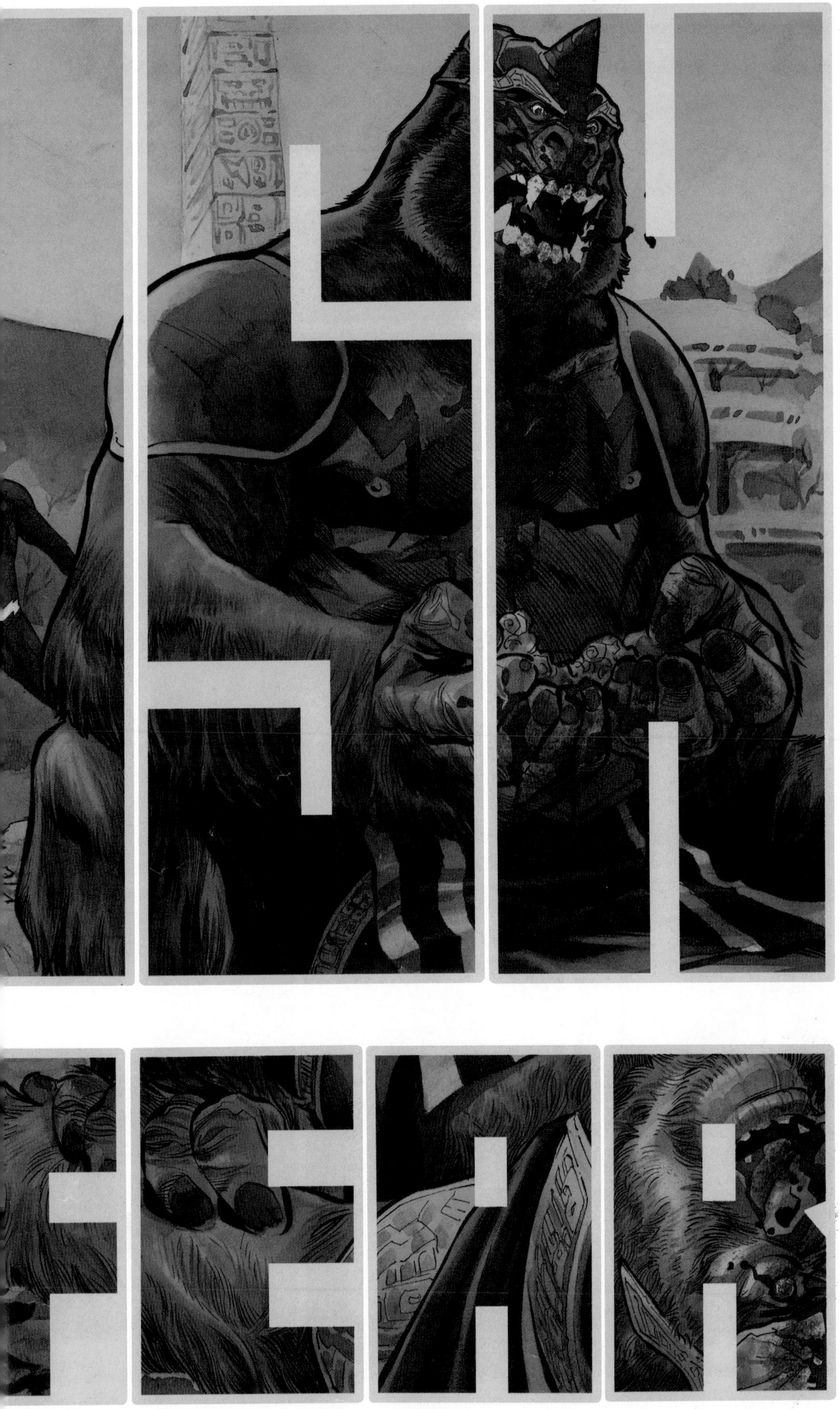
FEAR

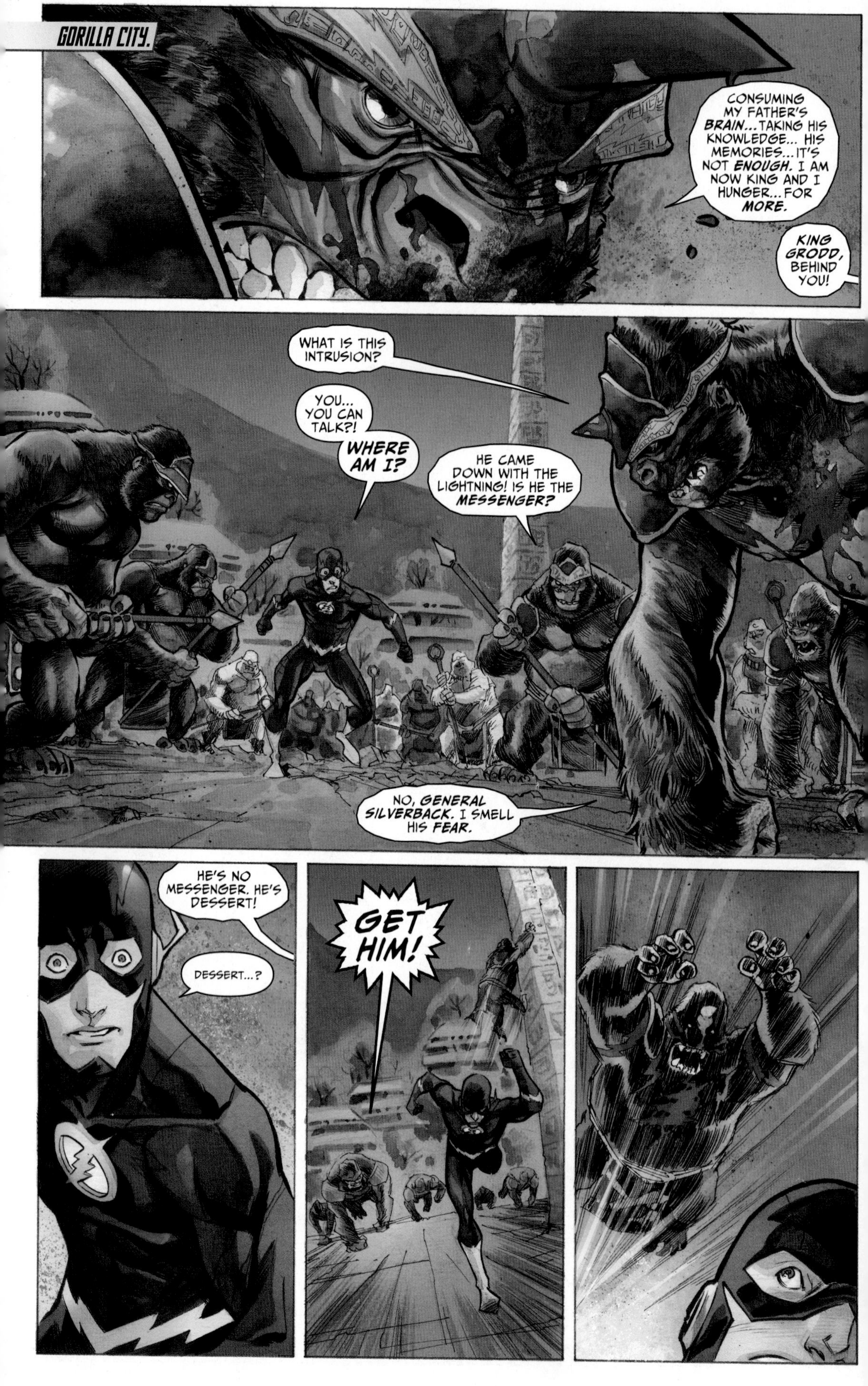

GORILLA CITY.
CONSUMING MY FATHER'S BRAIN... TAKING HIS KNOWLEDGE... HIS MEMORIES... IT'S NOT ENOUGH. I AM NOW KING AND I HUNGER... FOR MORE.
KING GRODD, BEHIND YOU!
WHAT IS THIS INTRUSION?
YOU... YOU CAN TALK?!
WHERE AM I?
HE CAME DOWN WITH THE LIGHTNING! IS HE THE MESSENGER?
NO, GENERAL SILVERBACK. I SMELL HIS FEAR.
HE'S NO MESSENGER. HE'S DESSERT!
DESSERT...?
GET HIM!

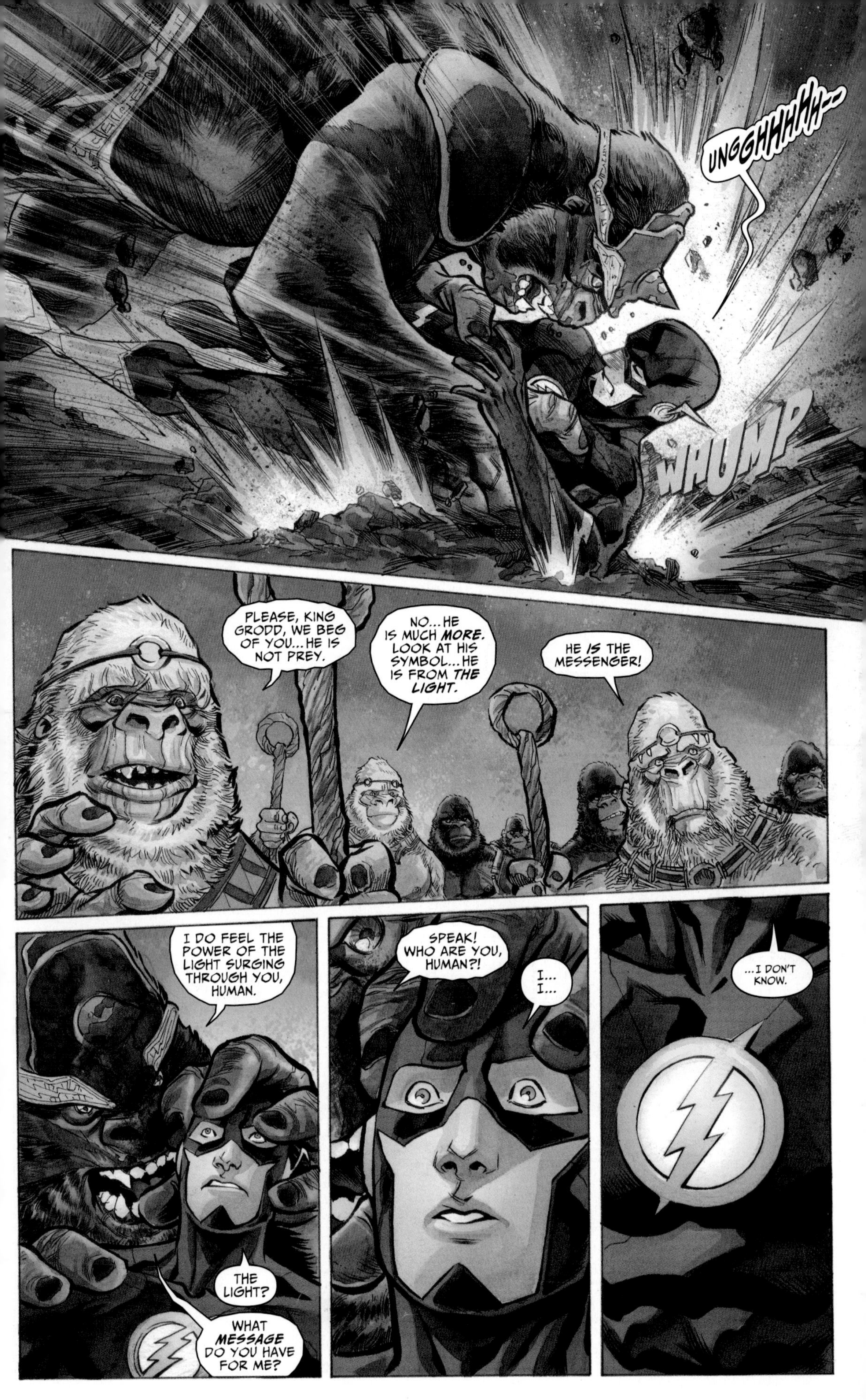
UNGGHHHHH--
WHUMP
PLEASE, KING GRODD, WE BEG OF YOU...HE IS NOT PREY.
NO...HE IS MUCH MORE. LOOK AT HIS SYMBOL...HE IS FROM THE LIGHT.
HE IS THE MESSENGER!
I DO FEEL THE POWER OF THE LIGHT SURGING THROUGH YOU, HUMAN.
THE LIGHT?
WHAT MESSAGE DO YOU HAVE FOR ME?
SPEAK! WHO ARE YOU, HUMAN?!
I... I...
...I DON'T KNOW.

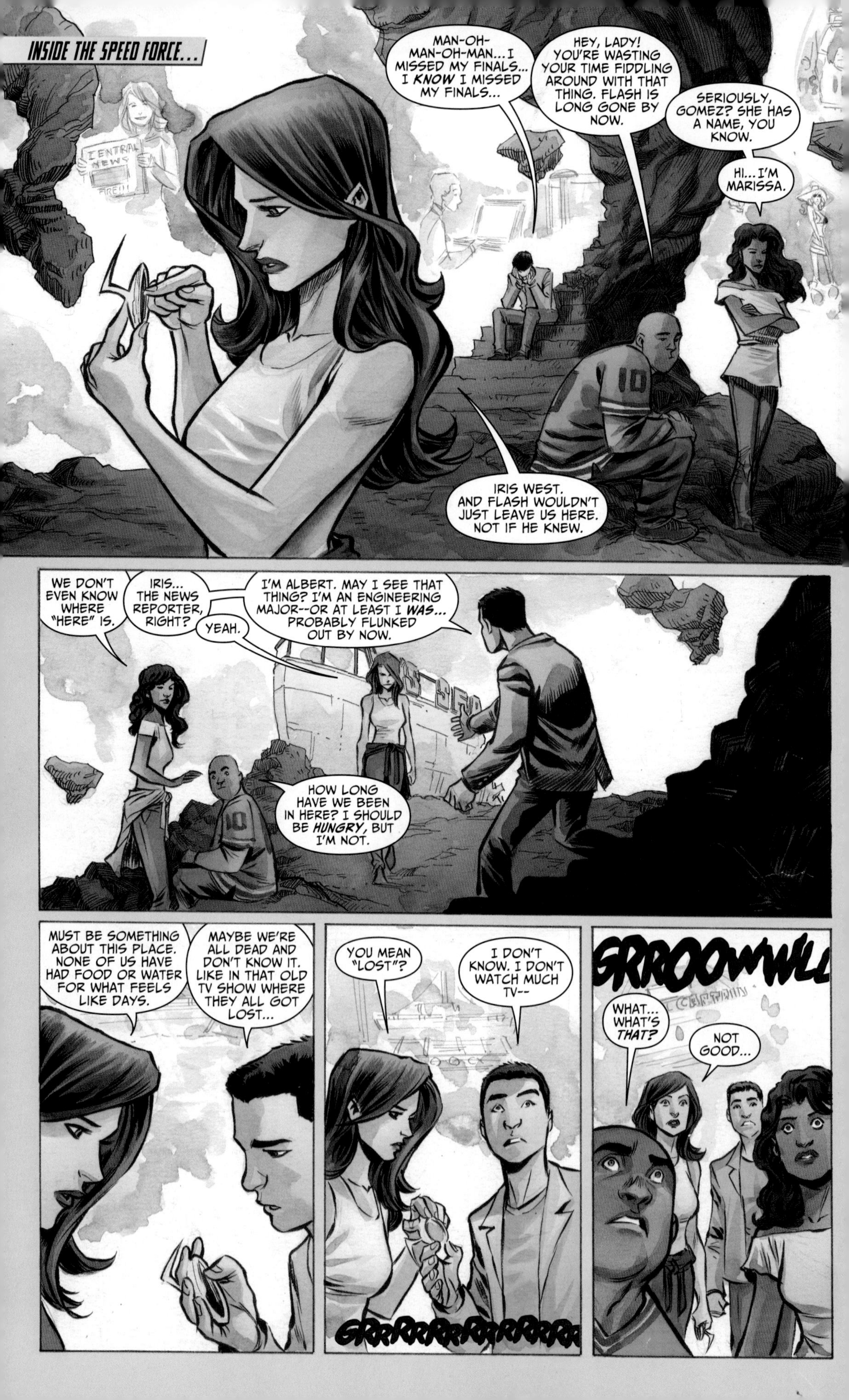
INSIDE THE SPEED FORCE...
MAN-OH-MAN-OH-MAN...I MISSED MY FINALS... I KNOW I MISSED MY FINALS...
HEY, LADY! YOU'RE WASTING YOUR TIME FIDDLING AROUND WITH THAT THING. FLASH IS LONG GONE BY NOW.
SERIOUSLY, GOMEZ? SHE HAS A NAME, YOU KNOW.
HI...I'M MARISSA.
IRIS WEST. AND FLASH WOULDN'T JUST LEAVE US HERE. NOT IF HE KNEW.
WE DON'T EVEN KNOW WHERE "HERE" IS.
IRIS... THE NEWS REPORTER, RIGHT?
YEAH.
I'M ALBERT. MAY I SEE THAT THING? I'M AN ENGINEERING MAJOR--OR AT LEAST I WAS... PROBABLY FLUNKED OUT BY NOW.
HOW LONG HAVE WE BEEN IN HERE? I SHOULD BE HUNGRY, BUT I'M NOT.
MUST BE SOMETHING ABOUT THIS PLACE. NONE OF US HAVE HAD FOOD OR WATER FOR WHAT FEELS LIKE DAYS.
MAYBE WE'RE ALL DEAD AND DON'T KNOW IT. LIKE IN THAT OLD TV SHOW WHERE THEY ALL GOT LOST...
YOU MEAN "LOST"?
I DON'T KNOW. I DON'T WATCH MUCH TV--
GRRRRRRRRRRRRRRRR
GRROOWWLL
WHAT... WHAT'S THAT?
NOT GOOD...

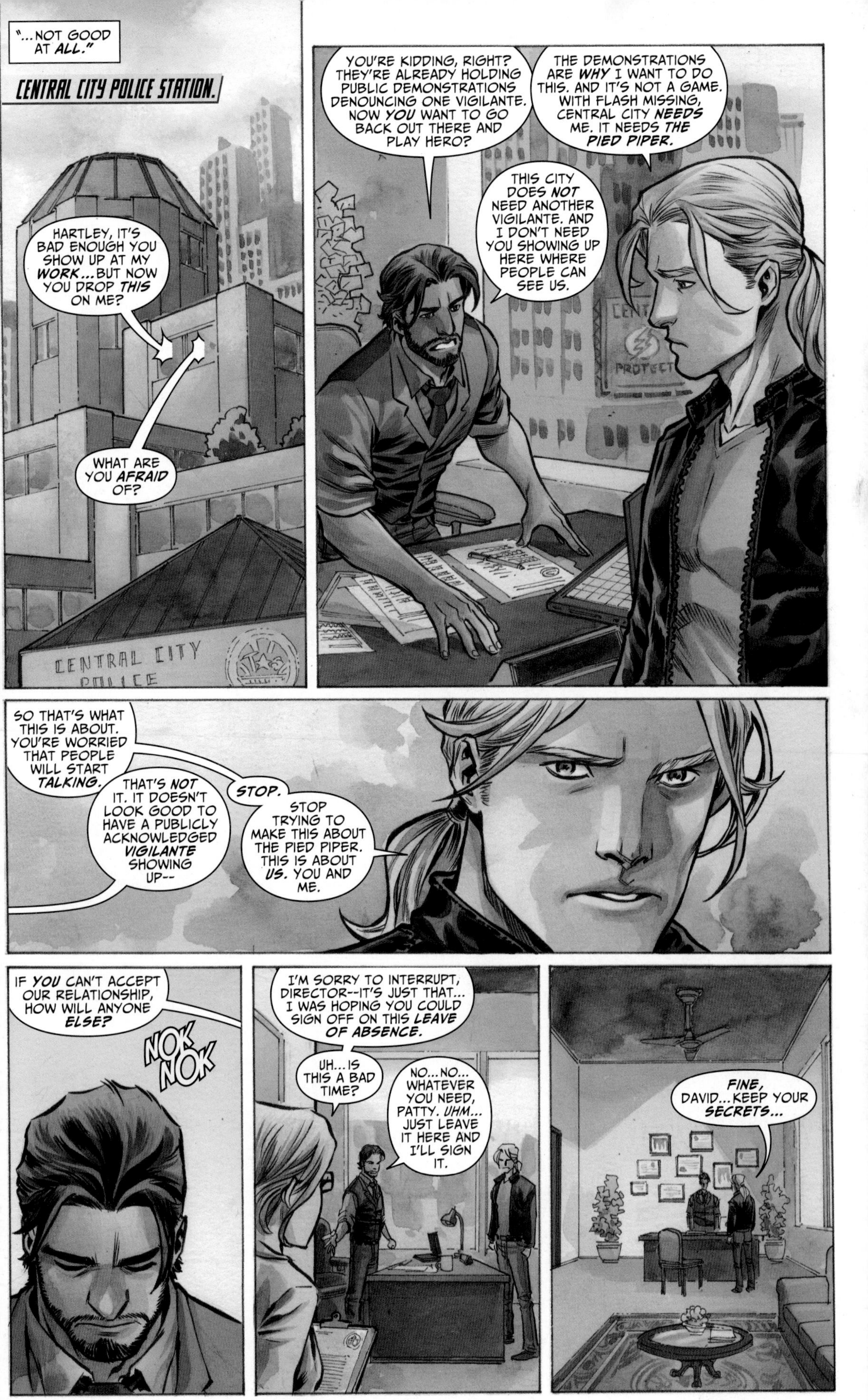
"...NOT GOOD AT ALL."
CENTRAL CITY POLICE STATION.
HARTLEY, IT'S BAD ENOUGH YOU SHOW UP AT MY WORK... BUT NOW YOU DROP THIS ON ME?
WHAT ARE YOU AFRAID OF?
CENTRAL CITY POLICE
YOU'RE KIDDING, RIGHT? THEY'RE ALREADY HOLDING PUBLIC DEMONSTRATIONS DENOUNCING ONE VIGILANTE. NOW YOU WANT TO GO BACK OUT THERE AND PLAY HERO?
THE DEMONSTRATIONS ARE WHY I WANT TO DO THIS. AND IT'S NOT A GAME. WITH FLASH MISSING, CENTRAL CITY NEEDS ME. IT NEEDS THE PIED PIPER.
THIS CITY DOES NOT NEED ANOTHER VIGILANTE. AND I DON'T NEED YOU SHOWING UP HERE WHERE PEOPLE CAN SEE US.
SO THAT'S WHAT THIS IS ABOUT. YOU'RE WORRIED THAT PEOPLE WILL START TALKING.
THAT'S NOT IT. IT DOESN'T LOOK GOOD TO HAVE A PUBLICLY ACKNOWLEDGED VIGILANTE SHOWING UP--
STOP.
STOP TRYING TO MAKE THIS ABOUT THE PIED PIPER. THIS IS ABOUT US. YOU AND ME.
IF YOU CAN'T ACCEPT OUR RELATIONSHIP, HOW WILL ANYONE ELSE?
NOK NOK
I'M SORRY TO INTERRUPT, DIRECTOR--IT'S JUST THAT... I WAS HOPING YOU COULD SIGN OFF ON THIS LEAVE OF ABSENCE.
UH... IS THIS A BAD TIME?
NO...NO... WHATEVER YOU NEED, PATTY. UHM... JUST LEAVE IT HERE AND I'LL SIGN IT.
FINE, DAVID... KEEP YOUR SECRETS...

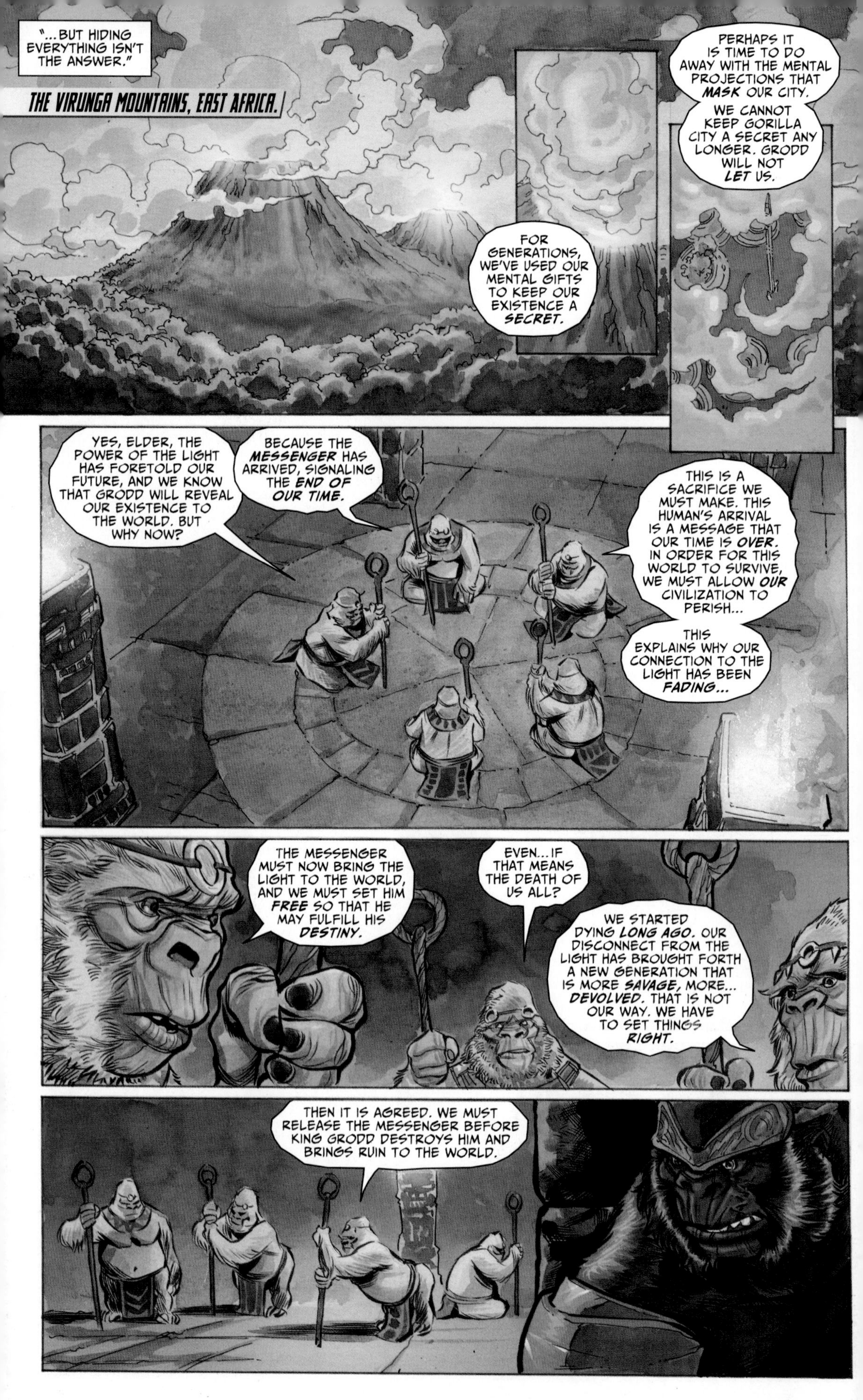
"...BUT HIDING EVERYTHING ISN'T THE ANSWER."
THE VIRUNGA MOUNTAINS, EAST AFRICA.
FOR GENERATIONS, WE'VE USED OUR MENTAL GIFTS TO KEEP OUR EXISTENCE A SECRET.
PERHAPS IT IS TIME TO DO AWAY WITH THE MENTAL PROJECTIONS THAT MASK OUR CITY.
WE CANNOT KEEP GORILLA CITY A SECRET ANY LONGER. GRODD WILL NOT LET US.
YES, ELDER, THE POWER OF THE LIGHT HAS FORETOLD OUR FUTURE, AND WE KNOW THAT GRODD WILL REVEAL OUR EXISTENCE TO THE WORLD. BUT WHY NOW?
BECAUSE THE MESSENGER HAS ARRIVED, SIGNALING THE END OF OUR TIME.
THIS IS A SACRIFICE WE MUST MAKE. THIS HUMAN'S ARRIVAL IS A MESSAGE THAT OUR TIME IS OVER. IN ORDER FOR THIS WORLD TO SURVIVE, WE MUST ALLOW OUR CIVILIZATION TO PERISH...
THIS EXPLAINS WHY OUR CONNECTION TO THE LIGHT HAS BEEN FADING...
THE MESSENGER MUST NOW BRING THE LIGHT TO THE WORLD, AND WE MUST SET HIM FREE SO THAT HE MAY FULFILL HIS DESTINY.
EVEN...IF THAT MEANS THE DEATH OF US ALL?
WE STARTED DYING LONG AGO. OUR DISCONNECT FROM THE LIGHT HAS BROUGHT FORTH A NEW GENERATION THAT IS MORE SAVAGE, MORE... DEVOLVED. THAT IS NOT OUR WAY. WE HAVE TO SET THINGS RIGHT.
THEN IT IS AGREED. WE MUST RELEASE THE MESSENGER BEFORE KING GRODD DESTROYS HIM AND BRINGS RUIN TO THE WORLD.

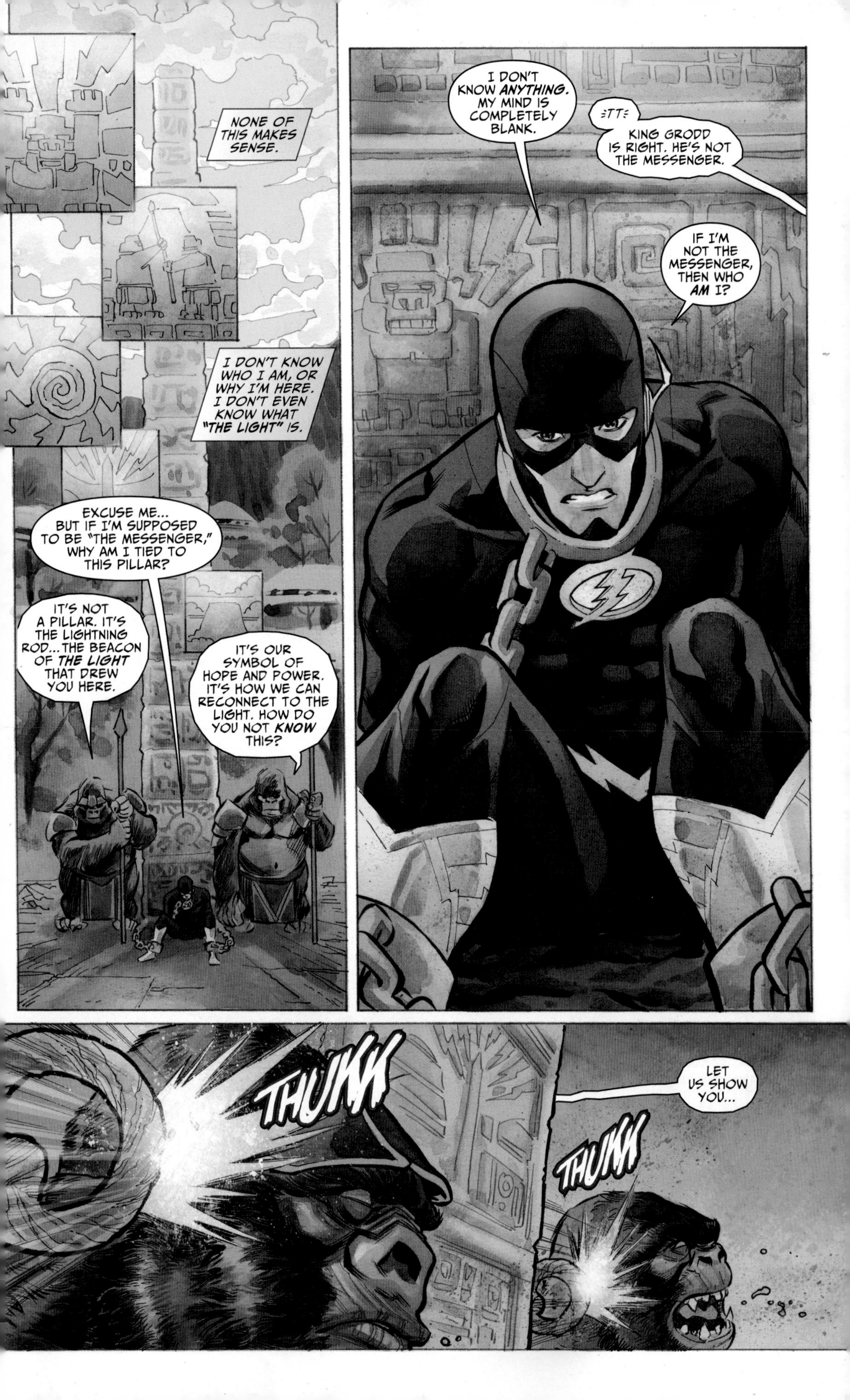
NONE OF THIS MAKES SENSE.
I DON'T KNOW WHO I AM, OR WHY I'M HERE. I DON'T EVEN KNOW WHAT "THE LIGHT" IS.
EXCUSE ME... BUT IF I'M SUPPOSED TO BE "THE MESSENGER," WHY AM I TIED TO THIS PILLAR?
IT'S NOT A PILLAR. IT'S THE LIGHTNING ROD...THE BEACON OF THE LIGHT THAT DREW YOU HERE.
IT'S OUR SYMBOL OF HOPE AND POWER. IT'S HOW WE CAN RECONNECT TO THE LIGHT. HOW DO YOU NOT KNOW THIS?
I DON'T KNOW ANYTHING. MY MIND IS COMPLETELY BLANK.
KING GRODD IS RIGHT. HE'S NOT THE MESSENGER.
IF I'M NOT THE MESSENGER, THEN WHO AM I?
THUKK
LET US SHOW YOU...
THUKK

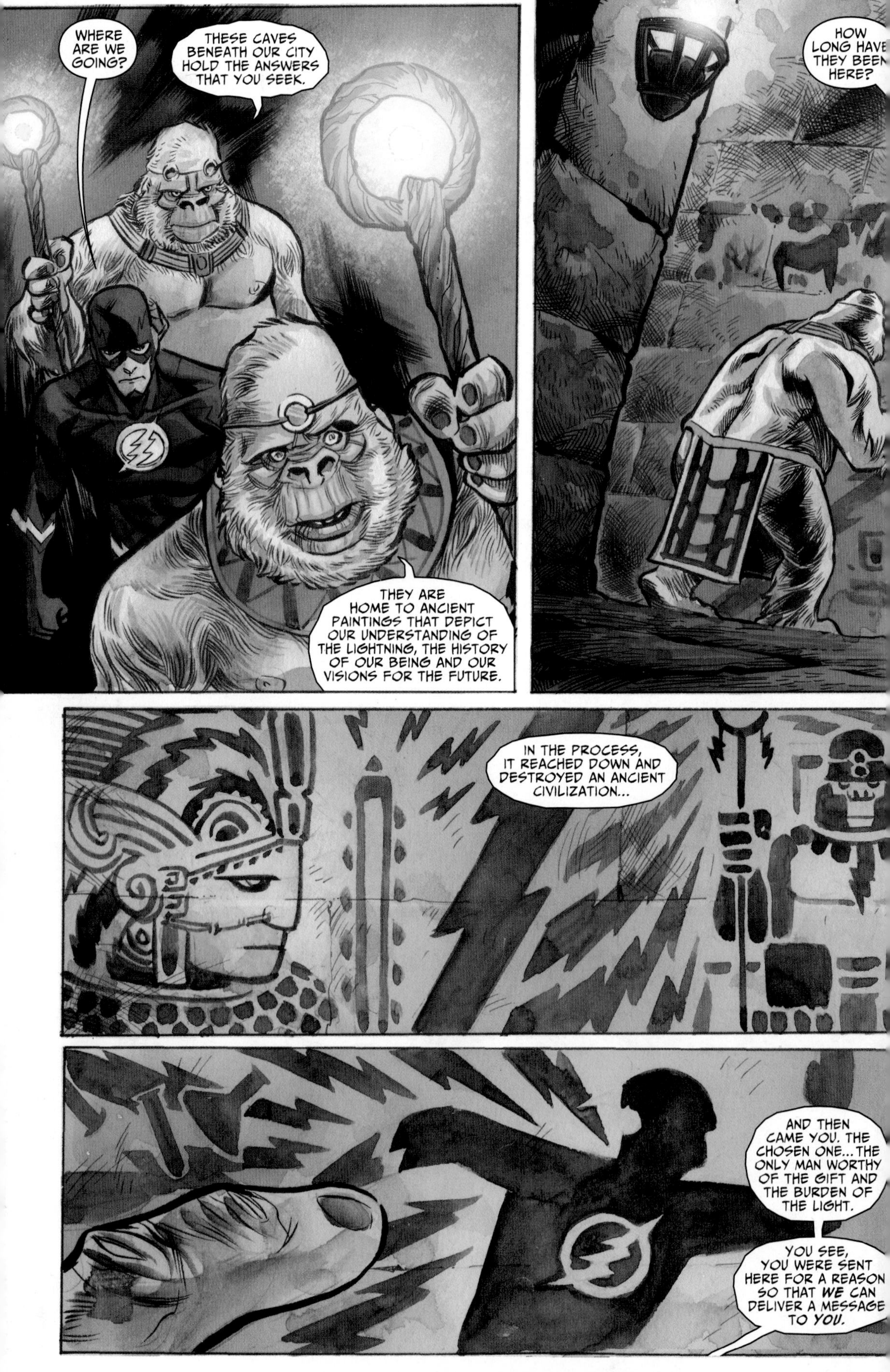
WHERE ARE WE GOING?
THESE CAVES BENEATH OUR CITY HOLD THE ANSWERS THAT YOU SEEK.
THEY ARE HOME TO ANCIENT PAINTINGS THAT DEPICT OUR UNDERSTANDING OF THE LIGHTNING, THE HISTORY OF OUR BEING AND OUR VISIONS FOR THE FUTURE.
HOW LONG HAVE THEY BEEN HERE?
IN THE PROCESS, IT REACHED DOWN AND DESTROYED AN ANCIENT CIVILIZATION...
AND THEN CAME YOU. THE CHOSEN ONE... THE ONLY MAN WORTHY OF THE GIFT AND THE BURDEN OF THE LIGHT.
YOU SEE, YOU WERE SENT HERE FOR A REASON SO THAT WE CAN DELIVER A MESSAGE TO YOU.

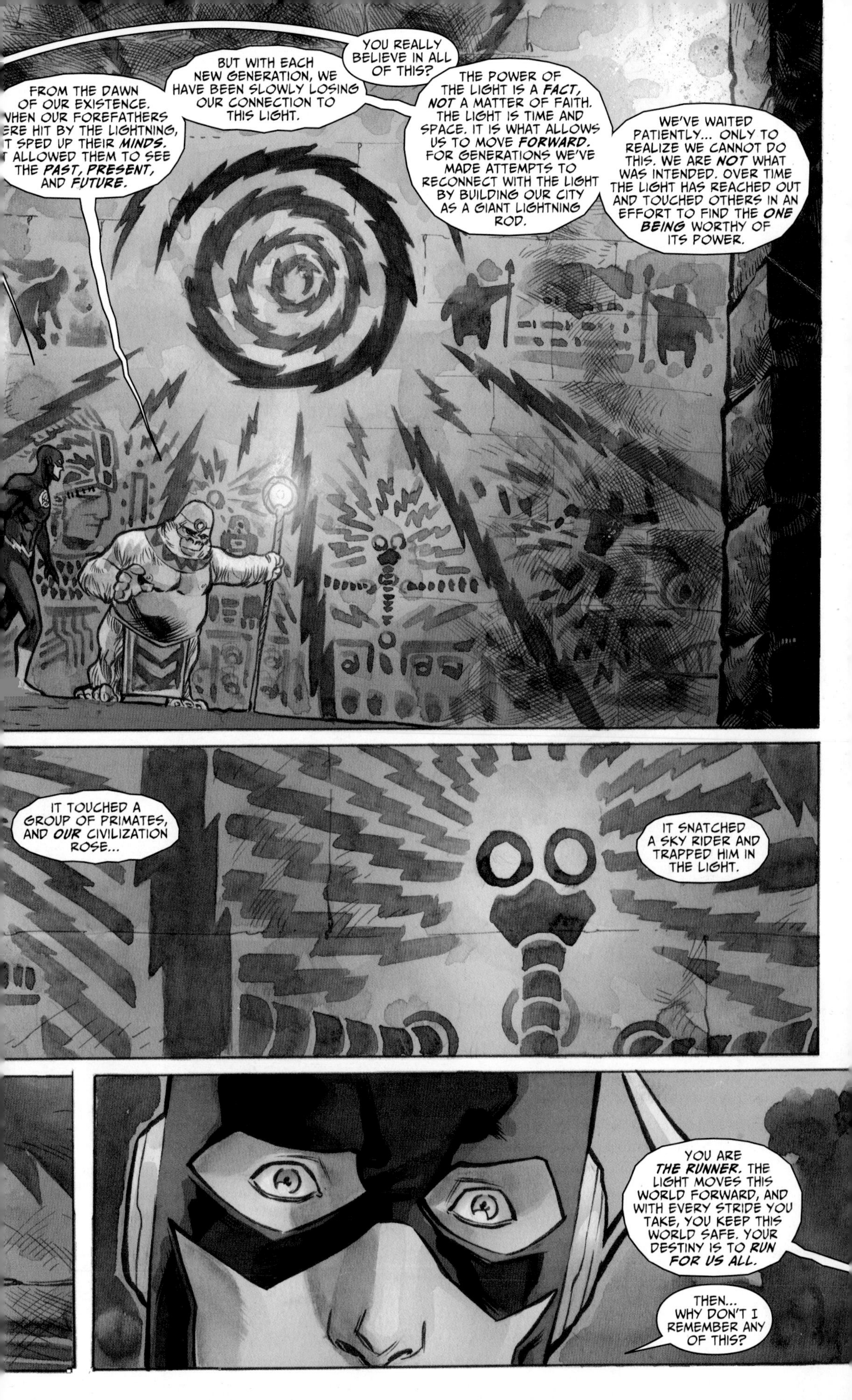
FROM THE DAWN OF OUR EXISTENCE. WHEN OUR FOREFATHERS WERE HIT BY THE LIGHTNING, IT SPED UP THEIR MINDS. IT ALLOWED THEM TO SEE THE PAST, PRESENT, AND FUTURE.
BUT WITH EACH NEW GENERATION, WE HAVE BEEN SLOWLY LOSING OUR CONNECTION TO THIS LIGHT.
YOU REALLY BELIEVE IN ALL OF THIS?
THE POWER OF THE LIGHT IS A FACT, NOT A MATTER OF FAITH. THE LIGHT IS TIME AND SPACE. IT IS WHAT ALLOWS US TO MOVE FORWARD. FOR GENERATIONS WE'VE MADE ATTEMPTS TO RECONNECT WITH THE LIGHT BY BUILDING OUR CITY AS A GIANT LIGHTNING ROD.
WE'VE WAITED PATIENTLY... ONLY TO REALIZE WE CANNOT DO THIS. WE ARE NOT WHAT WAS INTENDED. OVER TIME THE LIGHT HAS REACHED OUT AND TOUCHED OTHERS IN AN EFFORT TO FIND THE ONE BEING WORTHY OF ITS POWER.
IT TOUCHED A GROUP OF PRIMATES, AND OUR CIVILIZATION ROSE...
IT SNATCHED A SKY RIDER AND TRAPPED HIM IN THE LIGHT.
YOU ARE THE RUNNER. THE LIGHT MOVES THIS WORLD FORWARD, AND WITH EVERY STRIDE YOU TAKE, YOU KEEP THIS WORLD SAFE. YOUR DESTINY IS TO RUN FOR US ALL.
THEN... WHY DON'T I REMEMBER ANY OF THIS?

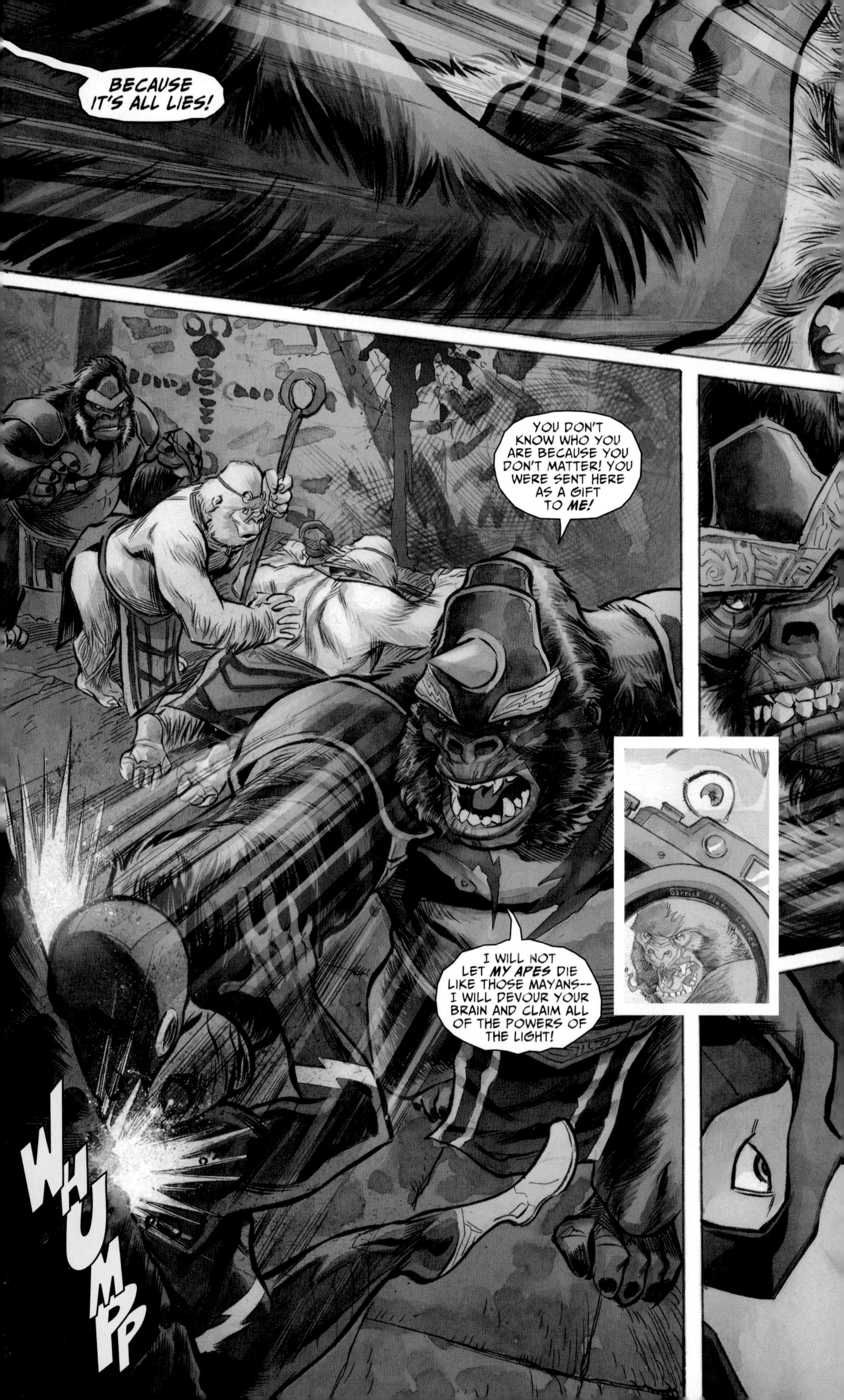
BECAUSE IT'S ALL LIES!
YOU DON'T KNOW WHO YOU ARE BECAUSE YOU DON'T MATTER! YOU WERE SENT HERE AS A GIFT TO ME!
I WILL NOT LET MY APES DIE LIKE THOSE MAYANS-- I WILL DEVOUR YOUR BRAIN AND CLAIM ALL OF THE POWERS OF THE LIGHT!
WHUMPP

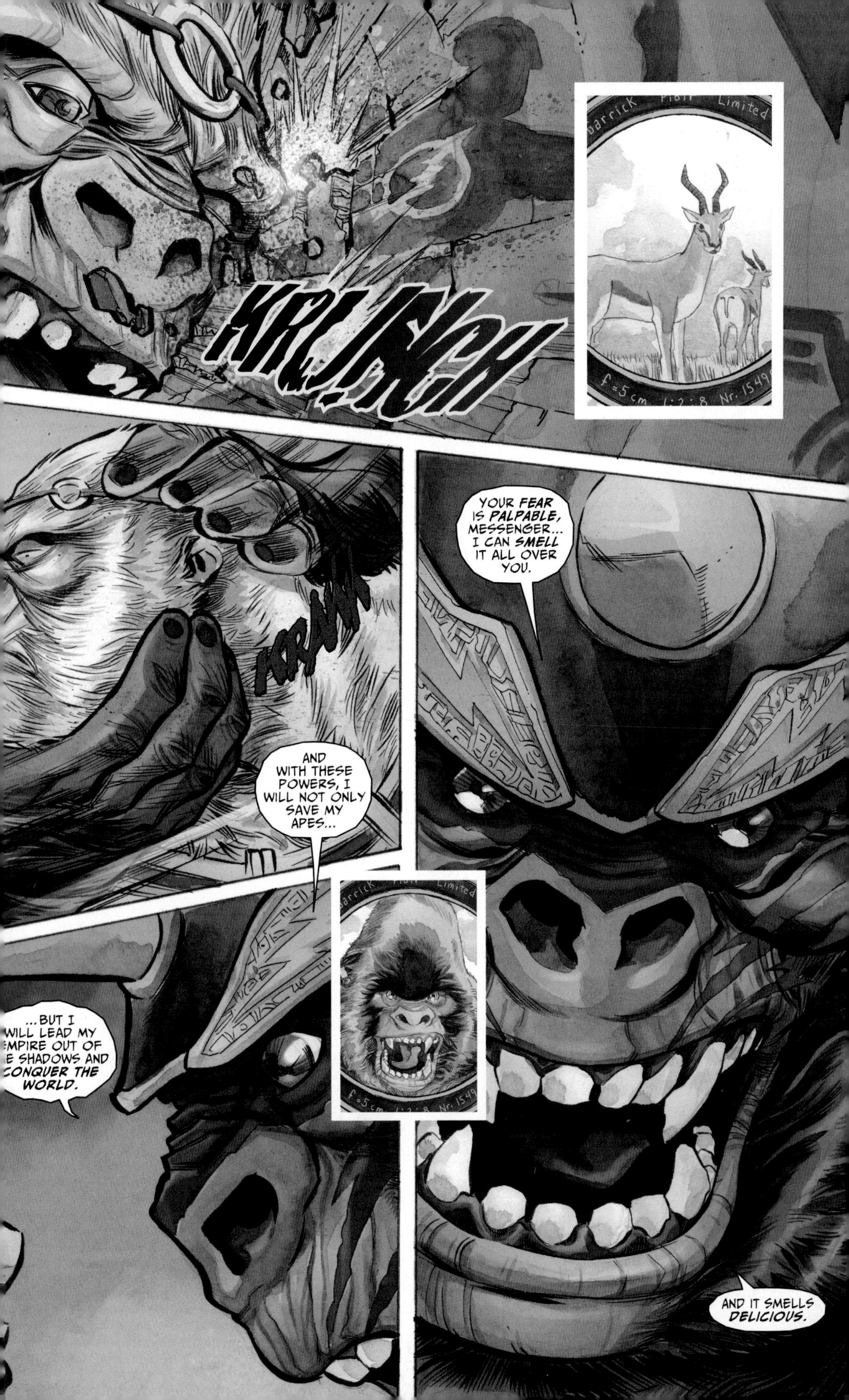
KRUNCH
Darrick Pratt Limited
f=5cm 1:2.8 Nr. 1549
KRAM
YOUR FEAR IS PALPABLE, MESSENGER... I CAN SMELL IT ALL OVER YOU.
AND WITH THESE POWERS, I WILL NOT ONLY SAVE MY APES...
...BUT I WILL LEAD MY EMPIRE OUT OF THE SHADOWS AND CONQUER THE WORLD.
AND IT SMELLS DELICIOUS.

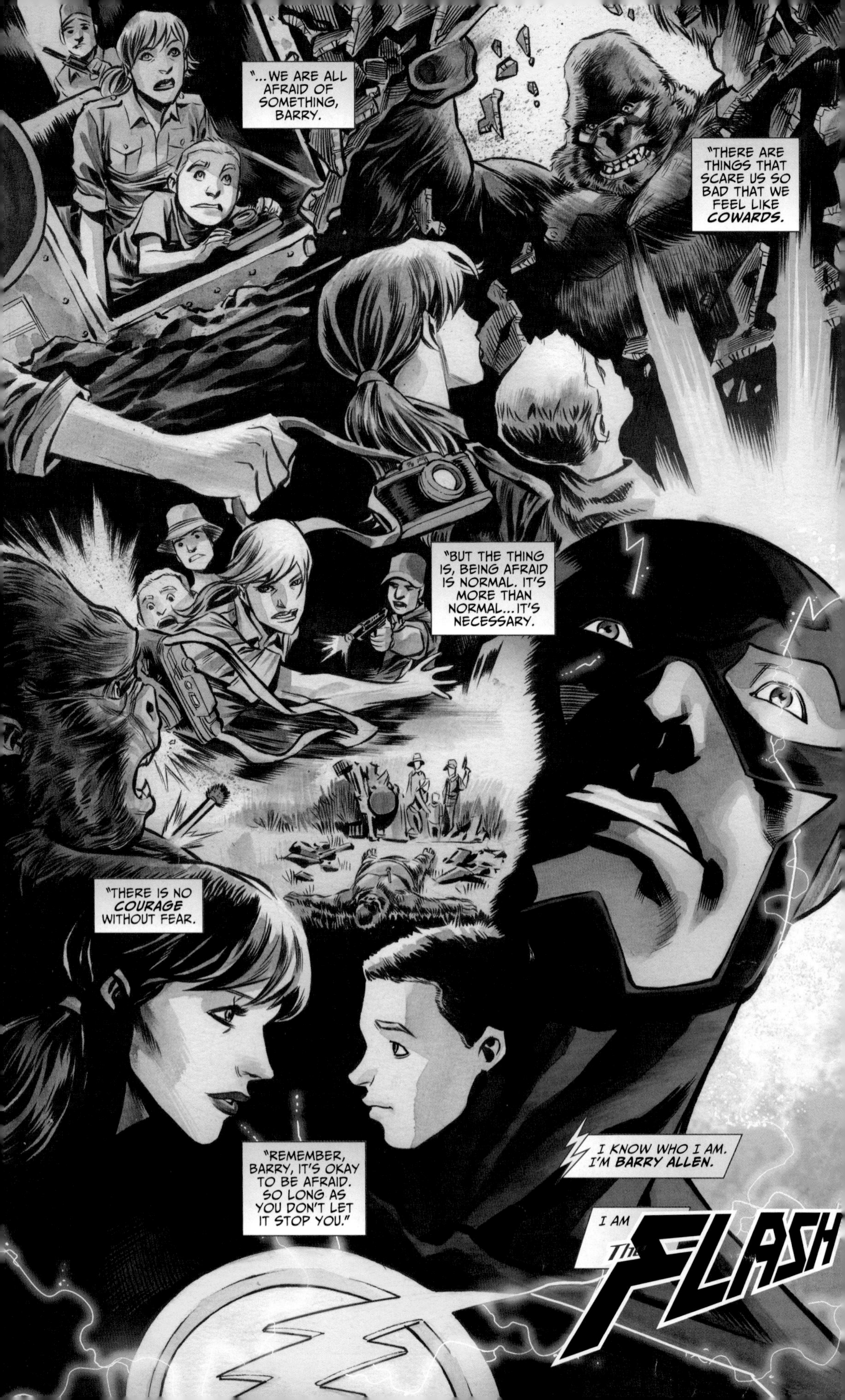
"...WE ARE ALL AFRAID OF SOMETHING, BARRY.
"THERE ARE THINGS THAT SCARE US SO BAD THAT WE FEEL LIKE COWARDS.
"BUT THE THING IS, BEING AFRAID IS NORMAL. IT'S MORE THAN NORMAL...IT'S NECESSARY.
"THERE IS NO COURAGE WITHOUT FEAR.
"REMEMBER, BARRY, IT'S OKAY TO BE AFRAID. SO LONG AS YOU DON'T LET IT STOP YOU."
I KNOW WHO I AM. I'M BARRY ALLEN.
I AM
THE FLASH

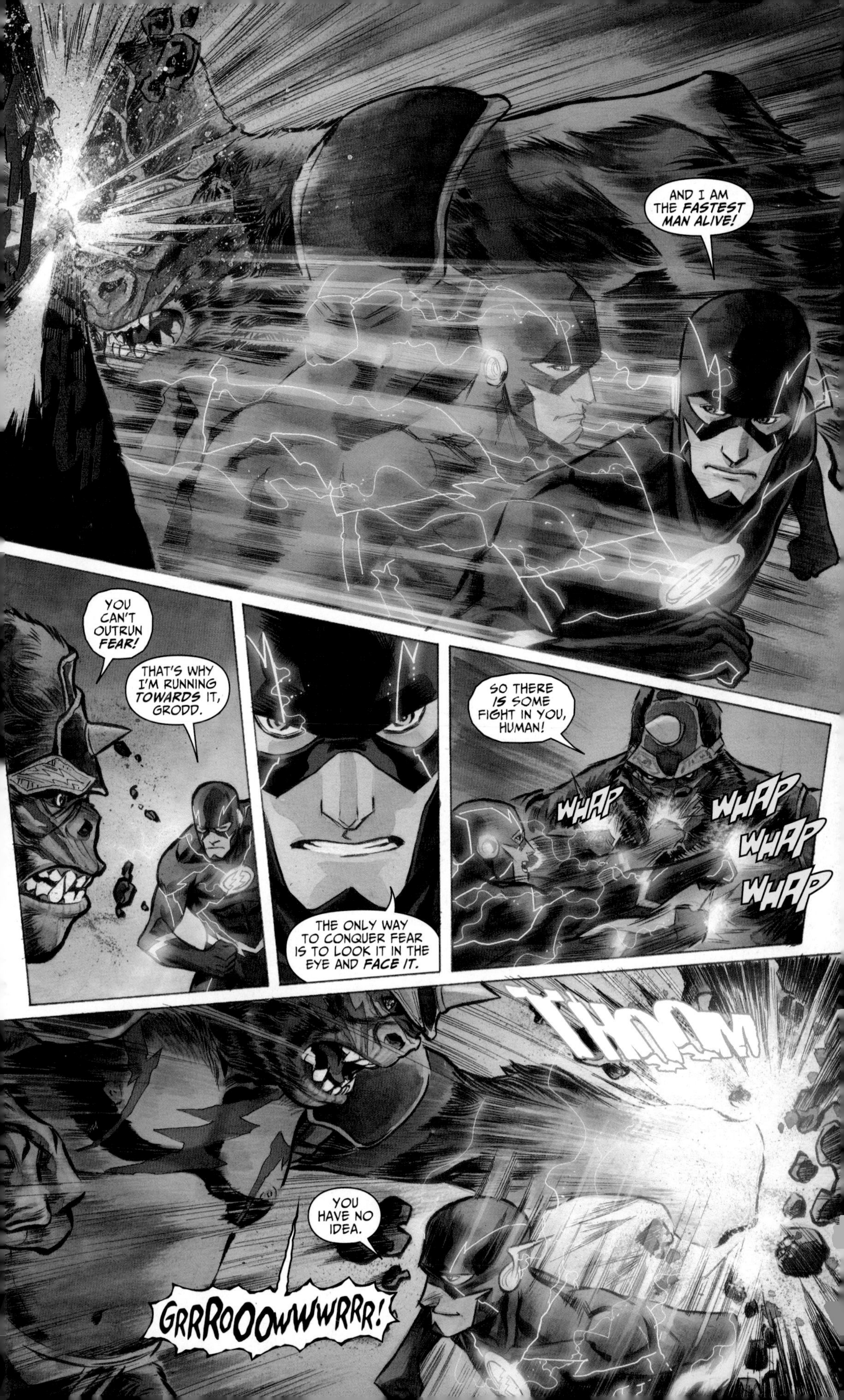
AND I AM THE FASTEST MAN ALIVE!
YOU CAN'T OUTRUN FEAR!
THAT'S WHY I'M RUNNING TOWARDS IT, GRODD.
THE ONLY WAY TO CONQUER FEAR IS TO LOOK IT IN THE EYE AND FACE IT.
SO THERE IS SOME FIGHT IN YOU, HUMAN!
WHAP
WHAP
WHAP
WHAP
THOOM
YOU HAVE NO IDEA.
GRRROOOWWWRRR!

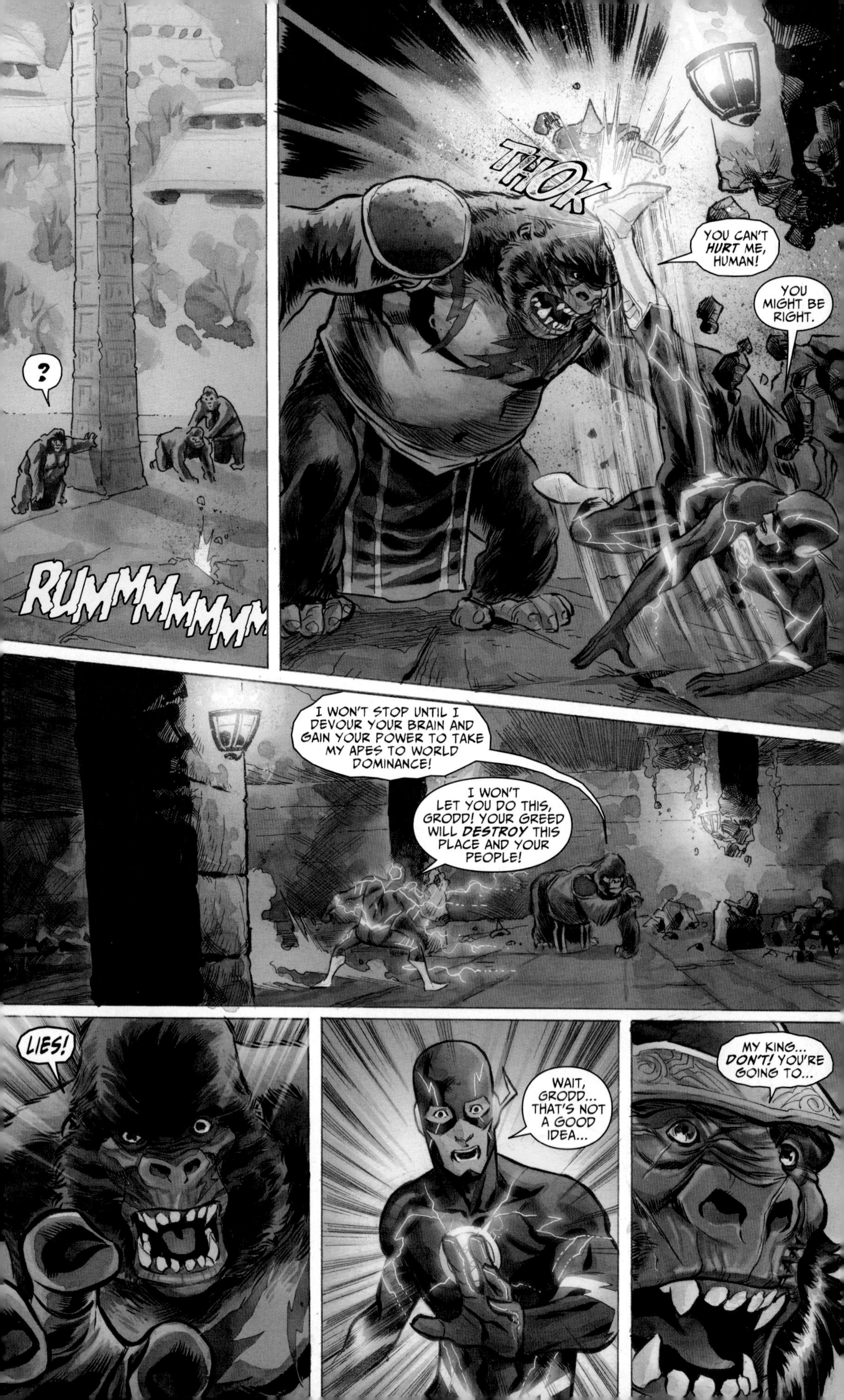
?
RUMMMMMMMM
THOK
YOU CAN'T HURT ME, HUMAN!
YOU MIGHT BE RIGHT.
I WON'T STOP UNTIL I DEVOUR YOUR BRAIN AND GAIN YOUR POWER TO TAKE MY APES TO WORLD DOMINANCE!
I WON'T LET YOU DO THIS, GRODD! YOUR GREED WILL DESTROY THIS PLACE AND YOUR PEOPLE!
LIES!
WAIT, GRODD... THAT'S NOT A GOOD IDEA...
MY KING... DON'T! YOU'RE GOING TO...

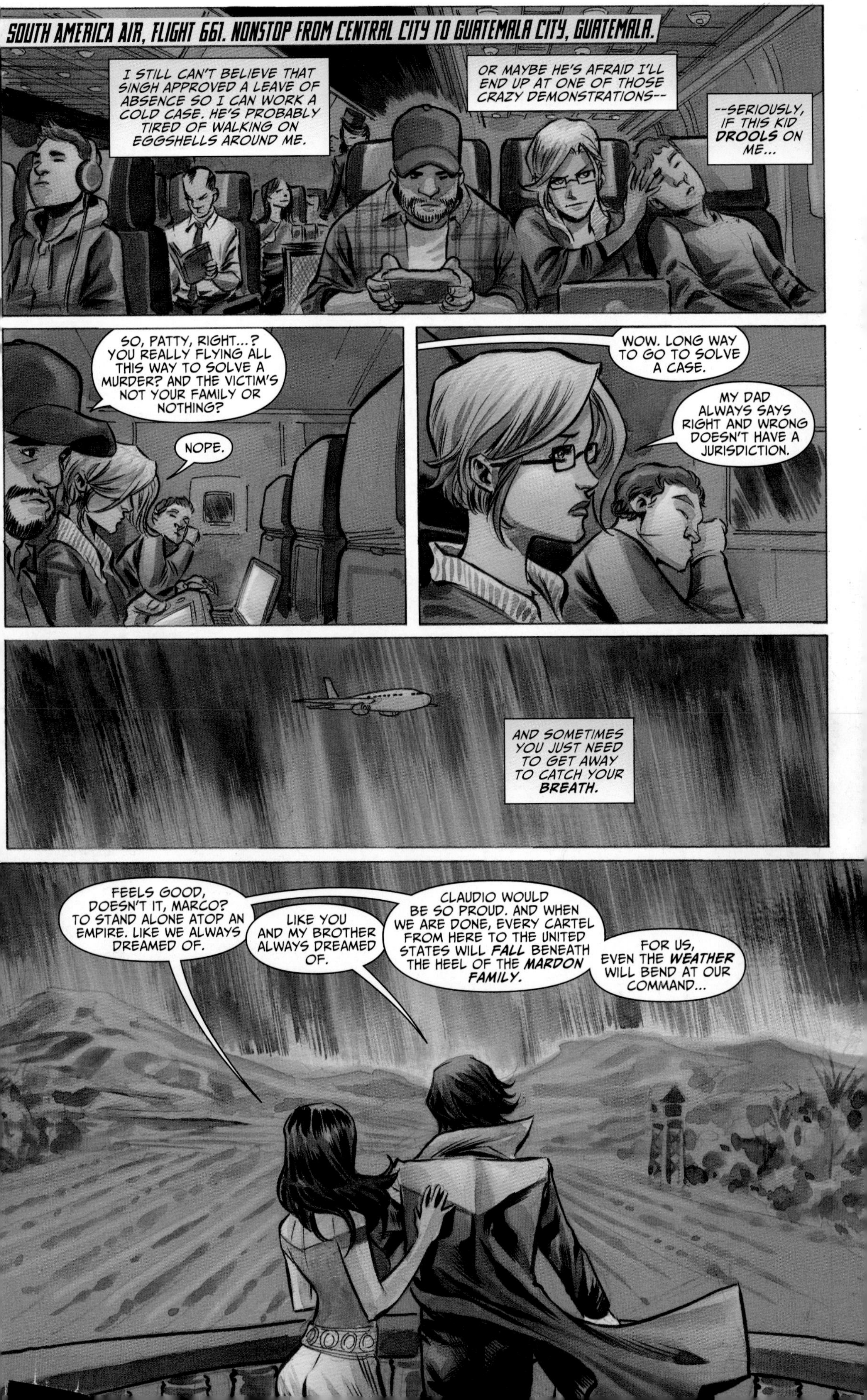
SOUTH AMERICA AIR, FLIGHT 661. NONSTOP FROM CENTRAL CITY TO GUATEMALA CITY, GUATEMALA.
I STILL CAN'T BELIEVE THAT SINGH APPROVED A LEAVE OF ABSENCE SO I CAN WORK A COLD CASE. HE'S PROBABLY TIRED OF WALKING ON EGGSHELLS AROUND ME.
OR MAYBE HE'S AFRAID I'LL END UP AT ONE OF THOSE CRAZY DEMONSTRATIONS--
--SERIOUSLY, IF THIS KID DROOLS ON ME...
SO, PATTY, RIGHT...? YOU REALLY FLYING ALL THIS WAY TO SOLVE A MURDER? AND THE VICTIM'S NOT YOUR FAMILY OR NOTHING?
NOPE.
WOW. LONG WAY TO GO TO SOLVE A CASE.
MY DAD ALWAYS SAYS RIGHT AND WRONG DOESN'T HAVE A JURISDICTION.
AND SOMETIMES YOU JUST NEED TO GET AWAY TO CATCH YOUR BREATH.
FEELS GOOD, DOESN'T IT, MARCO? TO STAND ALONE ATOP AN EMPIRE. LIKE WE ALWAYS DREAMED OF.
LIKE YOU AND MY BROTHER ALWAYS DREAMED OF.
CLAUDIO WOULD BE SO PROUD. AND WHEN WE ARE DONE, EVERY CARTEL FROM HERE TO THE UNITED STATES WILL FALL BENEATH THE HEEL OF THE MARDON FAMILY.
FOR US, EVEN THE WEATHER WILL BEND AT OUR COMMAND...

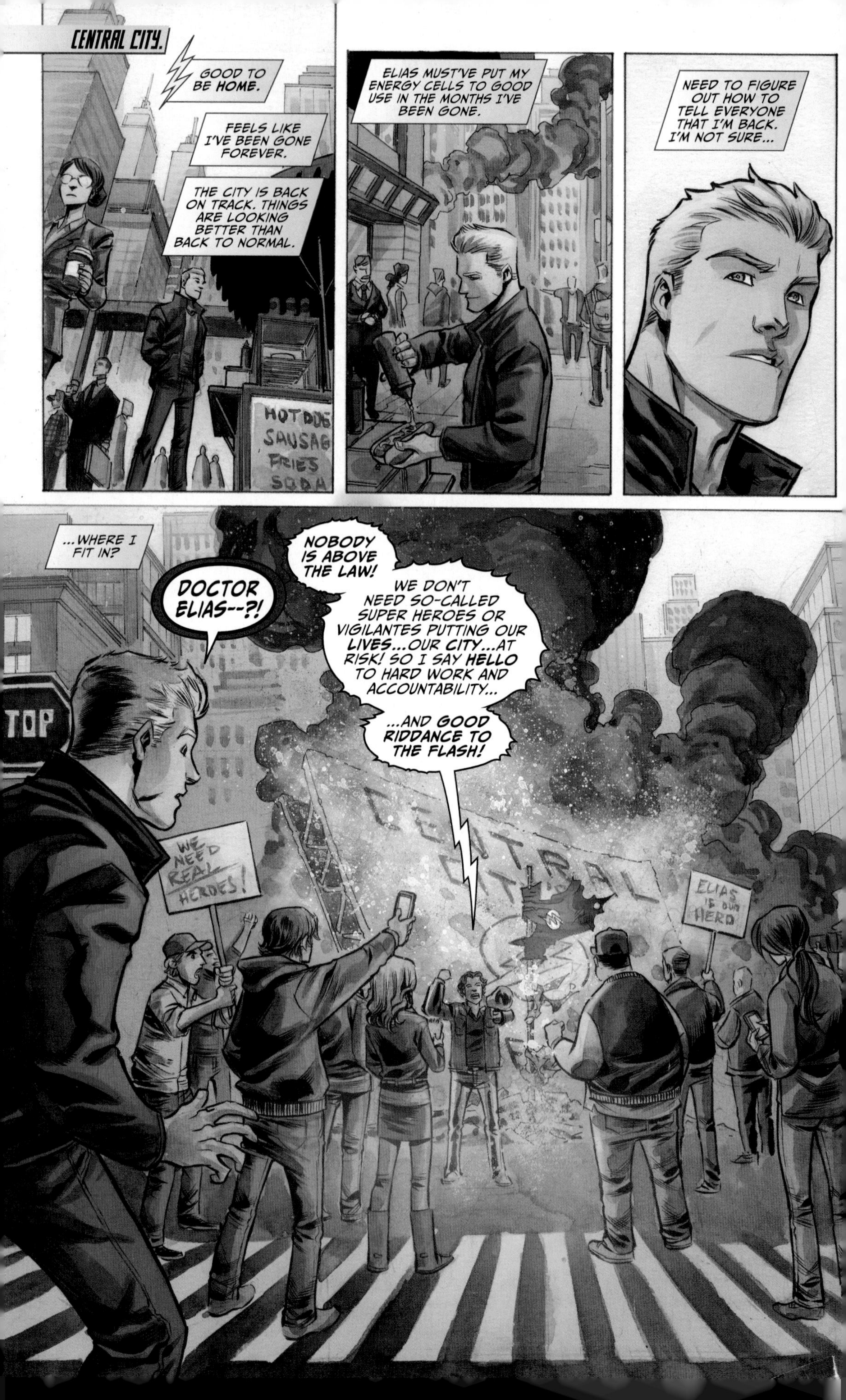
CENTRAL CITY.
GOOD TO BE HOME.
FEELS LIKE I'VE BEEN GONE FOREVER.
THE CITY IS BACK ON TRACK. THINGS ARE LOOKING BETTER THAN BACK TO NORMAL.
HOT DOG
SAUSAG
FRIES
SODA
ELIAS MUST'VE PUT MY ENERGY CELLS TO GOOD USE IN THE MONTHS I'VE BEEN GONE.
NEED TO FIGURE OUT HOW TO TELL EVERYONE THAT I'M BACK. I'M NOT SURE...
...WHERE I FIT IN?
DOCTOR ELIAS--?!
NOBODY IS ABOVE THE LAW!
WE DON'T NEED SO-CALLED SUPER HEROES OR VIGILANTES PUTTING OUR LIVES...OUR CITY...AT RISK! SO I SAY HELLO TO HARD WORK AND ACCOUNTABILITY...
...AND GOOD RIDDANCE TO THE FLASH!
WE NEED REAL HEROES!
ELIAS IS OUR HERO
TOP

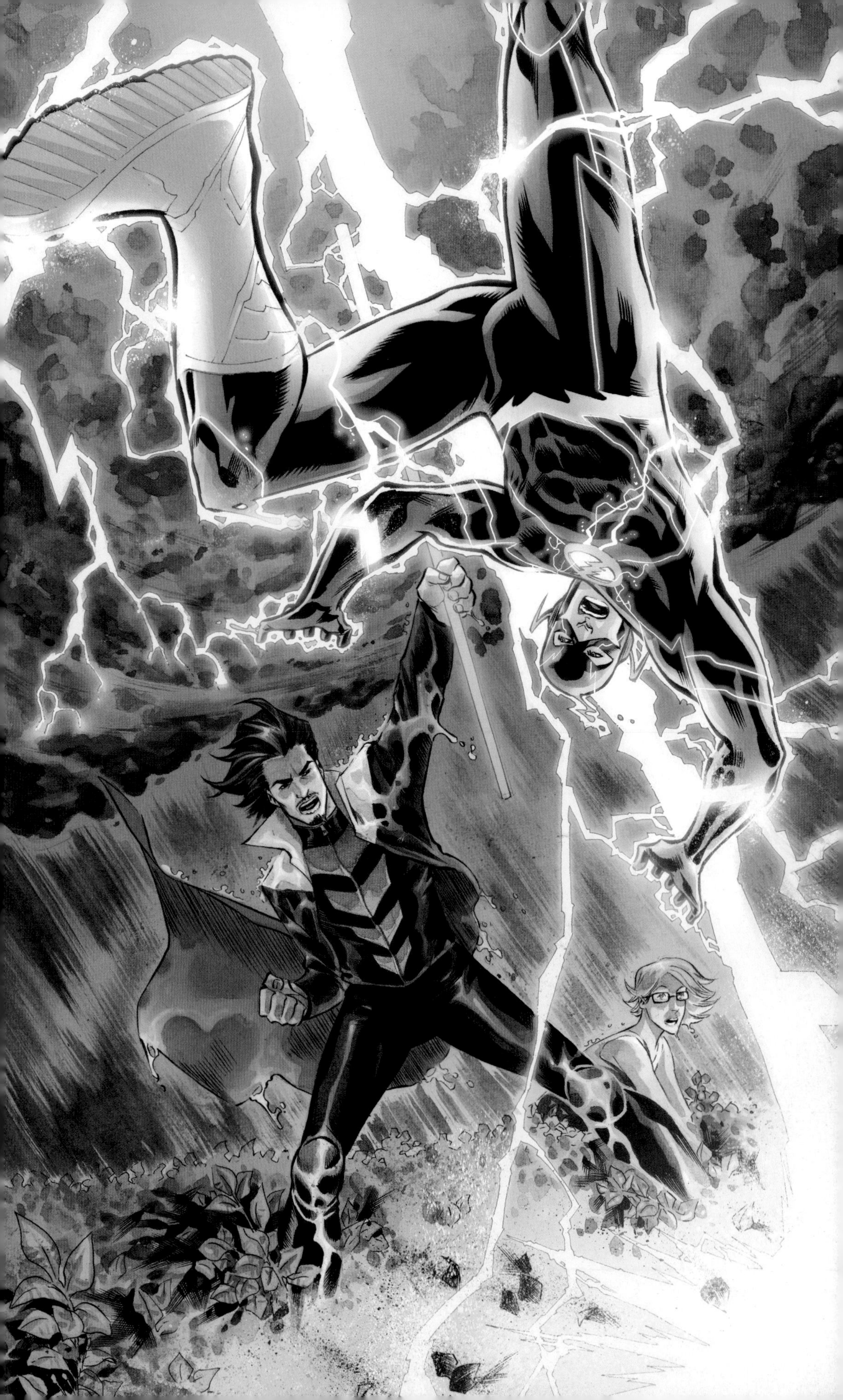

FRANCIS MANAPUL & BRIAN BUCCELLATO writers MARCUS TO penciler RAY McCARTHY inker

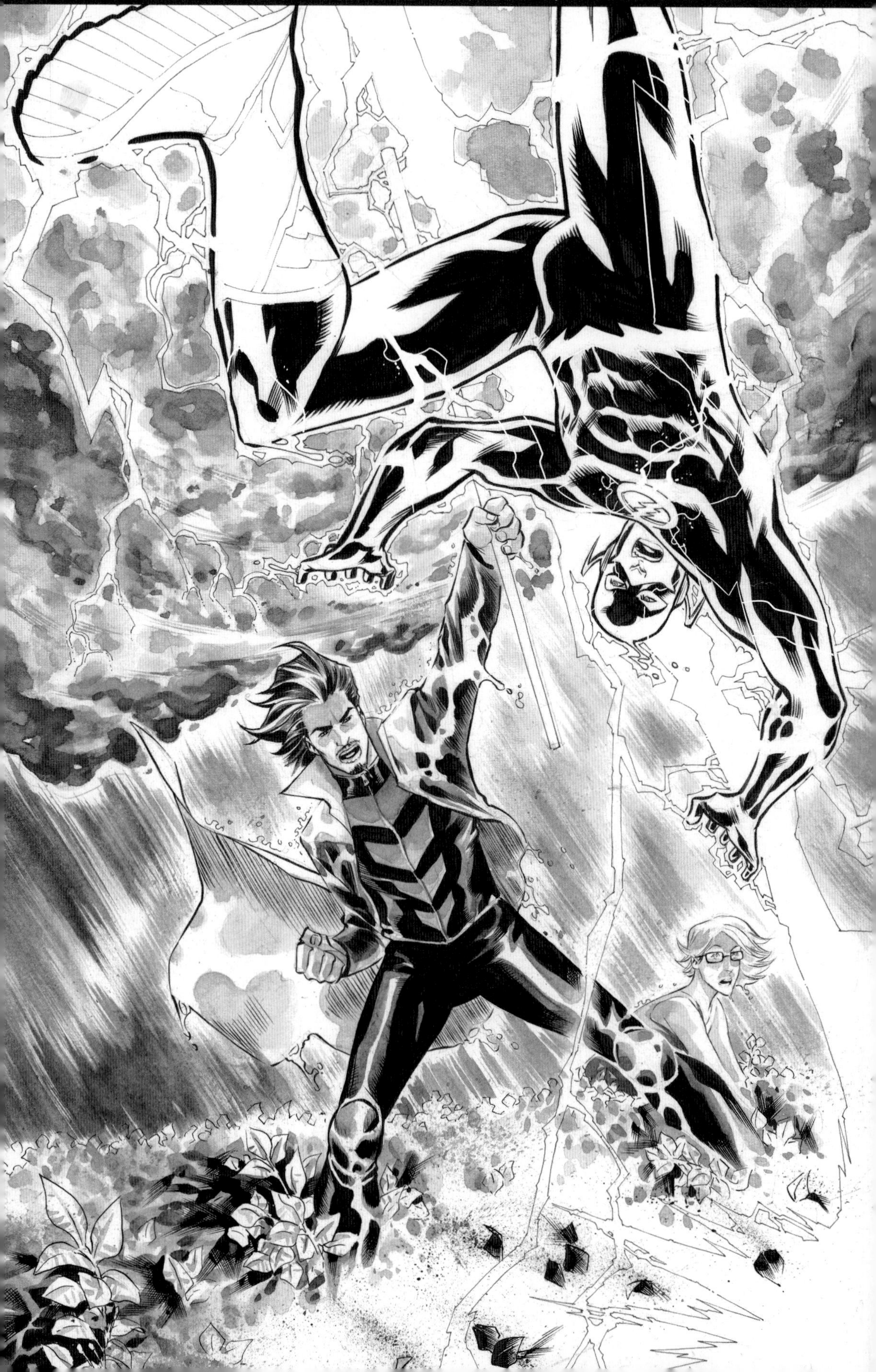

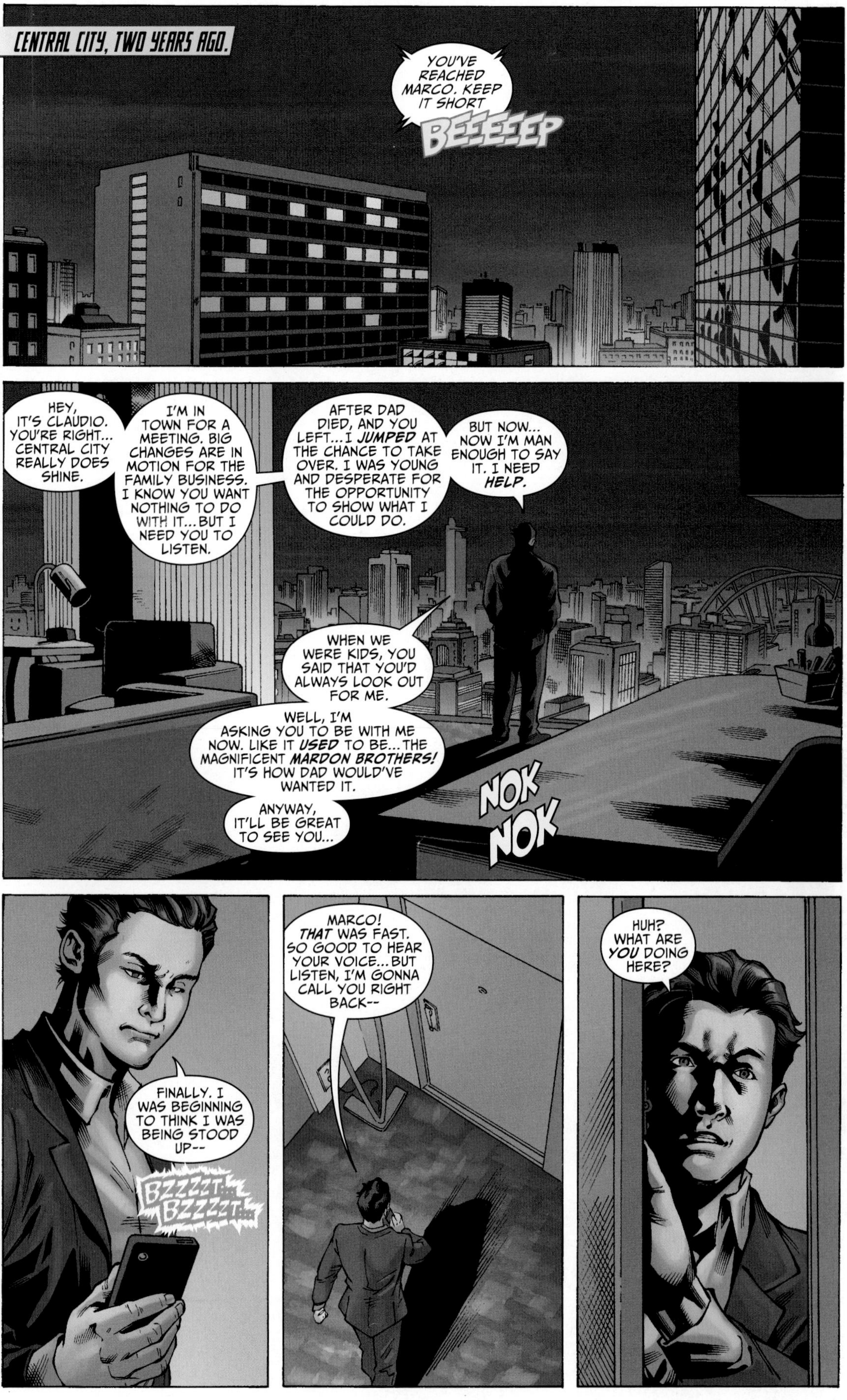
CENTRAL CITY, TWO YEARS AGO.
YOU'VE REACHED MARCO. KEEP IT SHORT
BEEEEEP
HEY, IT'S CLAUDIO. YOU'RE RIGHT... CENTRAL CITY REALLY DOES SHINE.
I'M IN TOWN FOR A MEETING. BIG CHANGES ARE IN MOTION FOR THE FAMILY BUSINESS. I KNOW YOU WANT NOTHING TO DO WITH IT...BUT I NEED YOU TO LISTEN.
AFTER DAD DIED, AND YOU LEFT...I JUMPED AT THE CHANCE TO TAKE OVER. I WAS YOUNG AND DESPERATE FOR THE OPPORTUNITY TO SHOW WHAT I COULD DO.
BUT NOW... NOW I'M MAN ENOUGH TO SAY IT. I NEED HELP.
WHEN WE WERE KIDS, YOU SAID THAT YOU'D ALWAYS LOOK OUT FOR ME.
WELL, I'M ASKING YOU TO BE WITH ME NOW. LIKE IT USED TO BE...THE MAGNIFICENT MARDON BROTHERS! IT'S HOW DAD WOULD'VE WANTED IT.
ANYWAY, IT'LL BE GREAT TO SEE YOU...
NOK NOK
FINALLY. I WAS BEGINNING TO THINK I WAS BEING STOOD UP--
BZZZZT... BZZZZT...
MARCO! THAT WAS FAST. SO GOOD TO HEAR YOUR VOICE...BUT LISTEN, I'M GONNA CALL YOU RIGHT BACK--
HUH? WHAT ARE YOU DOING HERE?

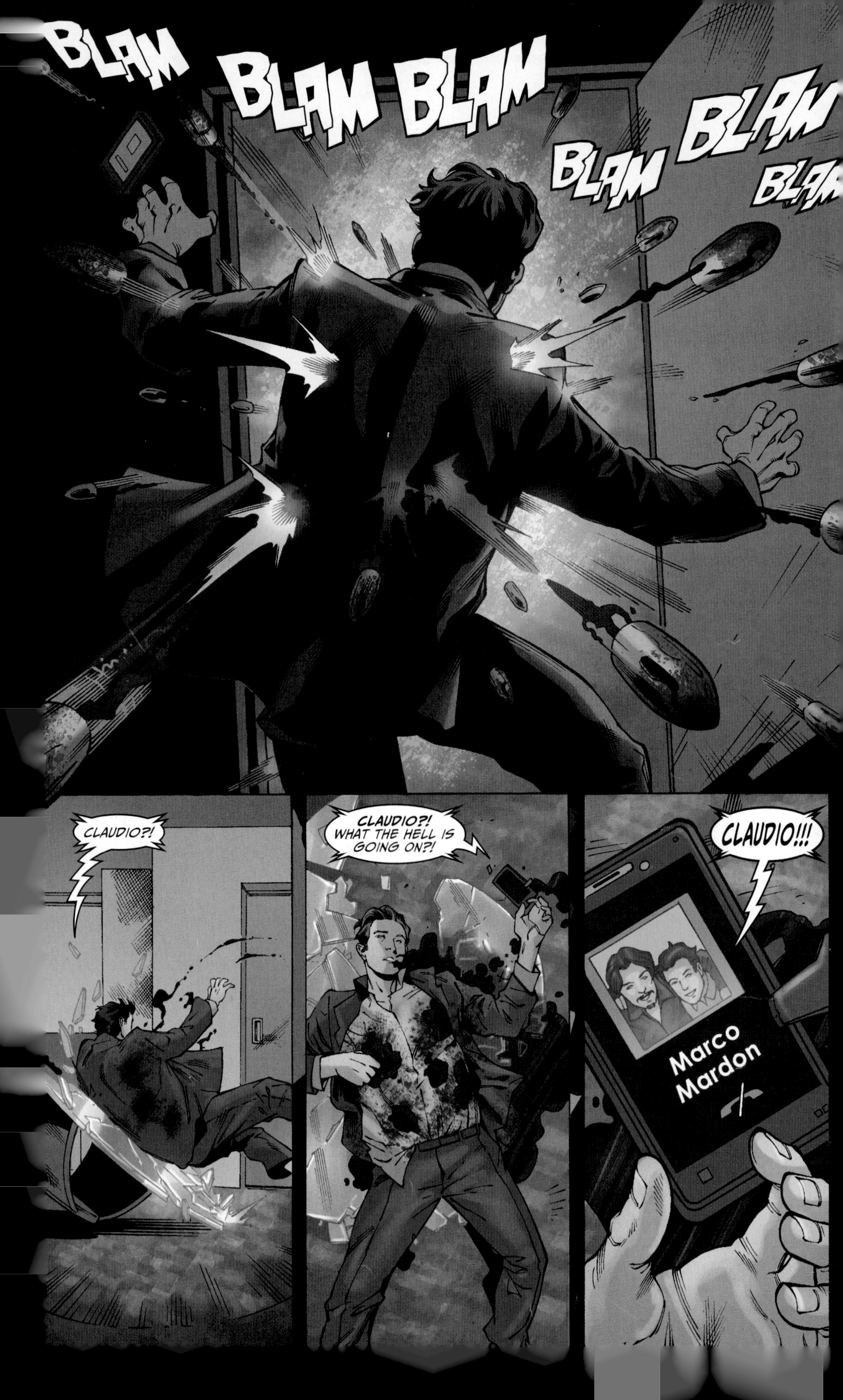
BLAM
BLAM BLAM
BLAM BLAM
BLAM
CLAUDIO?!
CLAUDIO?! WHAT THE HELL IS GOING ON?!
CLAUDIO!!!
Marco Mardon

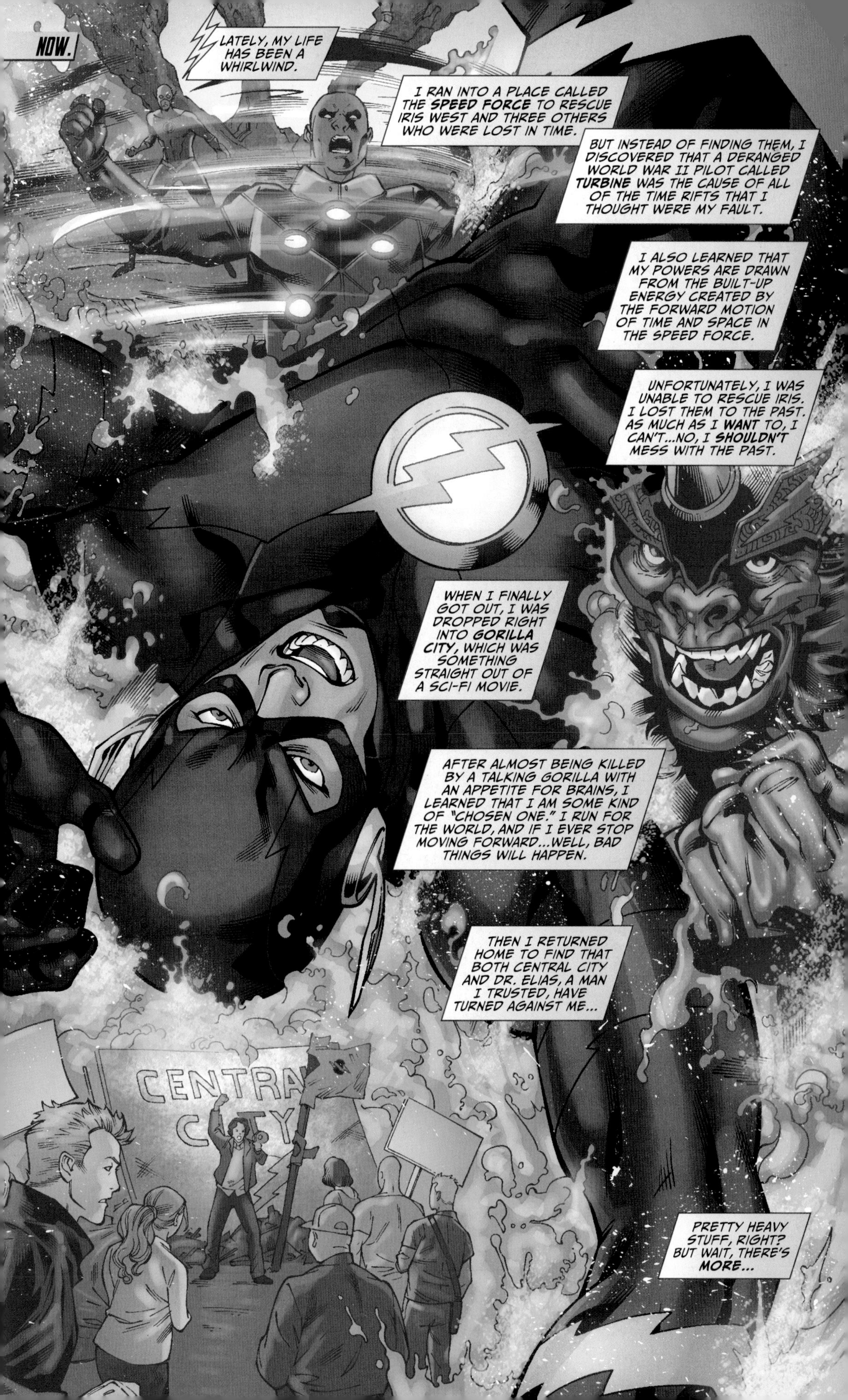
NOW.
LATELY, MY LIFE HAS BEEN A WHIRLWIND.
I RAN INTO A PLACE CALLED THE SPEED FORCE TO RESCUE IRIS WEST AND THREE OTHERS WHO WERE LOST IN TIME.
BUT INSTEAD OF FINDING THEM, I DISCOVERED THAT A DERANGED WORLD WAR II PILOT CALLED TURBINE WAS THE CAUSE OF ALL OF THE TIME RIFTS THAT I THOUGHT WERE MY FAULT.
I ALSO LEARNED THAT MY POWERS ARE DRAWN FROM THE BUILT-UP ENERGY CREATED BY THE FORWARD MOTION OF TIME AND SPACE IN THE SPEED FORCE.
UNFORTUNATELY, I WAS UNABLE TO RESCUE IRIS. I LOST THEM TO THE PAST. AS MUCH AS I WANT TO, I CAN'T...NO, I SHOULDN'T MESS WITH THE PAST.
WHEN I FINALLY GOT OUT, I WAS DROPPED RIGHT INTO GORILLA CITY, WHICH WAS SOMETHING STRAIGHT OUT OF A SCI-FI MOVIE.
AFTER ALMOST BEING KILLED BY A TALKING GORILLA WITH AN APPETITE FOR BRAINS, I LEARNED THAT I AM SOME KIND OF "CHOSEN ONE." I RUN FOR THE WORLD, AND IF I EVER STOP MOVING FORWARD...WELL, BAD THINGS WILL HAPPEN.
THEN I RETURNED HOME TO FIND THAT BOTH CENTRAL CITY AND DR. ELIAS, A MAN I TRUSTED, HAVE TURNED AGAINST ME...
PRETTY HEAVY STUFF, RIGHT? BUT WAIT, THERE'S MORE...

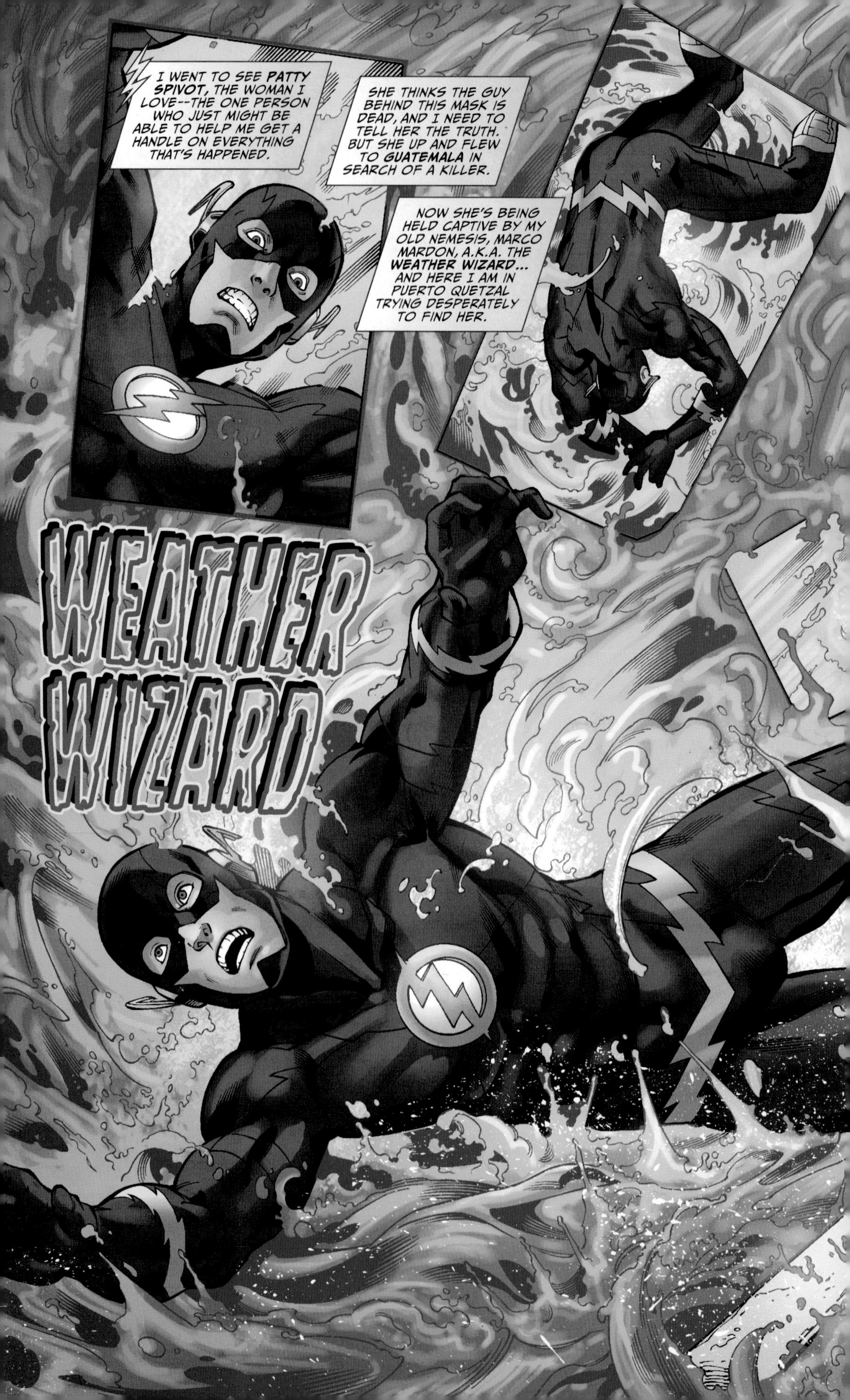
I WENT TO SEE PATTY SPIVOT, THE WOMAN I LOVE--THE ONE PERSON WHO JUST MIGHT BE ABLE TO HELP ME GET A HANDLE ON EVERYTHING THAT'S HAPPENED.
SHE THINKS THE GUY BEHIND THIS MASK IS DEAD, AND I NEED TO TELL HER THE TRUTH. BUT SHE UP AND FLEW TO GUATEMALA IN SEARCH OF A KILLER.
NOW SHE'S BEING HELD CAPTIVE BY MY OLD NEMESIS, MARCO MARDON, A.K.A. THE WEATHER WIZARD... AND HERE I AM IN PUERTO QUETZAL TRYING DESPERATELY TO FIND HER.
WEATHER WIZARD

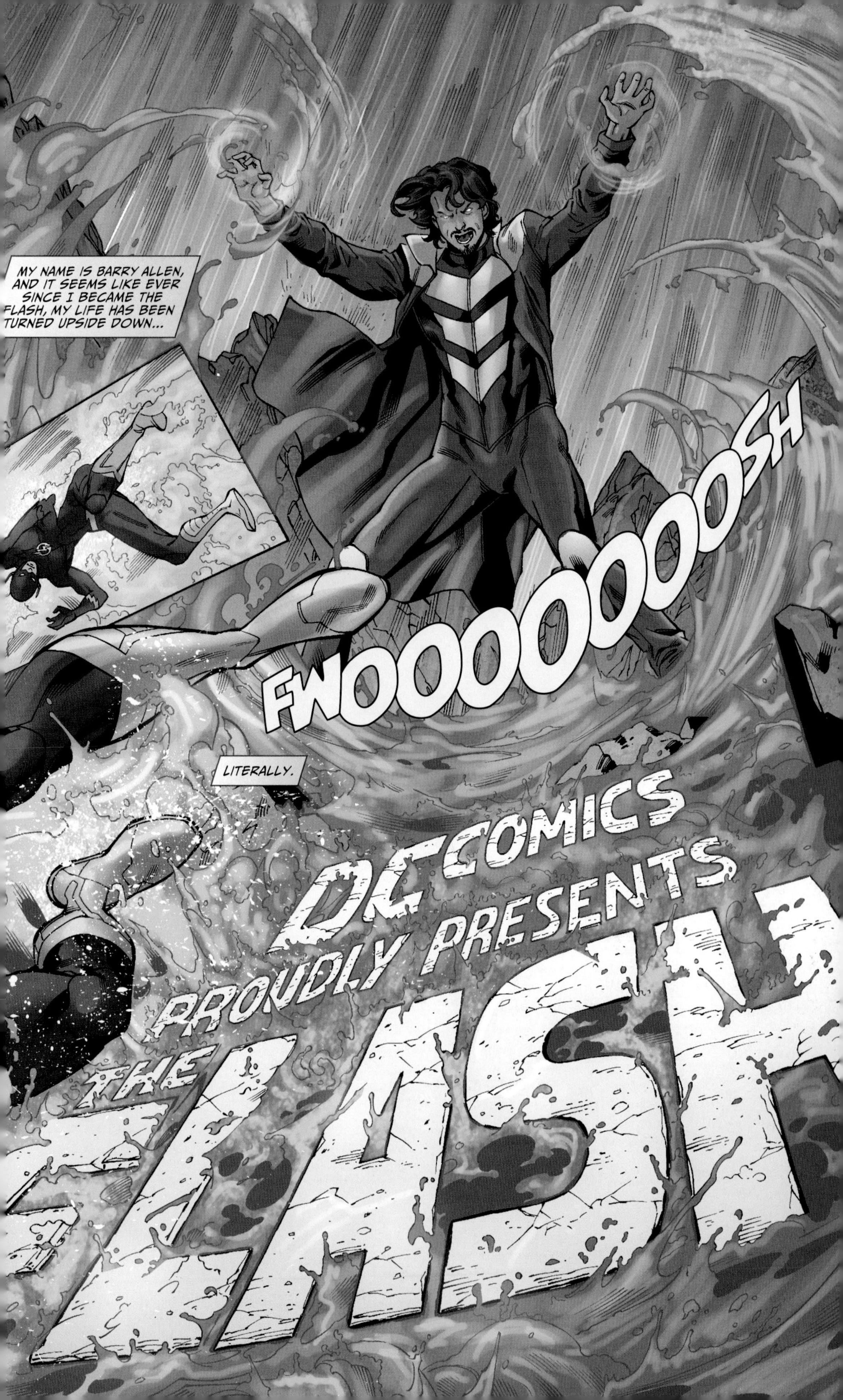

MY NAME IS BARRY ALLEN, AND IT SEEMS LIKE EVER SINCE I BECAME THE FLASH, MY LIFE HAS BEEN TURNED UPSIDE DOWN...
FWOOOOOOOOOSH
LITERALLY.
DC COMICS PROUDLY PRESENTS
THE FLASH

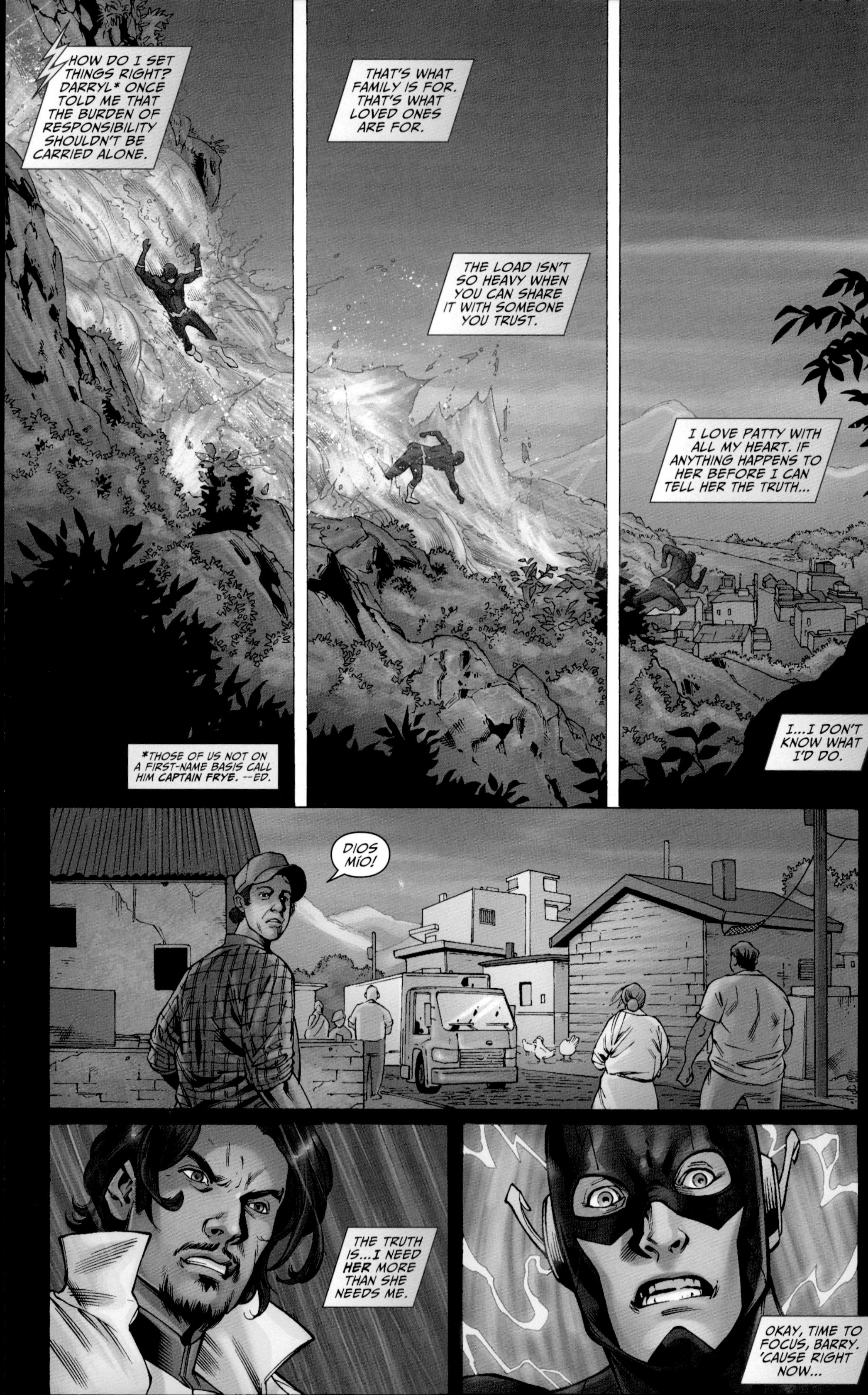
HOW DO I SET THINGS RIGHT? DARRYL* ONCE TOLD ME THAT THE BURDEN OF RESPONSIBILITY SHOULDN'T BE CARRIED ALONE.
*THOSE OF US NOT ON A FIRST-NAME BASIS CALL HIM CAPTAIN FRYE. --ED.
THAT'S WHAT FAMILY IS FOR. THAT'S WHAT LOVED ONES ARE FOR.
THE LOAD ISN'T SO HEAVY WHEN YOU CAN SHARE IT WITH SOMEONE YOU TRUST.
I LOVE PATTY WITH ALL MY HEART. IF ANYTHING HAPPENS TO HER BEFORE I CAN TELL HER THE TRUTH...
I...I DON'T KNOW WHAT I'D DO.
DIOS MÍO!
THE TRUTH IS...I NEED HER MORE THAN SHE NEEDS ME.
OKAY, TIME TO FOCUS, BARRY. 'CAUSE RIGHT NOW...

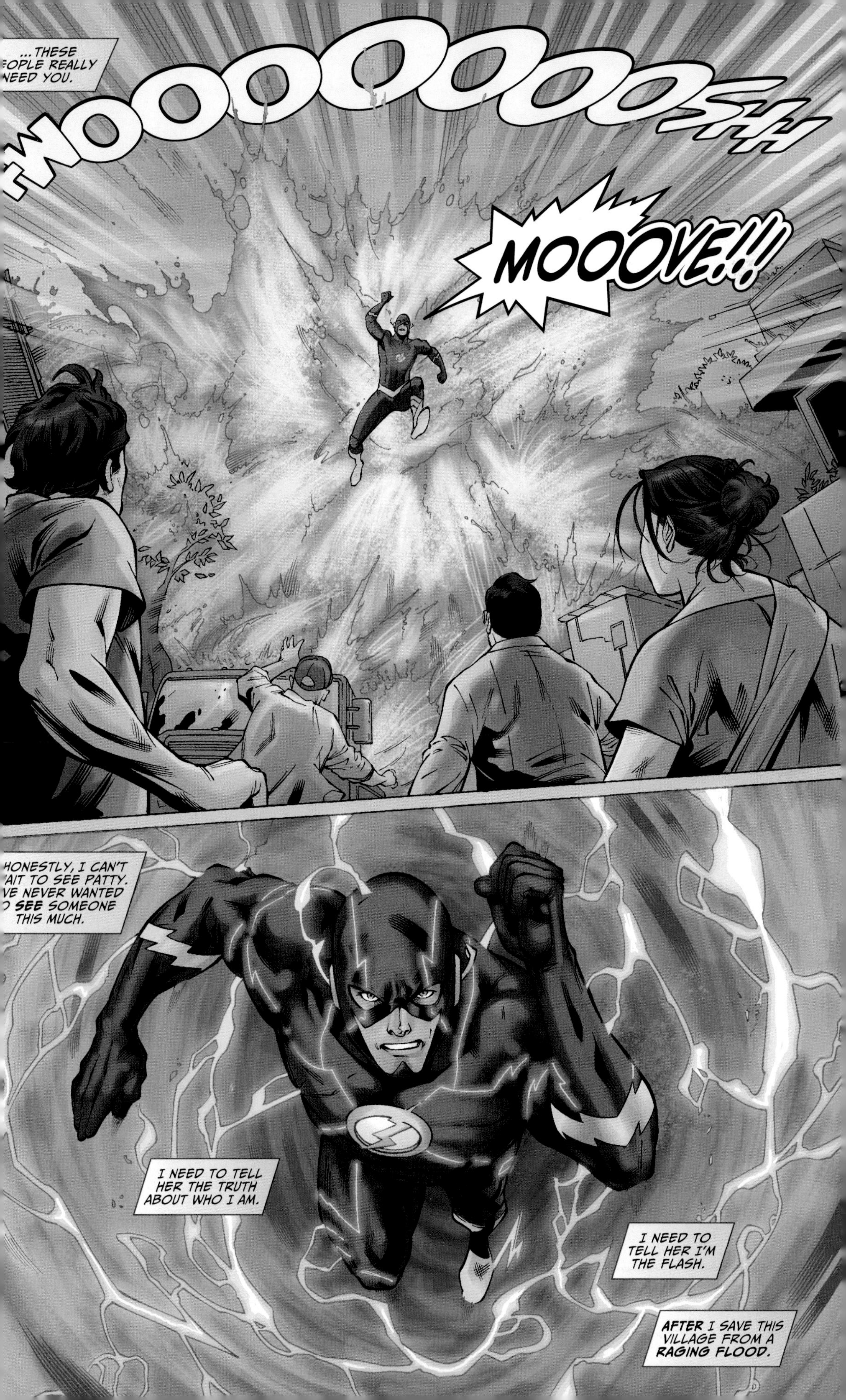
...THESE
EOPLE REALLY
NEED YOU.
WOOOOOOOOSH
MOOOVE!!
HONESTLY, I CAN'T
AIT TO SEE PATTY.
VE NEVER WANTED
O SEE SOMEONE
THIS MUCH.
I NEED TO TELL HER THE TRUTH ABOUT WHO I AM.
I NEED TO TELL HER I'M THE FLASH.
AFTER I SAVE THIS VILLAGE FROM A RAGING FLOOD.

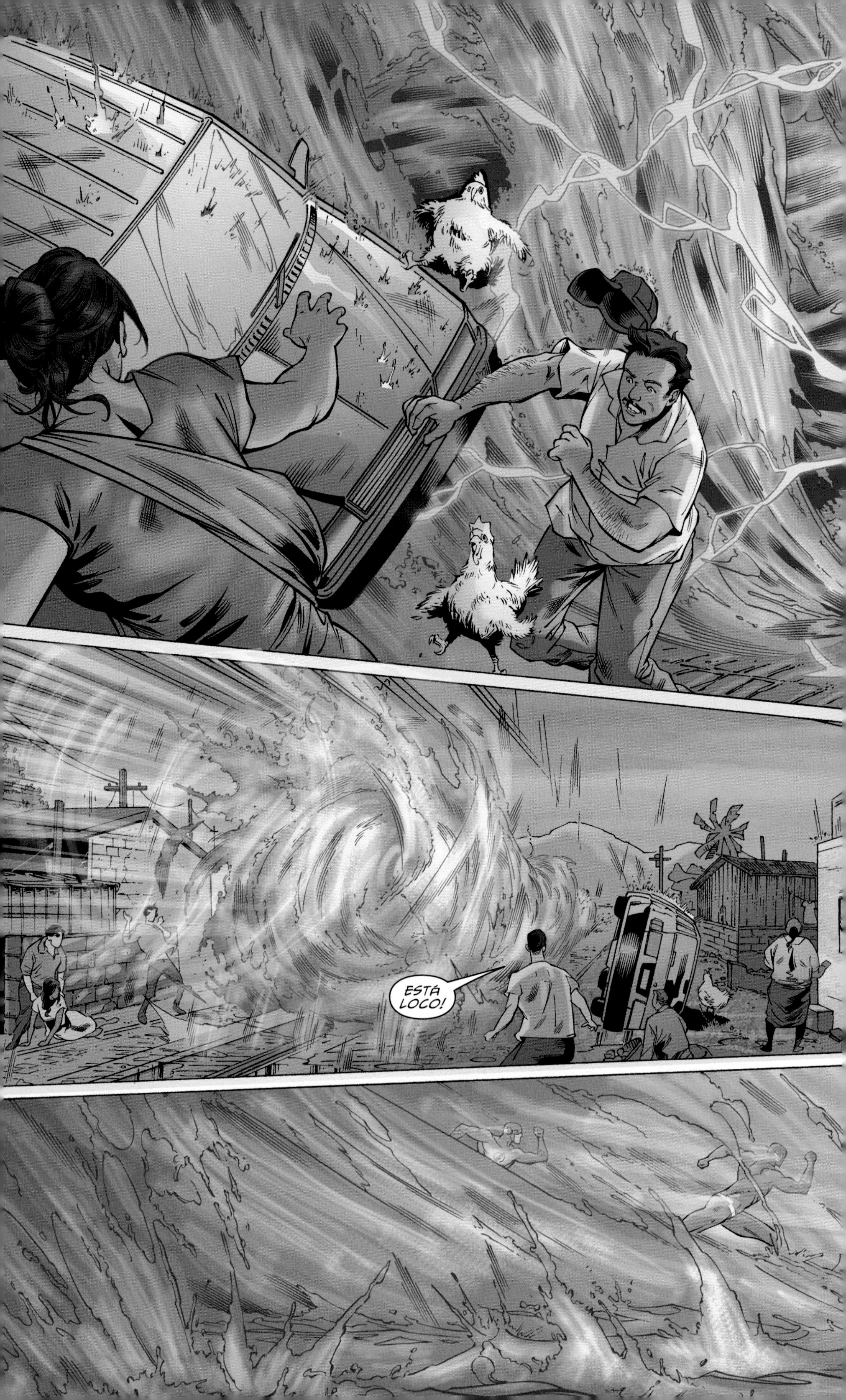
ESTÁ LOCO!

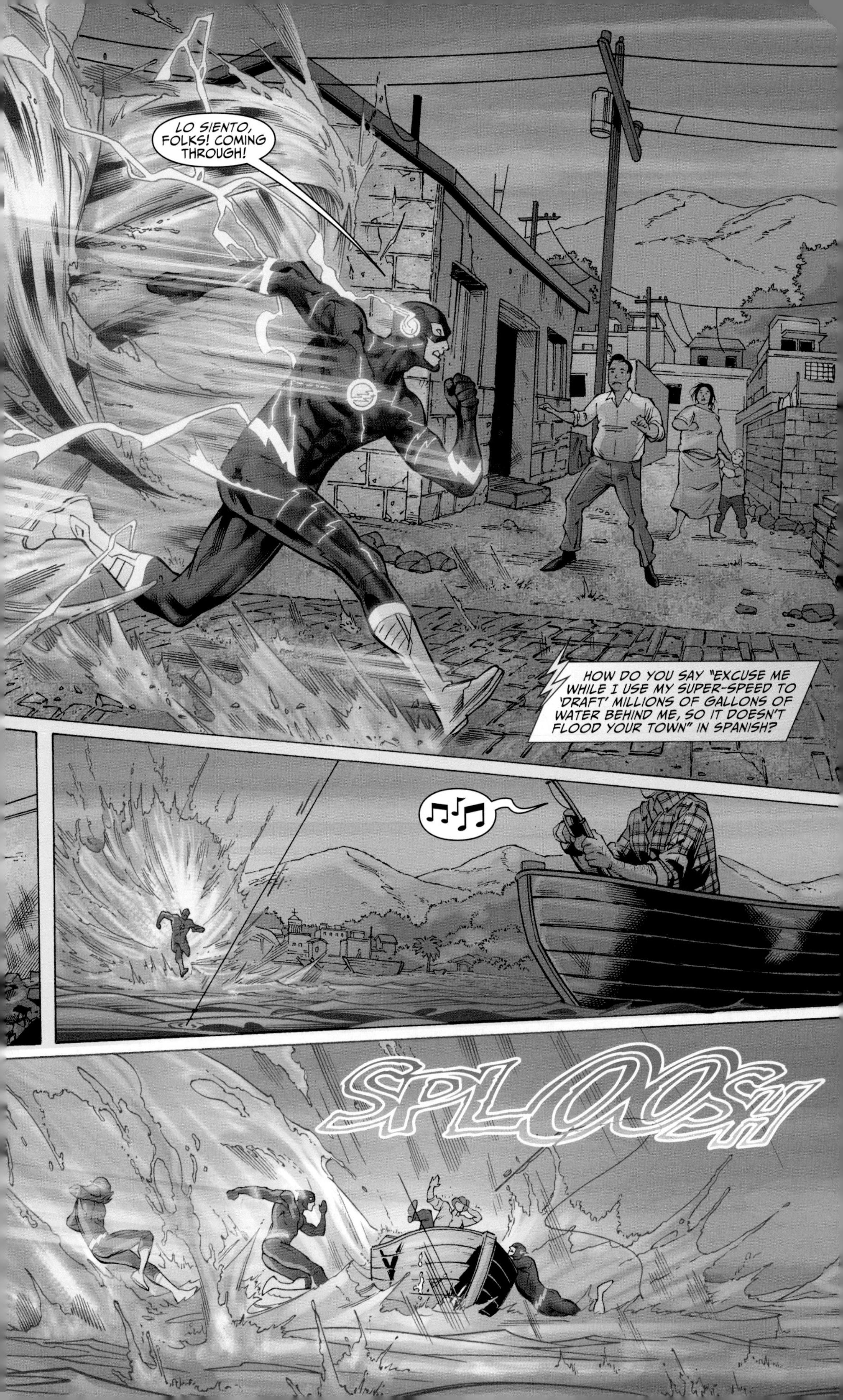
LO SIENTO, FOLKS! COMING THROUGH!
HOW DO YOU SAY "EXCUSE ME WHILE I USE MY SUPER-SPEED TO 'DRAFT' MILLIONS OF GALLONS OF WATER BEHIND ME, SO IT DOESN'T FLOOD YOUR TOWN" IN SPANISH?
SPLOOSH

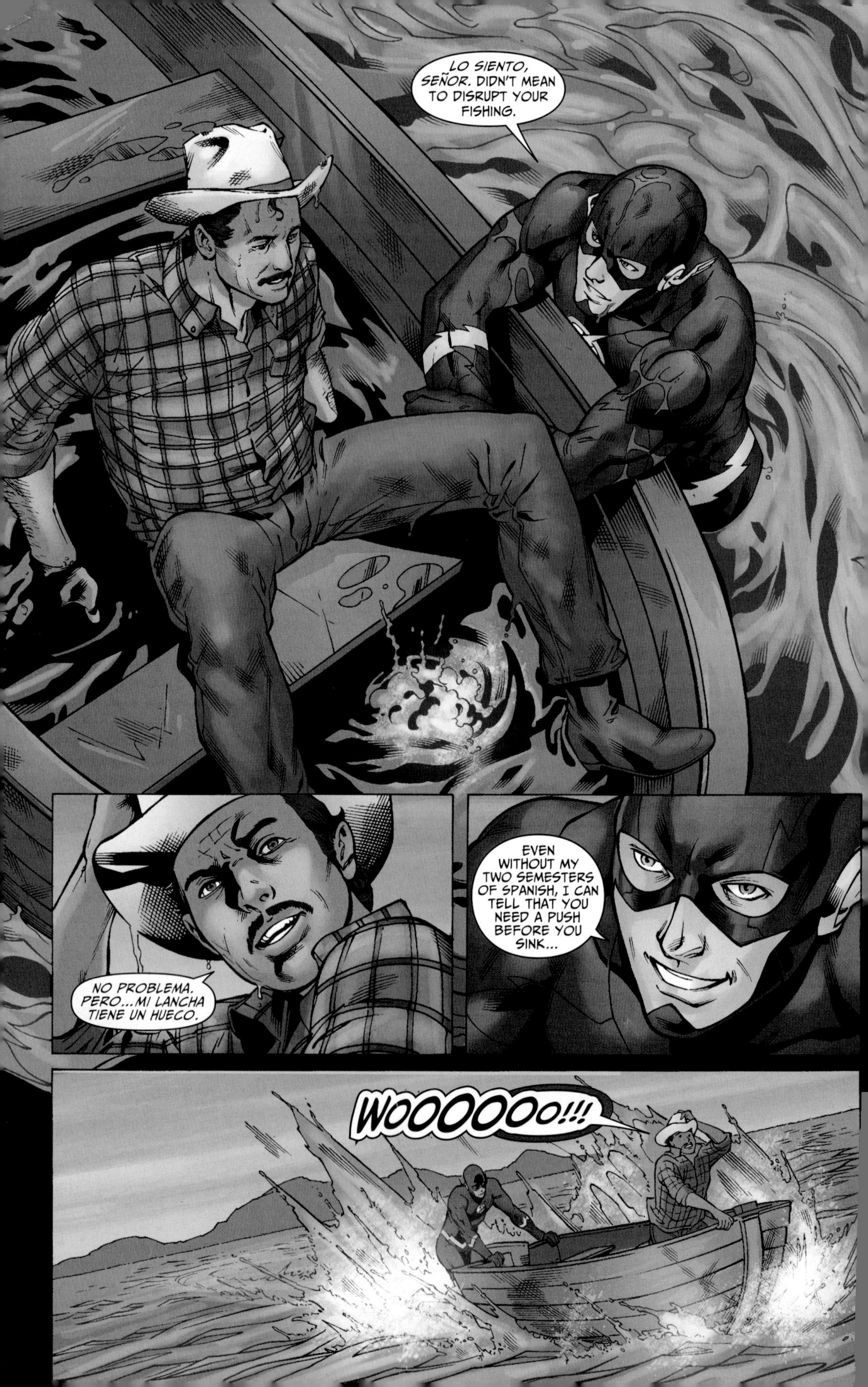
LO SIENTO, SEÑOR. DIDN'T MEAN TO DISRUPT YOUR FISHING.
NO PROBLEMA. PERO...MI LANCHA TIENE UN HUECO.
EVEN WITHOUT MY TWO SEMESTERS OF SPANISH, I CAN TELL THAT YOU NEED A PUSH BEFORE YOU SINK...
WOOOOOOO!!!

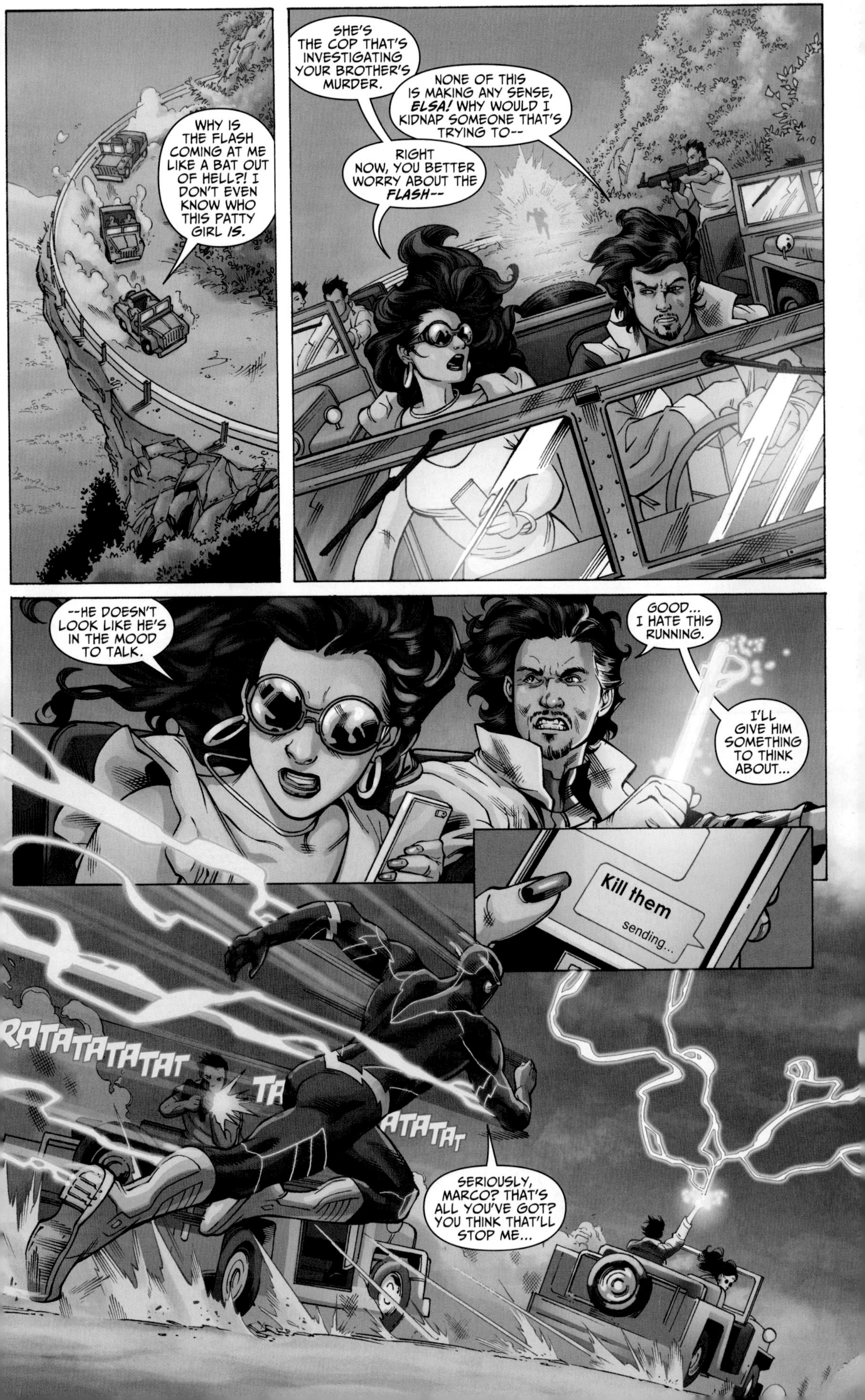

WHY IS THE FLASH COMING AT ME LIKE A BAT OUT OF HELL?! I DON'T EVEN KNOW WHO THIS PATTY GIRL IS.
SHE'S THE COP THAT'S INVESTIGATING YOUR BROTHER'S MURDER.
NONE OF THIS IS MAKING ANY SENSE, ELSA! WHY WOULD I KIDNAP SOMEONE THAT'S TRYING TO--
RIGHT NOW, YOU BETTER WORRY ABOUT THE FLASH--
--HE DOESN'T LOOK LIKE HE'S IN THE MOOD TO TALK.
GOOD... I HATE THIS RUNNING.
I'LL GIVE HIM SOMETHING TO THINK ABOUT...
Kill them
sending...
RATATATATAT
TA
ATATAT
SERIOUSLY, MARCO? THAT'S ALL YOU'VE GOT? YOU THINK THAT'LL STOP ME...

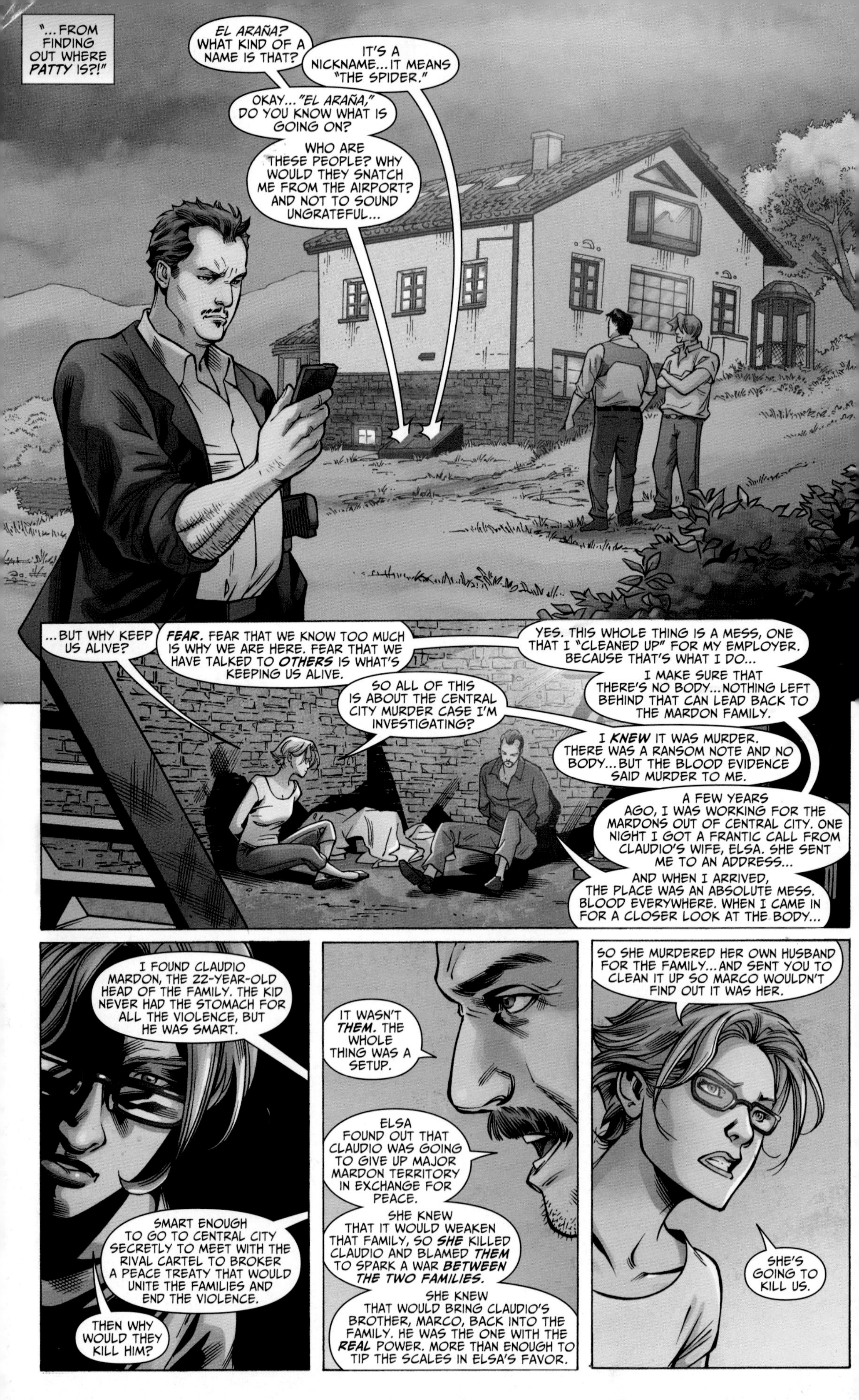
"...FROM FINDING OUT WHERE *PATTY* IS?!"
EL ARAÑA? WHAT KIND OF A NAME IS THAT?
IT'S A NICKNAME...IT MEANS "THE SPIDER."
OKAY..."*EL ARAÑA,*" DO YOU KNOW WHAT IS GOING ON?
WHO ARE THESE PEOPLE? WHY WOULD THEY SNATCH ME FROM THE AIRPORT? AND NOT TO SOUND UNGRATEFUL...
...BUT WHY KEEP US ALIVE?
FEAR. FEAR THAT WE KNOW TOO MUCH IS WHY WE ARE HERE. FEAR THAT WE HAVE TALKED TO ***OTHERS*** IS WHAT'S KEEPING US ALIVE.
SO ALL OF THIS IS ABOUT THE CENTRAL CITY MURDER CASE I'M INVESTIGATING?
YES. THIS WHOLE THING IS A MESS, ONE THAT I "CLEANED UP" FOR MY EMPLOYER. BECAUSE THAT'S WHAT I DO...
I MAKE SURE THAT THERE'S NO BODY...NOTHING LEFT BEHIND THAT CAN LEAD BACK TO THE MARDON FAMILY.
I ***KNEW*** IT WAS MURDER. THERE WAS A RANSOM NOTE AND NO BODY...BUT THE BLOOD EVIDENCE SAID MURDER TO ME.
A FEW YEARS AGO, I WAS WORKING FOR THE MARDONS OUT OF CENTRAL CITY. ONE NIGHT I GOT A FRANTIC CALL FROM CLAUDIO'S WIFE, ELSA. SHE SENT ME TO AN ADDRESS...
AND WHEN I ARRIVED, THE PLACE WAS AN ABSOLUTE MESS. BLOOD EVERYWHERE. WHEN I CAME IN FOR A CLOSER LOOK AT THE BODY...
I FOUND CLAUDIO MARDON, THE 22-YEAR-OLD HEAD OF THE FAMILY. THE KID NEVER HAD THE STOMACH FOR ALL THE VIOLENCE, BUT HE WAS SMART.
SMART ENOUGH TO GO TO CENTRAL CITY SECRETLY TO MEET WITH THE RIVAL CARTEL TO BROKER A PEACE TREATY THAT WOULD UNITE THE FAMILIES AND END THE VIOLENCE.
THEN WHY WOULD THEY KILL HIM?
IT WASN'T ***THEM.*** THE WHOLE THING WAS A SETUP.
ELSA FOUND OUT THAT CLAUDIO WAS GOING TO GIVE UP MAJOR MARDON TERRITORY IN EXCHANGE FOR PEACE.
SHE KNEW THAT IT WOULD WEAKEN THAT FAMILY, SO ***SHE*** KILLED CLAUDIO AND BLAMED ***THEM*** TO SPARK A WAR ***BETWEEN THE TWO FAMILIES.***
SHE KNEW THAT WOULD BRING CLAUDIO'S BROTHER, MARCO, BACK INTO THE FAMILY. HE WAS THE ONE WITH THE ***REAL*** POWER. MORE THAN ENOUGH TO TIP THE SCALES IN ELSA'S FAVOR.
SO SHE MURDERED HER OWN HUSBAND FOR THE FAMILY...AND SENT YOU TO CLEAN IT UP SO MARCO WOULDN'T FIND OUT IT WAS HER.
SHE'S GOING TO KILL US.

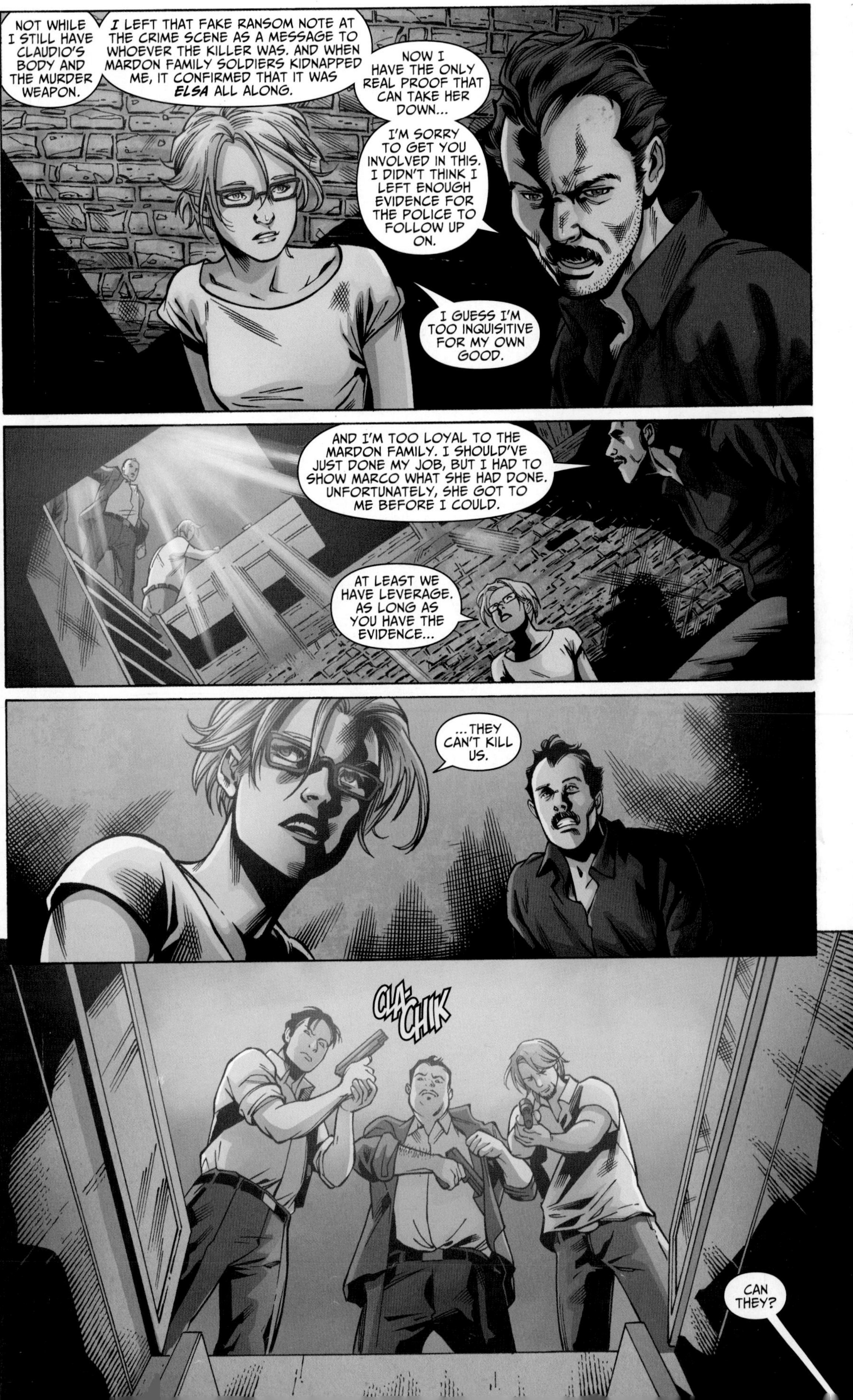
NOT WHILE I STILL HAVE CLAUDIO'S BODY AND THE MURDER WEAPON.
I LEFT THAT FAKE RANSOM NOTE AT THE CRIME SCENE AS A MESSAGE TO WHOEVER THE KILLER WAS. AND WHEN MARDON FAMILY SOLDIERS KIDNAPPED ME, IT CONFIRMED THAT IT WAS ELSA ALL ALONG.
NOW I HAVE THE ONLY REAL PROOF THAT CAN TAKE HER DOWN...
I'M SORRY TO GET YOU INVOLVED IN THIS. I DIDN'T THINK I LEFT ENOUGH EVIDENCE FOR THE POLICE TO FOLLOW UP ON.
I GUESS I'M TOO INQUISITIVE FOR MY OWN GOOD.
AND I'M TOO LOYAL TO THE MARDON FAMILY. I SHOULD'VE JUST DONE MY JOB, BUT I HAD TO SHOW MARCO WHAT SHE HAD DONE. UNFORTUNATELY, SHE GOT TO ME BEFORE I COULD.
AT LEAST WE HAVE LEVERAGE. AS LONG AS YOU HAVE THE EVIDENCE...
...THEY CAN'T KILL US.
CLA-CHIK
CAN THEY?

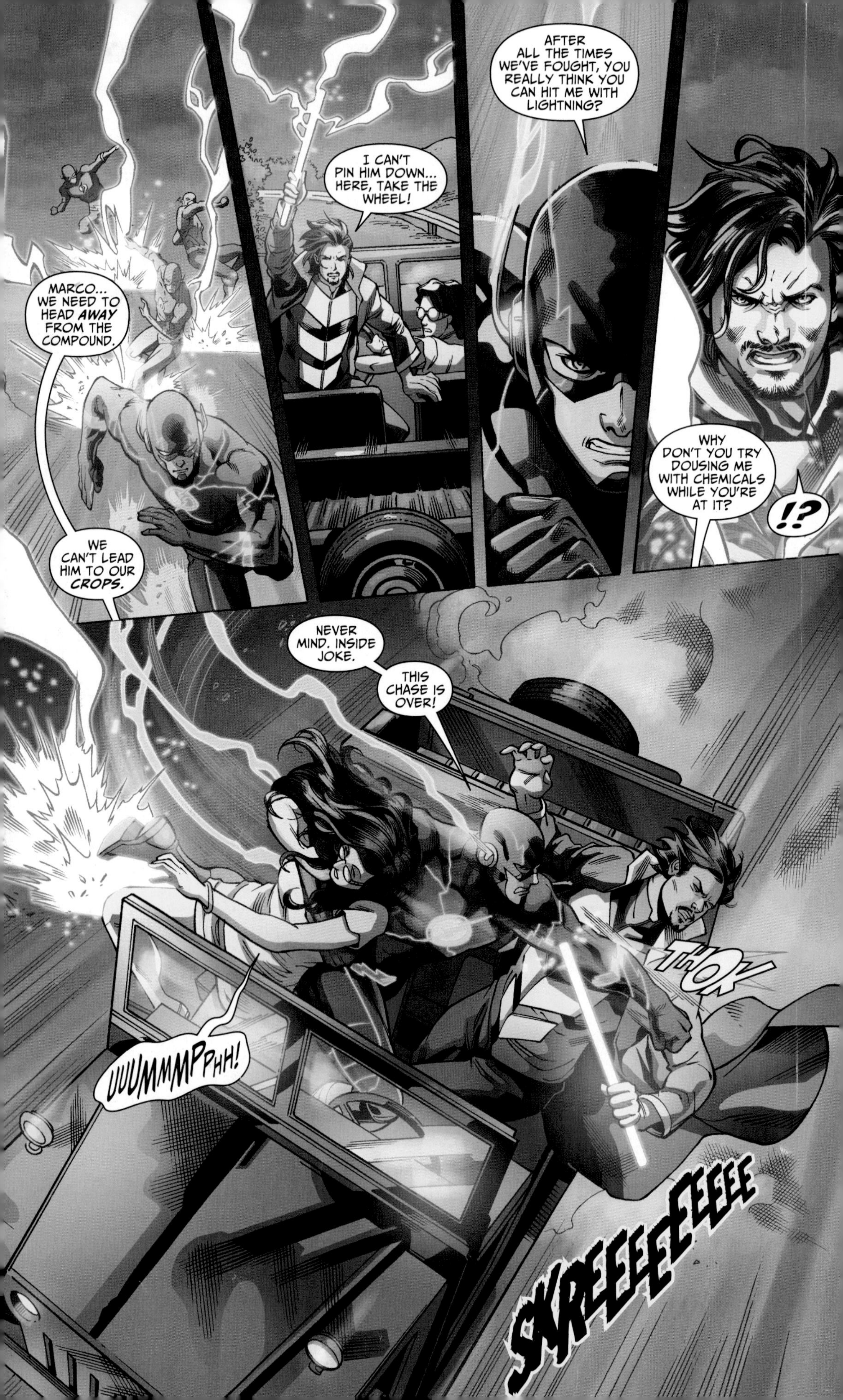

MARCO... WE NEED TO HEAD AWAY FROM THE COMPOUND.
WE CAN'T LEAD HIM TO OUR CROPS.
I CAN'T PIN HIM DOWN... HERE, TAKE THE WHEEL!
AFTER ALL THE TIMES WE'VE FOUGHT, YOU REALLY THINK YOU CAN HIT ME WITH LIGHTNING?
WHY DON'T YOU TRY DOUSING ME WITH CHEMICALS WHILE YOU'RE AT IT?
!?
NEVER MIND. INSIDE JOKE.
THIS CHASE IS OVER!
THOK
UUUMMMPHH!
SKREEEEEEEEE

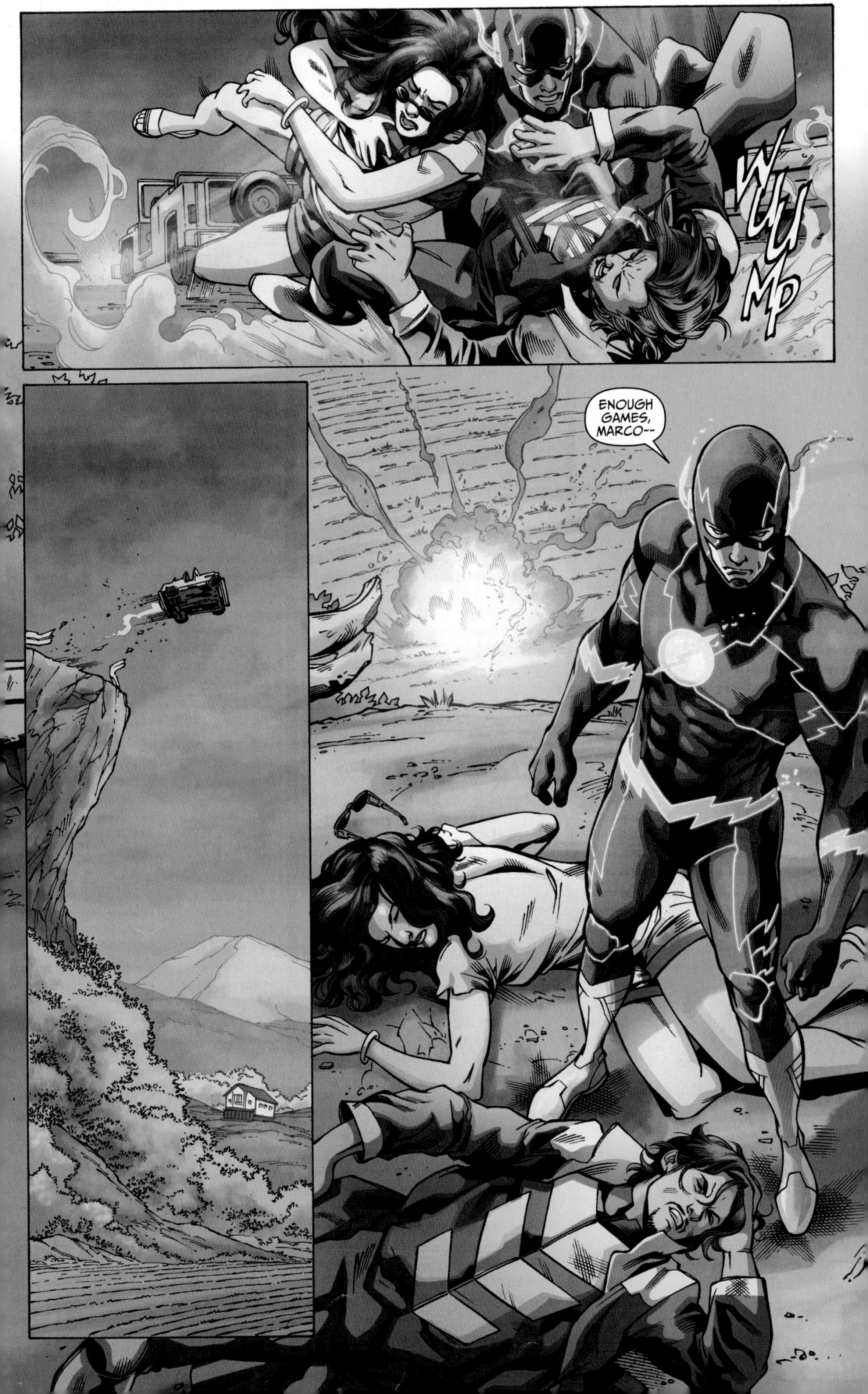
WUUMP
ENOUGH GAMES, MARCO--

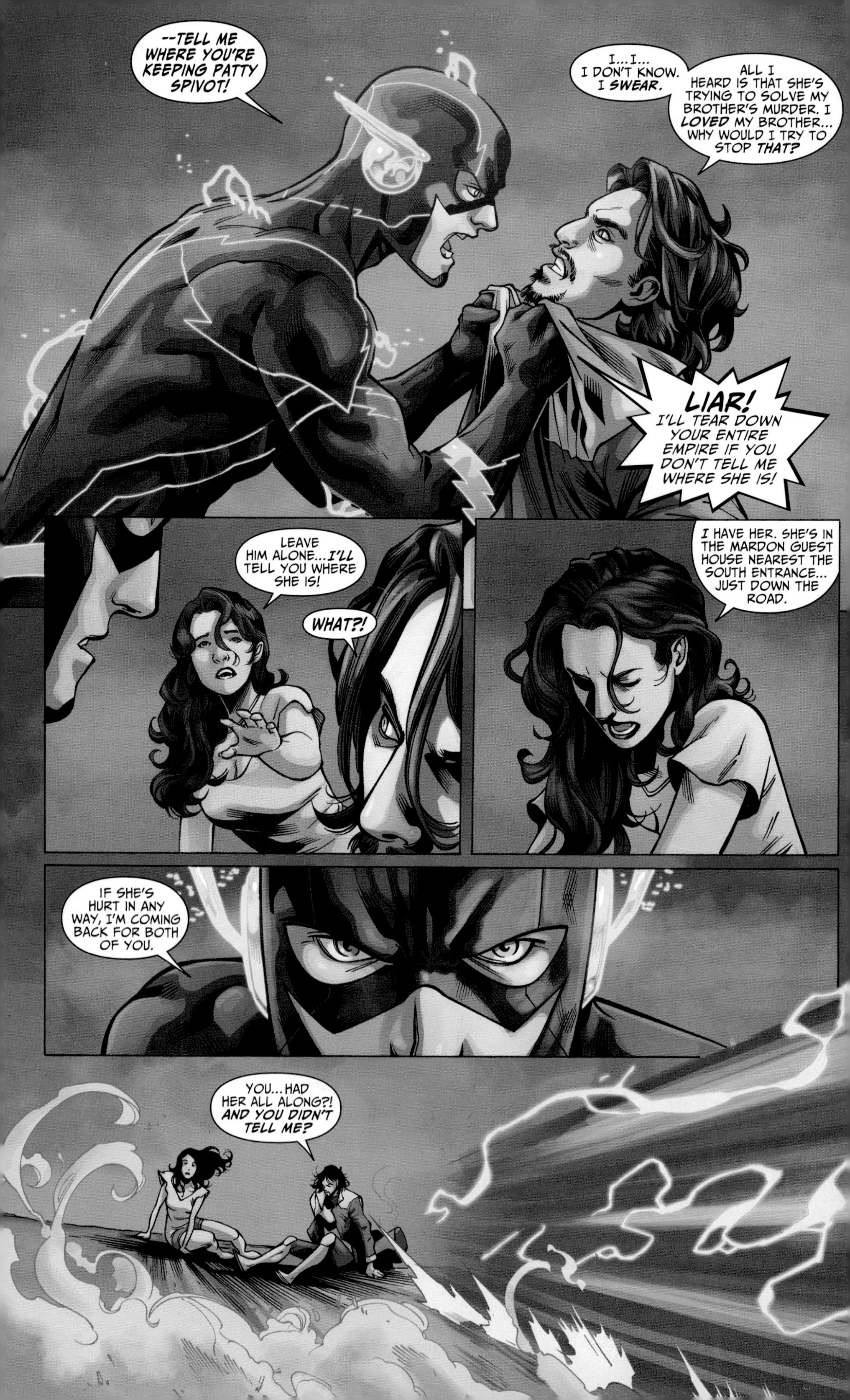
--TELL ME WHERE YOU'RE KEEPING PATTY SPIVOT!
I...I... I DON'T KNOW. I SWEAR.
ALL I HEARD IS THAT SHE'S TRYING TO SOLVE MY BROTHER'S MURDER. I LOVED MY BROTHER... WHY WOULD I TRY TO STOP THAT?
LIAR! I'LL TEAR DOWN YOUR ENTIRE EMPIRE IF YOU DON'T TELL ME WHERE SHE IS!
LEAVE HIM ALONE...I'LL TELL YOU WHERE SHE IS!
WHAT?!
I HAVE HER. SHE'S IN THE MARDON GUEST HOUSE NEAREST THE SOUTH ENTRANCE... JUST DOWN THE ROAD.
IF SHE'S HURT IN ANY WAY, I'M COMING BACK FOR BOTH OF YOU.
YOU...HAD HER ALL ALONG?! AND YOU DIDN'T TELL ME?

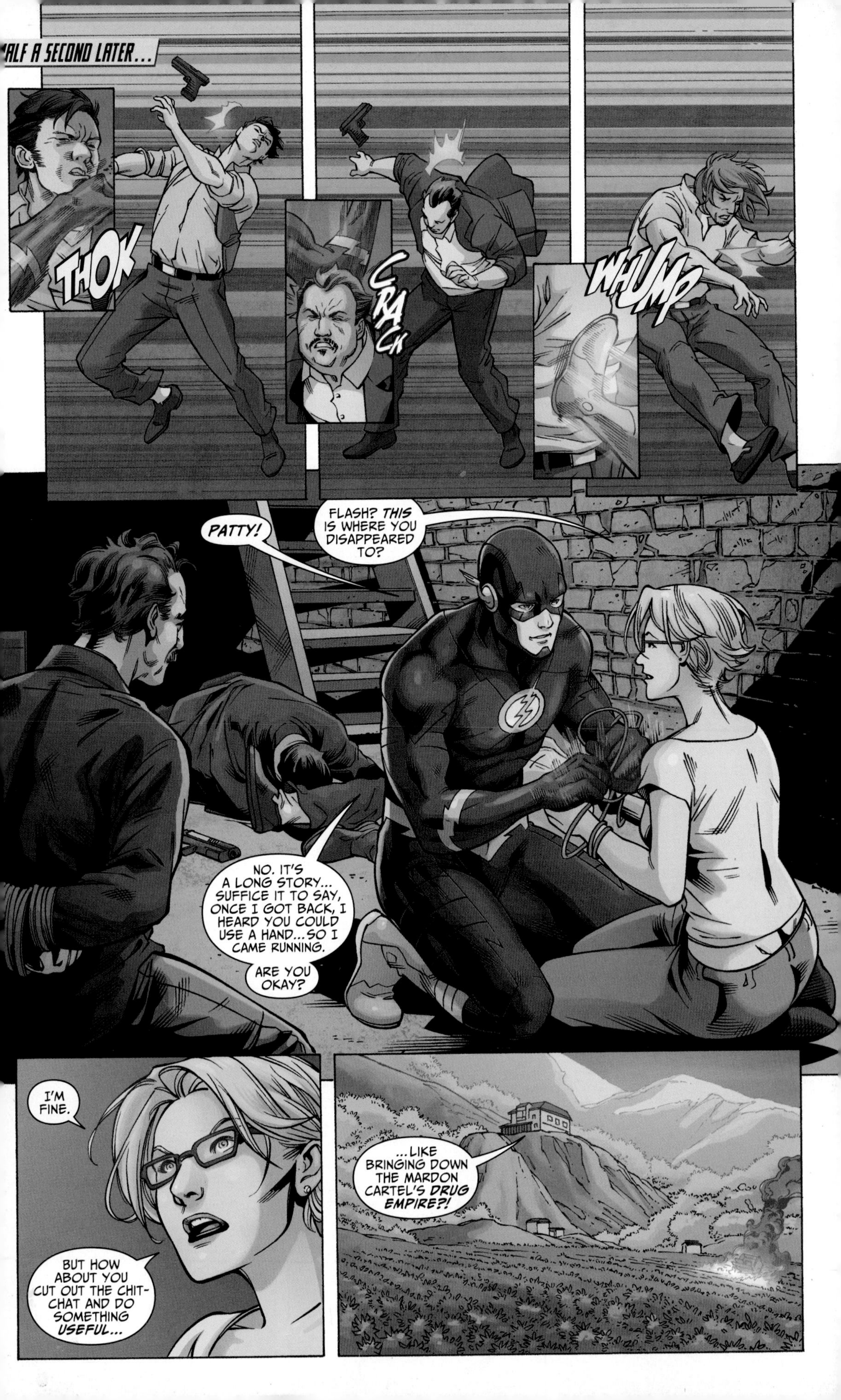
ALF A SECOND LATER...
THOK
CRACK
WHUMP
PATTY!
FLASH? THIS IS WHERE YOU DISAPPEARED TO?
NO. IT'S A LONG STORY... SUFFICE IT TO SAY, ONCE I GOT BACK, I HEARD YOU COULD USE A HAND...SO I CAME RUNNING.
ARE YOU OKAY?
I'M FINE.
BUT HOW ABOUT YOU CUT OUT THE CHIT-CHAT AND DO SOMETHING USEFUL...
...LIKE BRINGING DOWN THE MARDON CARTEL'S DRUG EMPIRE?!

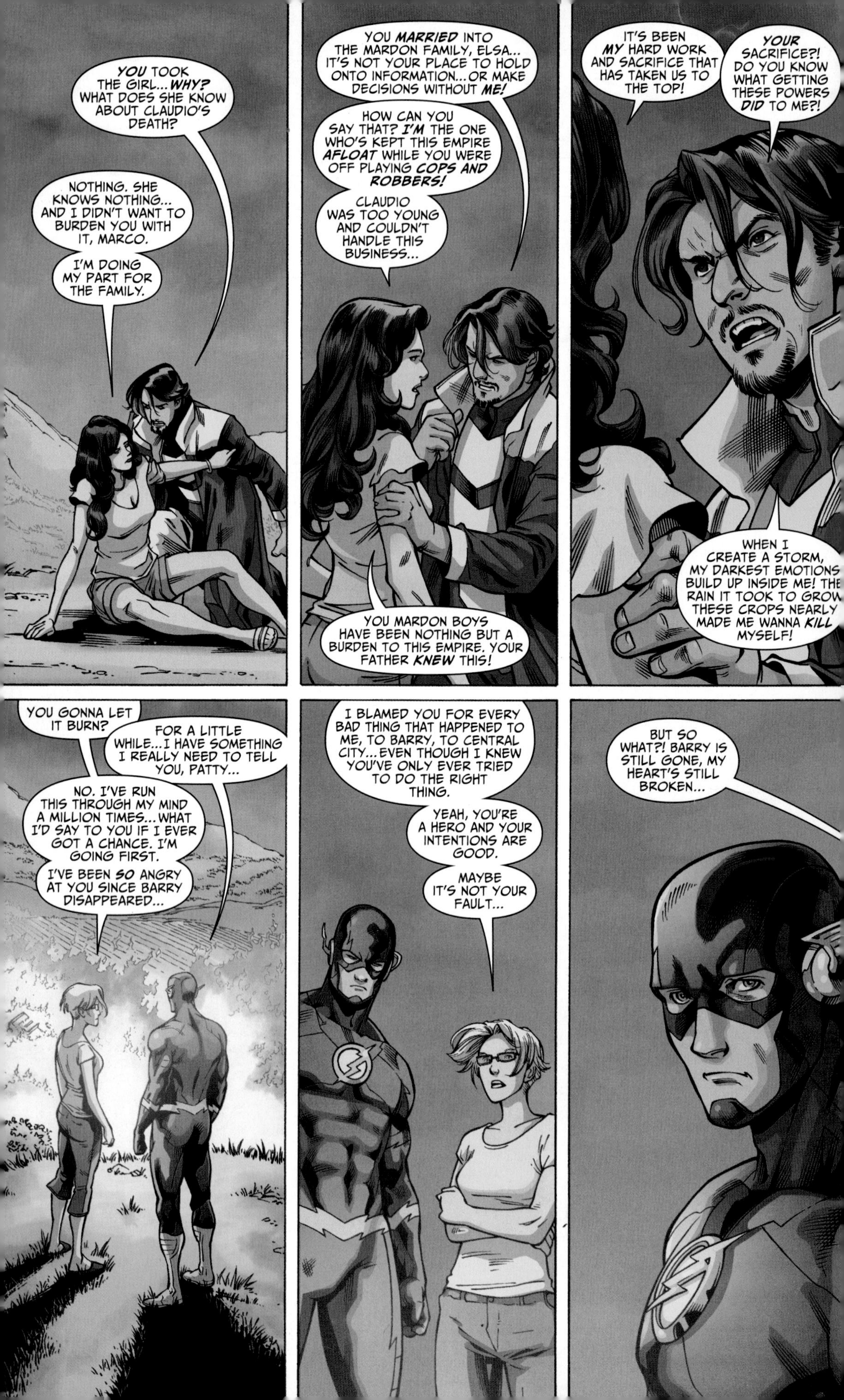
YOU TOOK THE GIRL... WHY? WHAT DOES SHE KNOW ABOUT CLAUDIO'S DEATH?
NOTHING. SHE KNOWS NOTHING... AND I DIDN'T WANT TO BURDEN YOU WITH IT, MARCO.
I'M DOING MY PART FOR THE FAMILY.
YOU MARRIED INTO THE MARDON FAMILY, ELSA... IT'S NOT YOUR PLACE TO HOLD ONTO INFORMATION...OR MAKE DECISIONS WITHOUT ME!
HOW CAN YOU SAY THAT? I'M THE ONE WHO'S KEPT THIS EMPIRE AFLOAT WHILE YOU WERE OFF PLAYING COPS AND ROBBERS!
CLAUDIO WAS TOO YOUNG AND COULDN'T HANDLE THIS BUSINESS...
YOU MARDON BOYS HAVE BEEN NOTHING BUT A BURDEN TO THIS EMPIRE. YOUR FATHER KNEW THIS!
IT'S BEEN MY HARD WORK AND SACRIFICE THAT HAS TAKEN US TO THE TOP!
YOUR SACRIFICE?! DO YOU KNOW WHAT GETTING THESE POWERS DID TO ME?!
WHEN I CREATE A STORM, MY DARKEST EMOTIONS BUILD UP INSIDE ME! THE RAIN IT TOOK TO GROW THESE CROPS NEARLY MADE ME WANNA KILL MYSELF!
YOU GONNA LET IT BURN?
FOR A LITTLE WHILE...I HAVE SOMETHING I REALLY NEED TO TELL YOU, PATTY...
NO. I'VE RUN THIS THROUGH MY MIND A MILLION TIMES...WHAT I'D SAY TO YOU IF I EVER GOT A CHANCE. I'M GOING FIRST.
I'VE BEEN SO ANGRY AT YOU SINCE BARRY DISAPPEARED...
I BLAMED YOU FOR EVERY BAD THING THAT HAPPENED TO ME, TO BARRY, TO CENTRAL CITY...EVEN THOUGH I KNEW YOU'VE ONLY EVER TRIED TO DO THE RIGHT THING.
YEAH, YOU'RE A HERO AND YOUR INTENTIONS ARE GOOD.
MAYBE IT'S NOT YOUR FAULT...
BUT SO WHAT?! BARRY IS STILL GONE, MY HEART'S STILL BROKEN...

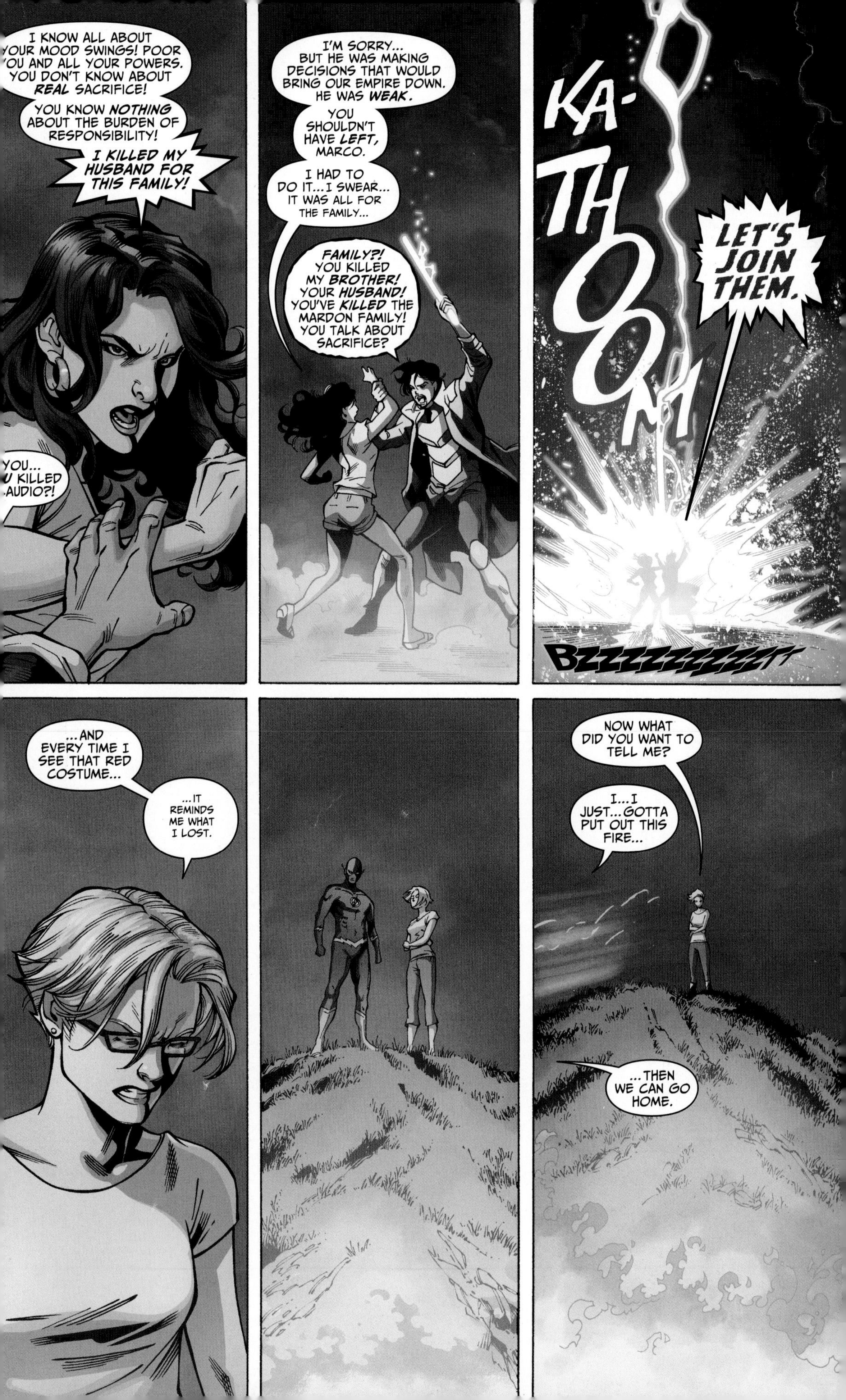

I KNOW ALL ABOUT YOUR MOOD SWINGS! POOR YOU AND ALL YOUR POWERS. YOU DON'T KNOW ABOUT REAL SACRIFICE!
YOU KNOW NOTHING ABOUT THE BURDEN OF RESPONSIBILITY!
I KILLED MY HUSBAND FOR THIS FAMILY!
YOU... U KILLED AUDIO?!
I'M SORRY... BUT HE WAS MAKING DECISIONS THAT WOULD BRING OUR EMPIRE DOWN. HE WAS WEAK.
YOU SHOULDN'T HAVE LEFT, MARCO.
I HAD TO DO IT...I SWEAR... IT WAS ALL FOR THE FAMILY...
FAMILY?! YOU KILLED MY BROTHER! YOUR HUSBAND! YOU'VE KILLED THE MARDON FAMILY! YOU TALK ABOUT SACRIFICE?
KA-THOOM
LET'S JOIN THEM.
BZZZZZZZZZZZT
...AND EVERY TIME I SEE THAT RED COSTUME...
...IT REMINDS ME WHAT I LOST.
NOW WHAT DID YOU WANT TO TELL ME?
I...I JUST...GOTTA PUT OUT THIS FIRE...
...THEN WE CAN GO HOME.

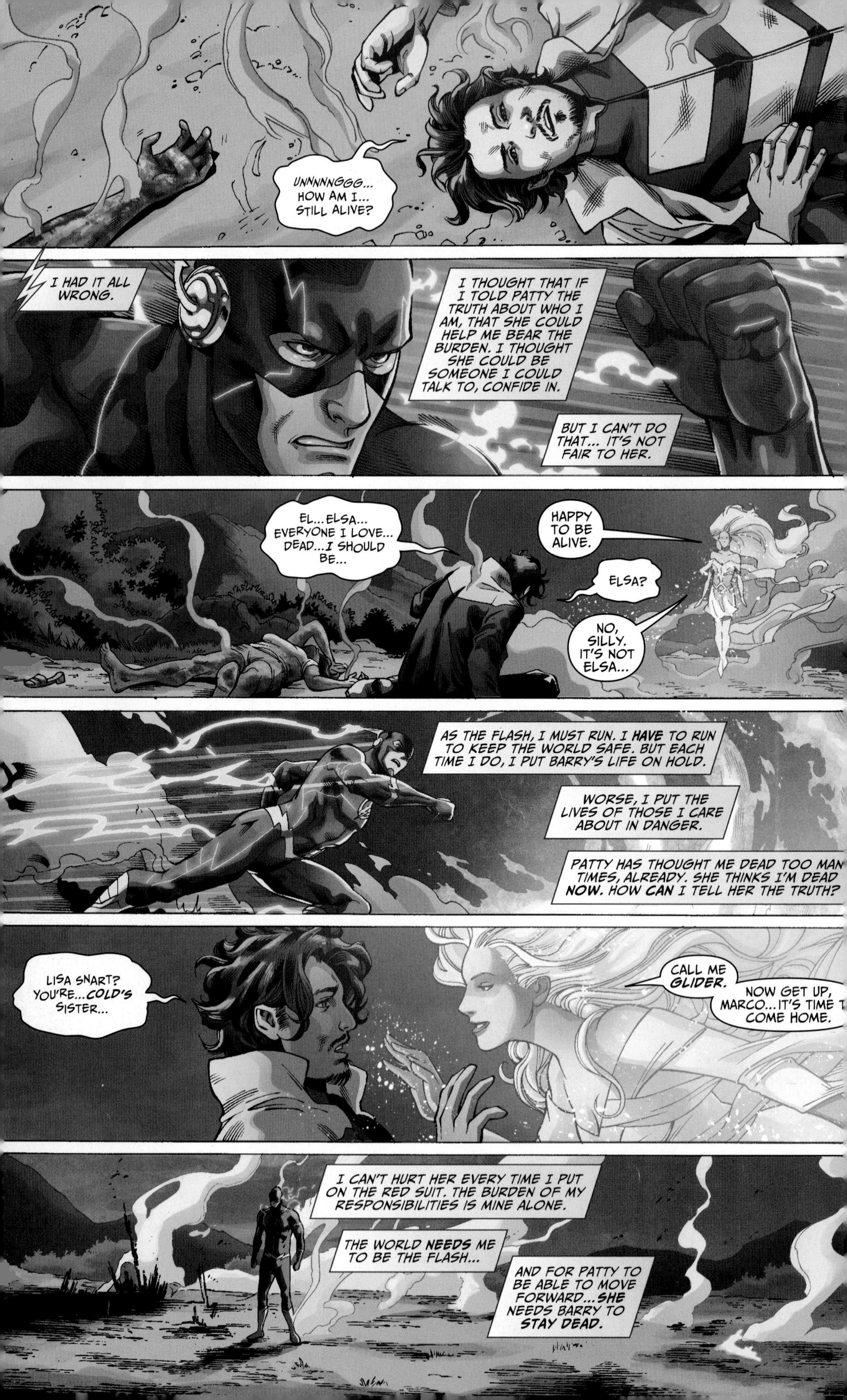
UNNNNNGGG... HOW AM I... STILL ALIVE?
I HAD IT ALL WRONG.
I THOUGHT THAT IF I TOLD PATTY THE TRUTH ABOUT WHO I AM, THAT SHE COULD HELP ME BEAR THE BURDEN. I THOUGHT SHE COULD BE SOMEONE I COULD TALK TO, CONFIDE IN.
BUT I CAN'T DO THAT... IT'S NOT FAIR TO HER.
EL...ELSA... EVERYONE I LOVE... DEAD...I SHOULD BE...
HAPPY TO BE ALIVE.
ELSA?
NO, SILLY. IT'S NOT ELSA...
AS THE FLASH, I MUST RUN. I HAVE TO RUN TO KEEP THE WORLD SAFE. BUT EACH TIME I DO, I PUT BARRY'S LIFE ON HOLD.
WORSE, I PUT THE LIVES OF THOSE I CARE ABOUT IN DANGER.
PATTY HAS THOUGHT ME DEAD TOO MAN TIMES, ALREADY. SHE THINKS I'M DEAD NOW. HOW CAN I TELL HER THE TRUTH?
LISA SNART? YOU'RE...COLD'S SISTER...
CALL ME GLIDER.
NOW GET UP, MARCO...IT'S TIME T COME HOME.
I CAN'T HURT HER EVERY TIME I PUT ON THE RED SUIT. THE BURDEN OF MY RESPONSIBILITIES IS MINE ALONE.
THE WORLD NEEDS ME TO BE THE FLASH...
AND FOR PATTY TO BE ABLE TO MOVE FORWARD...SHE NEEDS BARRY TO STAY DEAD.

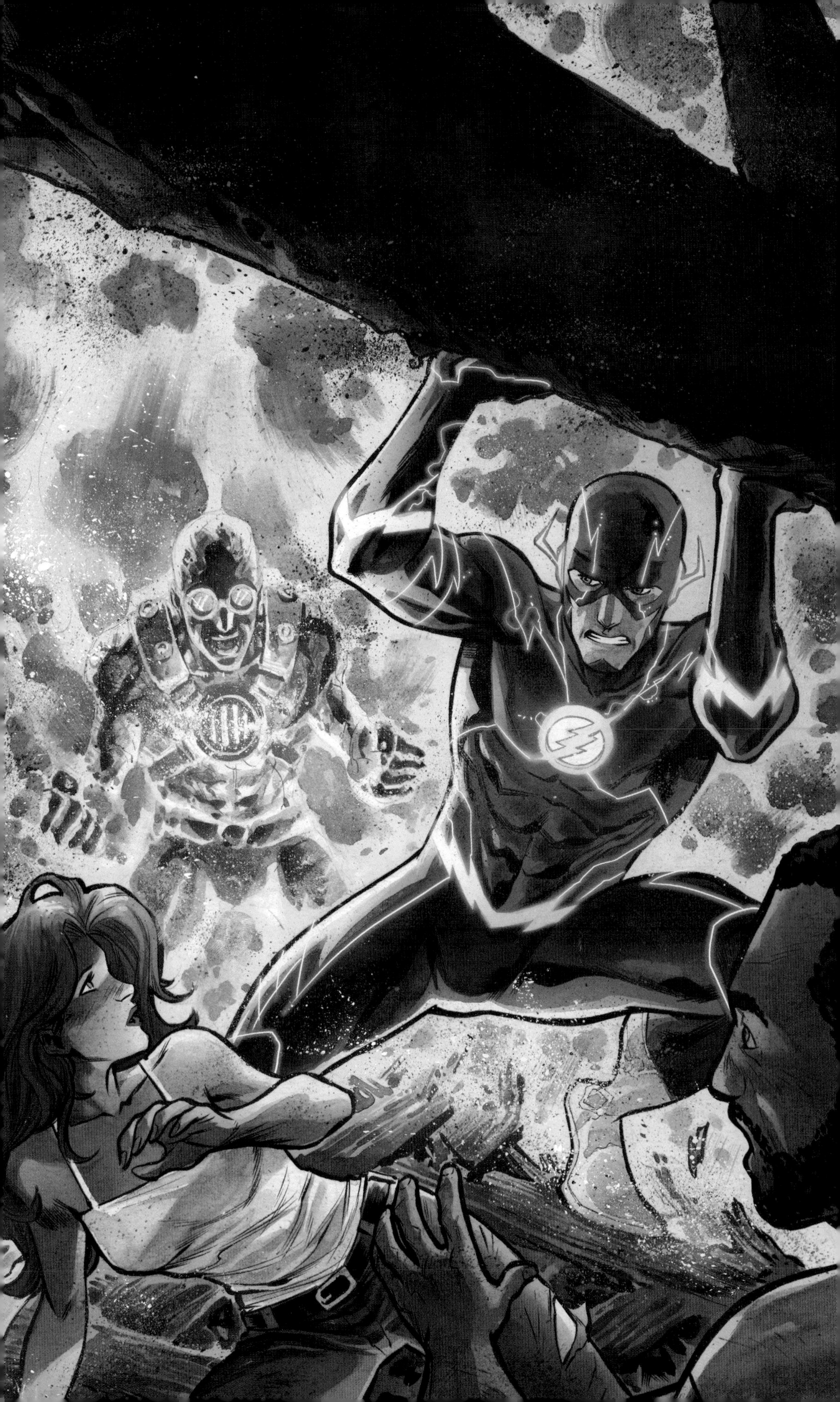

FRANCIS MANAPUL & BRIAN BUCCELLATO writers MARCUS TO penciller RAY McCARTHY inker

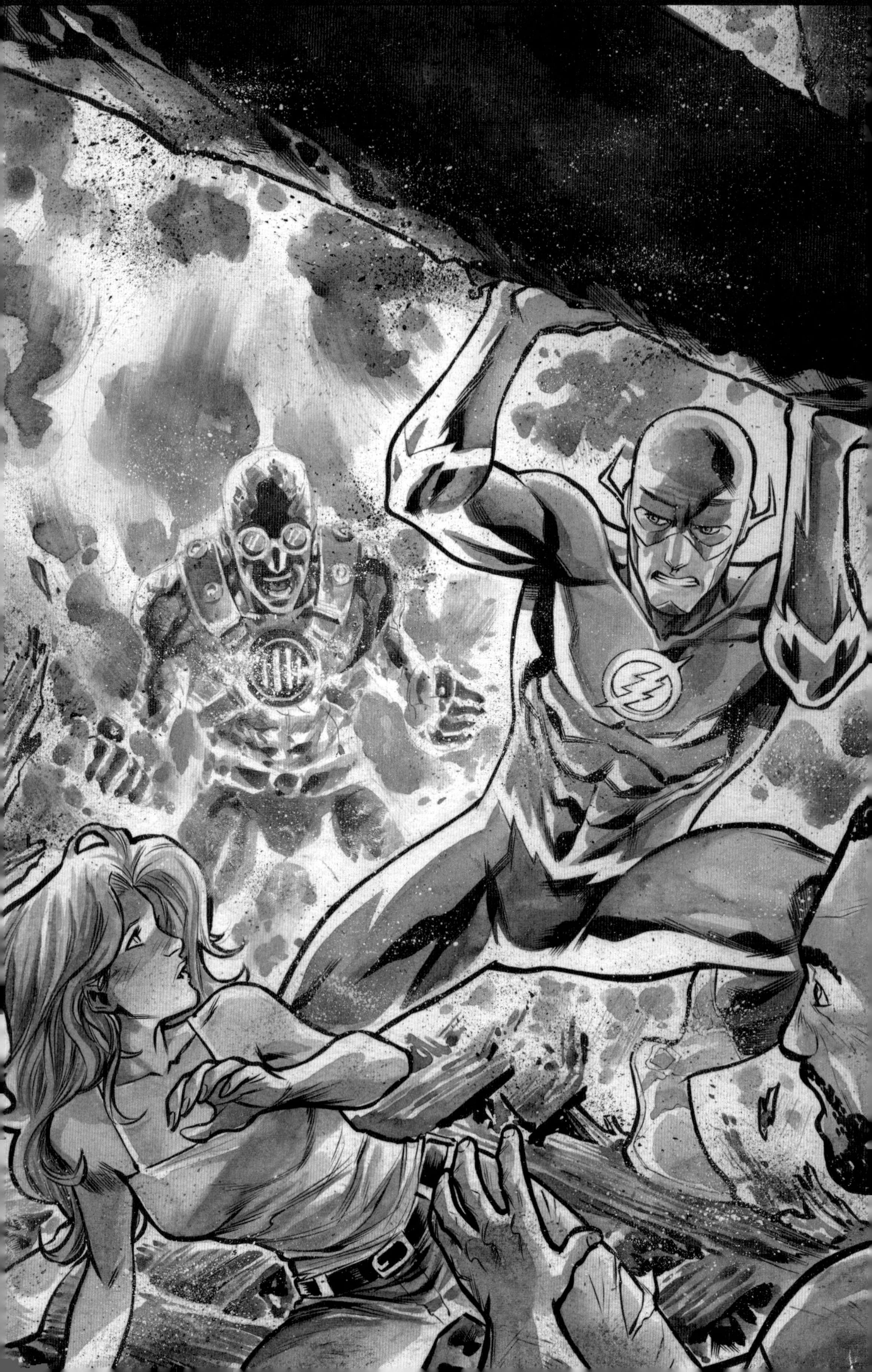

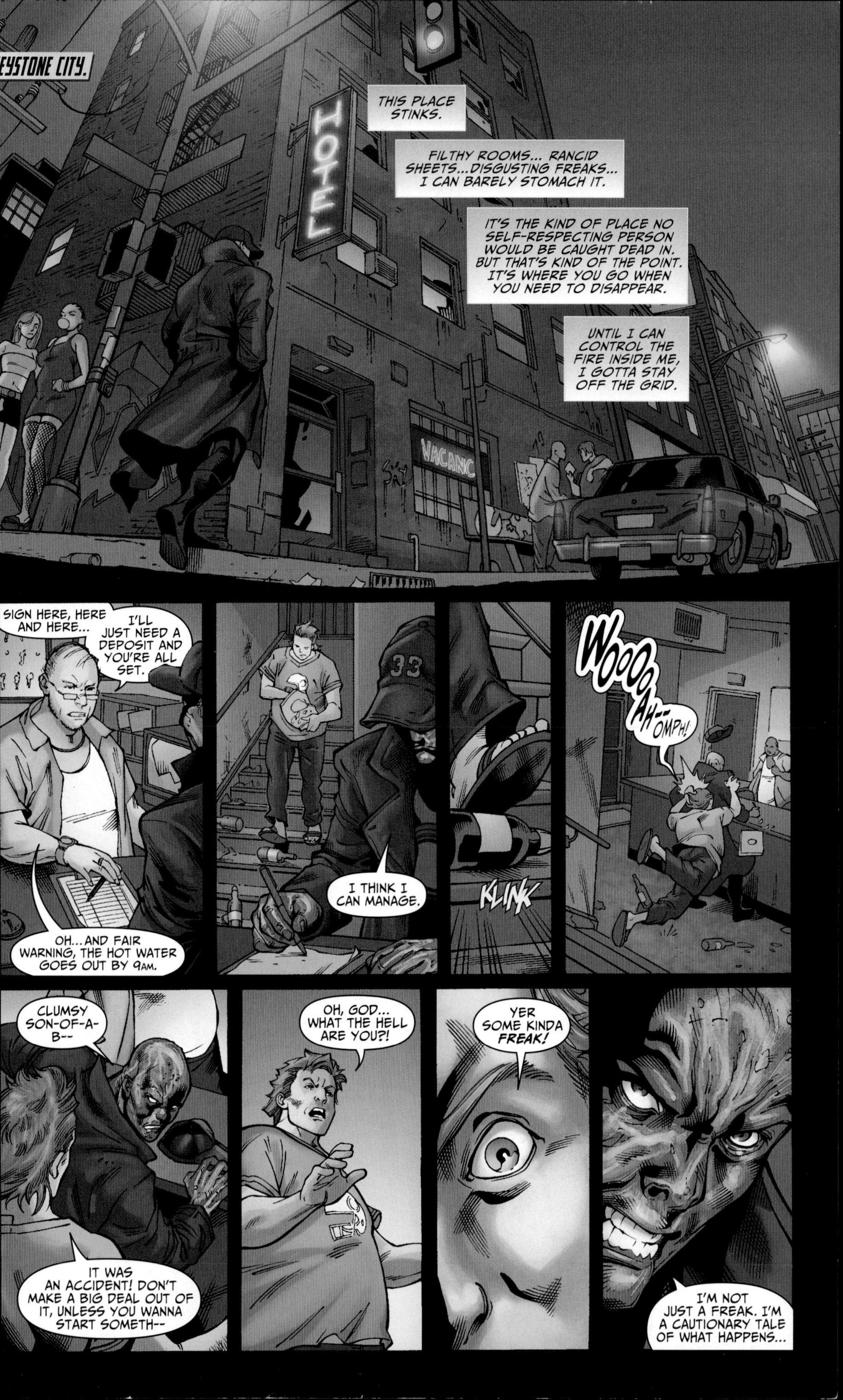

EYSTONE CITY.
THIS PLACE STINKS.
FILTHY ROOMS... RANCID SHEETS...DISGUSTING FREAKS... I CAN BARELY STOMACH IT.
IT'S THE KIND OF PLACE NO SELF-RESPECTING PERSON WOULD BE CAUGHT DEAD IN. BUT THAT'S KIND OF THE POINT. IT'S WHERE YOU GO WHEN YOU NEED TO DISAPPEAR.
UNTIL I CAN CONTROL THE FIRE INSIDE ME, I GOTTA STAY OFF THE GRID.
HOTEL
VACANC
SIGN HERE, HERE AND HERE...
I'LL JUST NEED A DEPOSIT AND YOU'RE ALL SET.
OH...AND FAIR WARNING, THE HOT WATER GOES OUT BY 9AM.
I THINK I CAN MANAGE.
KLINK
WOOOOAH--
OMPH!
CLUMSY SON-OF-A-B--
IT WAS AN ACCIDENT! DON'T MAKE A BIG DEAL OUT OF IT, UNLESS YOU WANNA START SOMETH--
OH, GOD... WHAT THE HELL ARE YOU?!
YER SOME KINDA FREAK!
I'M NOT JUST A FREAK. I'M A CAUTIONARY TALE OF WHAT HAPPENS...

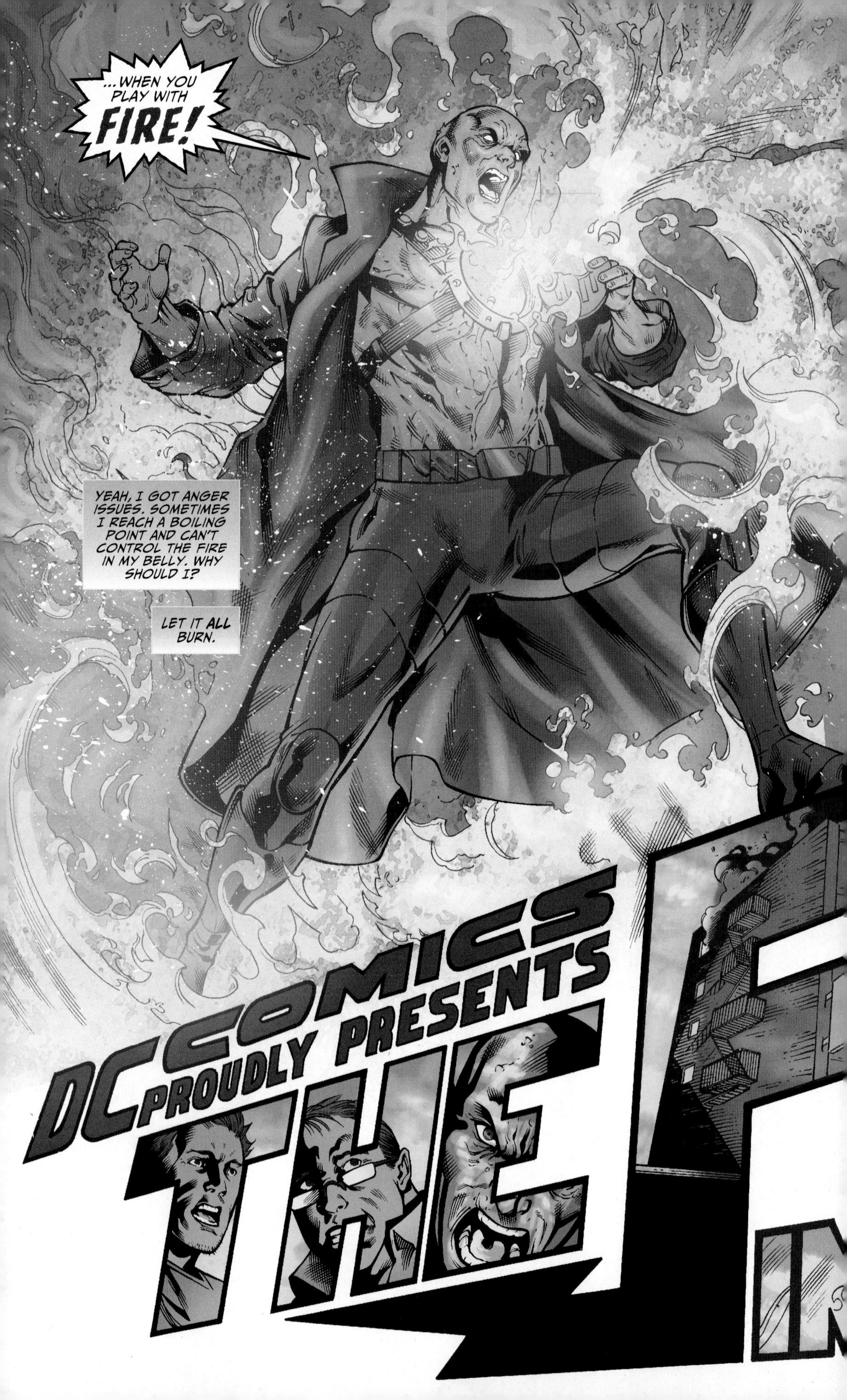
...WHEN YOU PLAY WITH FIRE!
YEAH, I GOT ANGER ISSUES. SOMETIMES I REACH A BOILING POINT AND CAN'T CONTROL THE FIRE IN MY BELLY. WHY SHOULD I?
LET IT ALL BURN.
DC COMICS PROUDLY PRESENTS
THE

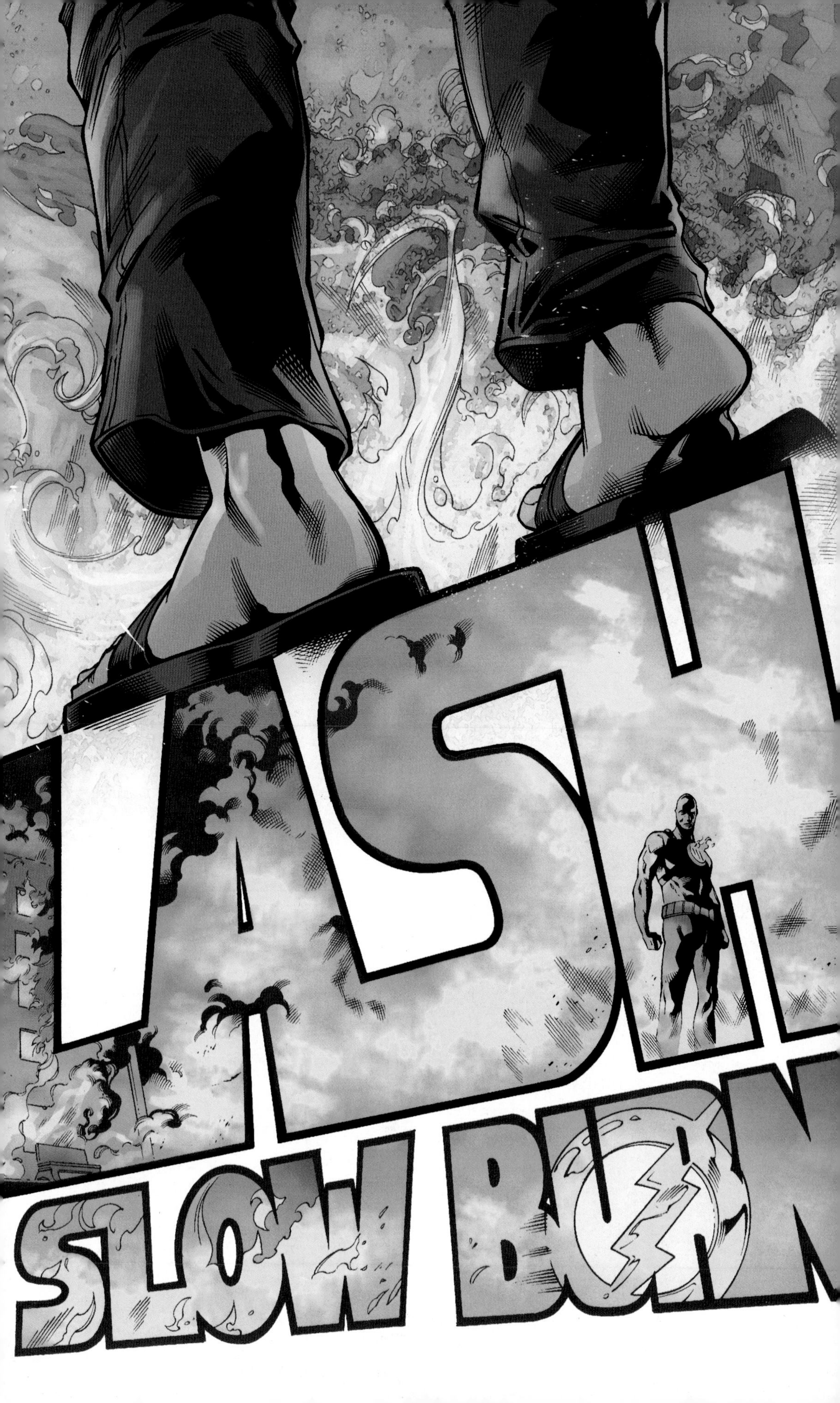
SLOW

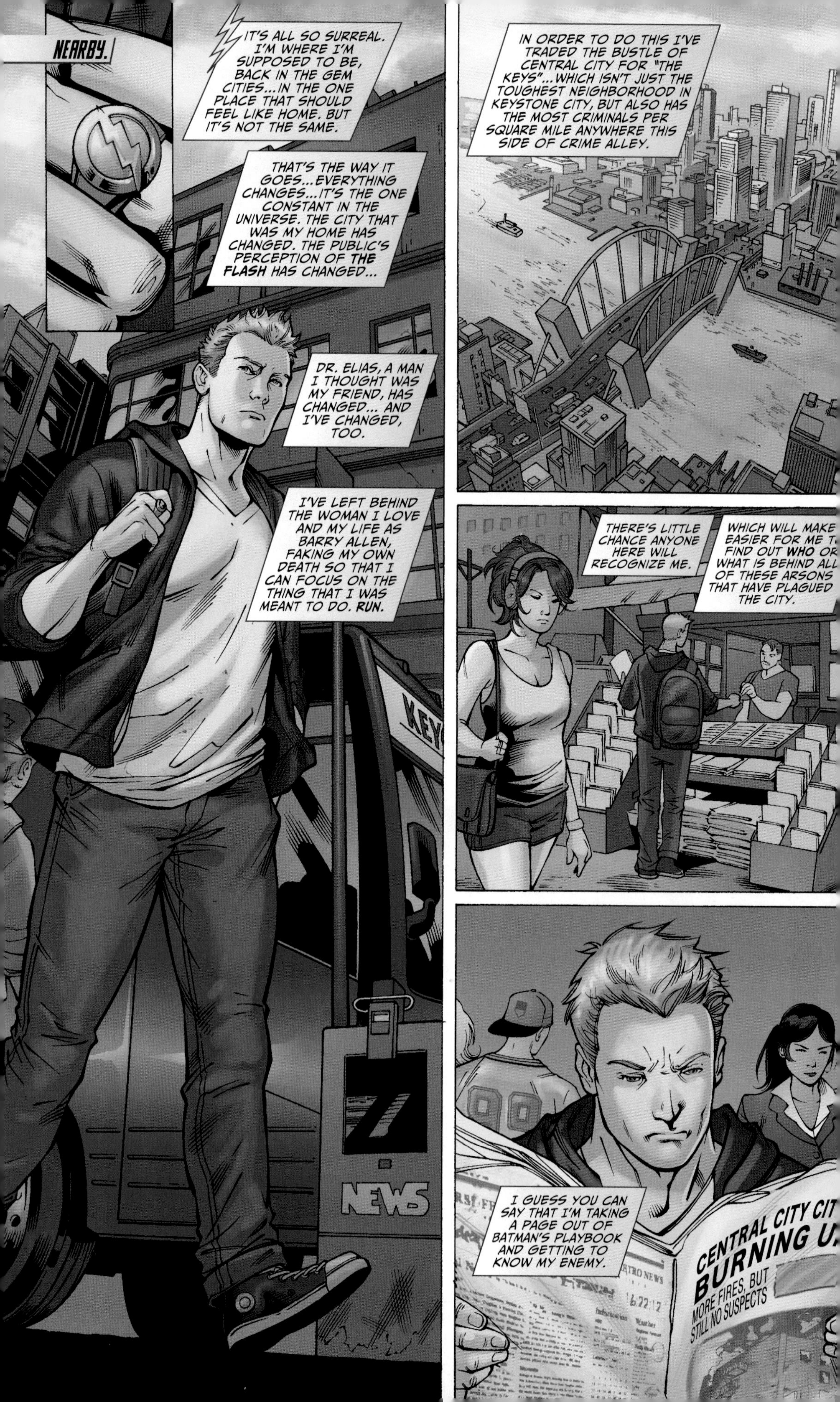
NEARBY.
IT'S ALL SO SURREAL. I'M WHERE I'M SUPPOSED TO BE, BACK IN THE GEM CITIES...IN THE ONE PLACE THAT SHOULD FEEL LIKE HOME. BUT IT'S NOT THE SAME.
THAT'S THE WAY IT GOES...EVERYTHING CHANGES...IT'S THE ONE CONSTANT IN THE UNIVERSE. THE CITY THAT WAS MY HOME HAS CHANGED. THE PUBLIC'S PERCEPTION OF THE FLASH HAS CHANGED...
DR. ELIAS, A MAN I THOUGHT WAS MY FRIEND, HAS CHANGED... AND I'VE CHANGED, TOO.
I'VE LEFT BEHIND THE WOMAN I LOVE AND MY LIFE AS BARRY ALLEN, FAKING MY OWN DEATH SO THAT I CAN FOCUS ON THE THING THAT I WAS MEANT TO DO. RUN.
NEWS
IN ORDER TO DO THIS I'VE TRADED THE BUSTLE OF CENTRAL CITY FOR "THE KEYS"...WHICH ISN'T JUST THE TOUGHEST NEIGHBORHOOD IN KEYSTONE CITY, BUT ALSO HAS THE MOST CRIMINALS PER SQUARE MILE ANYWHERE THIS SIDE OF CRIME ALLEY.
THERE'S LITTLE CHANCE ANYONE HERE WILL RECOGNIZE ME.
WHICH WILL MAKE EASIER FOR ME T FIND OUT WHO OR WHAT IS BEHIND ALL OF THESE ARSONS THAT HAVE PLAGUED THE CITY.
I GUESS YOU CAN SAY THAT I'M TAKING A PAGE OUT OF BATMAN'S PLAYBOOK AND GETTING TO KNOW MY ENEMY.
CENTRAL CITY CIT
BURNING U
MORE FIRES, BUT STILL NO SUSPECTS

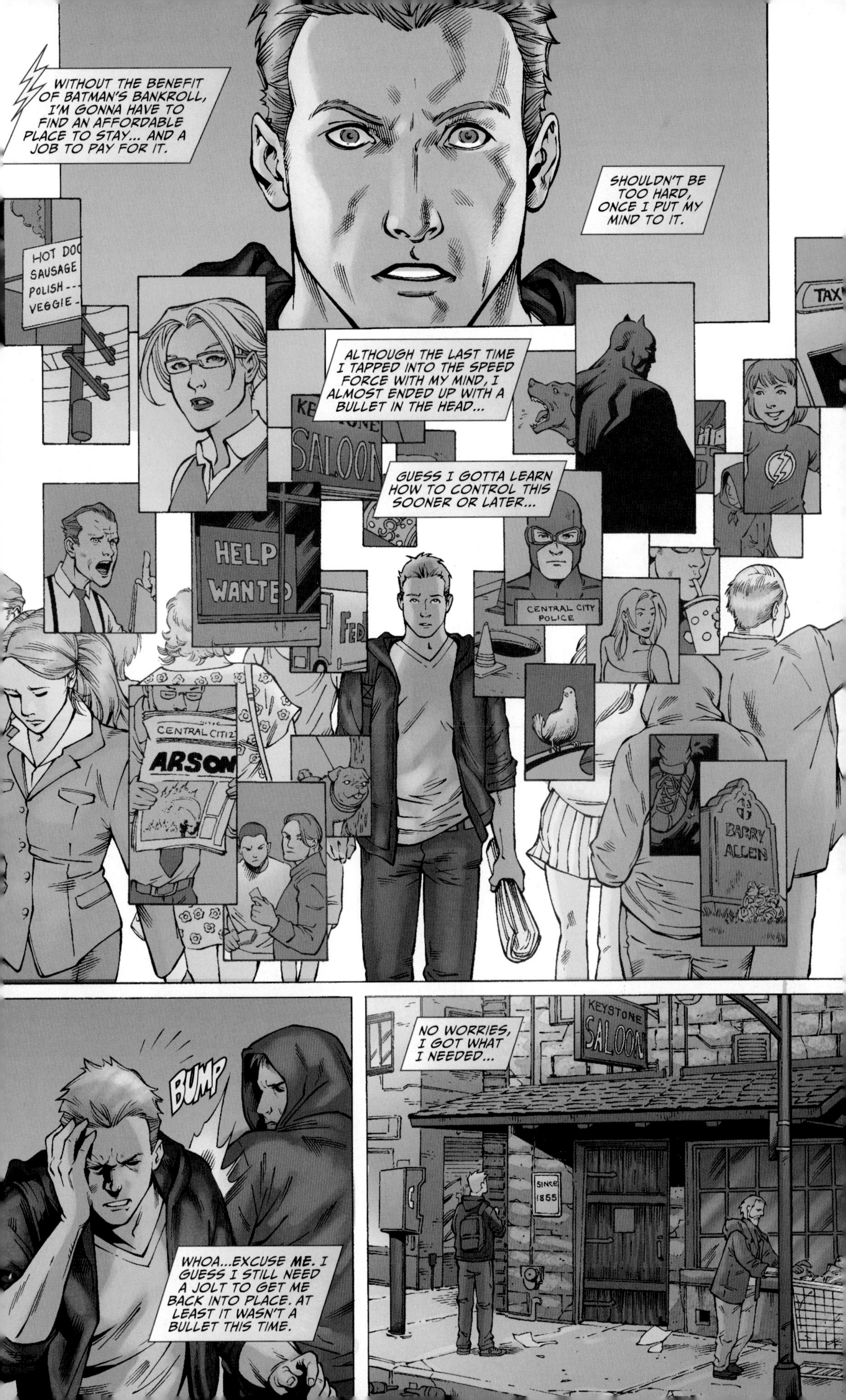

WITHOUT THE BENEFIT OF BATMAN'S BANKROLL, I'M GONNA HAVE TO FIND AN AFFORDABLE PLACE TO STAY... AND A JOB TO PAY FOR IT.
SHOULDN'T BE TOO HARD, ONCE I PUT MY MIND TO IT.
HOT DOG
SAUSAGE
POLISH
VEGGIE
TAXI
ALTHOUGH THE LAST TIME I TAPPED INTO THE SPEED FORCE WITH MY MIND, I ALMOST ENDED UP WITH A BULLET IN THE HEAD...
KEYSTONE SALOON
GUESS I GOTTA LEARN HOW TO CONTROL THIS SOONER OR LATER...
HELP WANTED
CENTRAL CITY POLICE
CENTRAL CITIZ
ARSON
BARRY ALLEN
BUMP
WHOA...EXCUSE **ME.** I GUESS I STILL NEED A JOLT TO GET ME BACK INTO PLACE. AT LEAST IT WASN'T A BULLET THIS TIME.
NO WORRIES, I GOT WHAT I NEEDED...
KEYSTONE SALOON
SINCE 1855

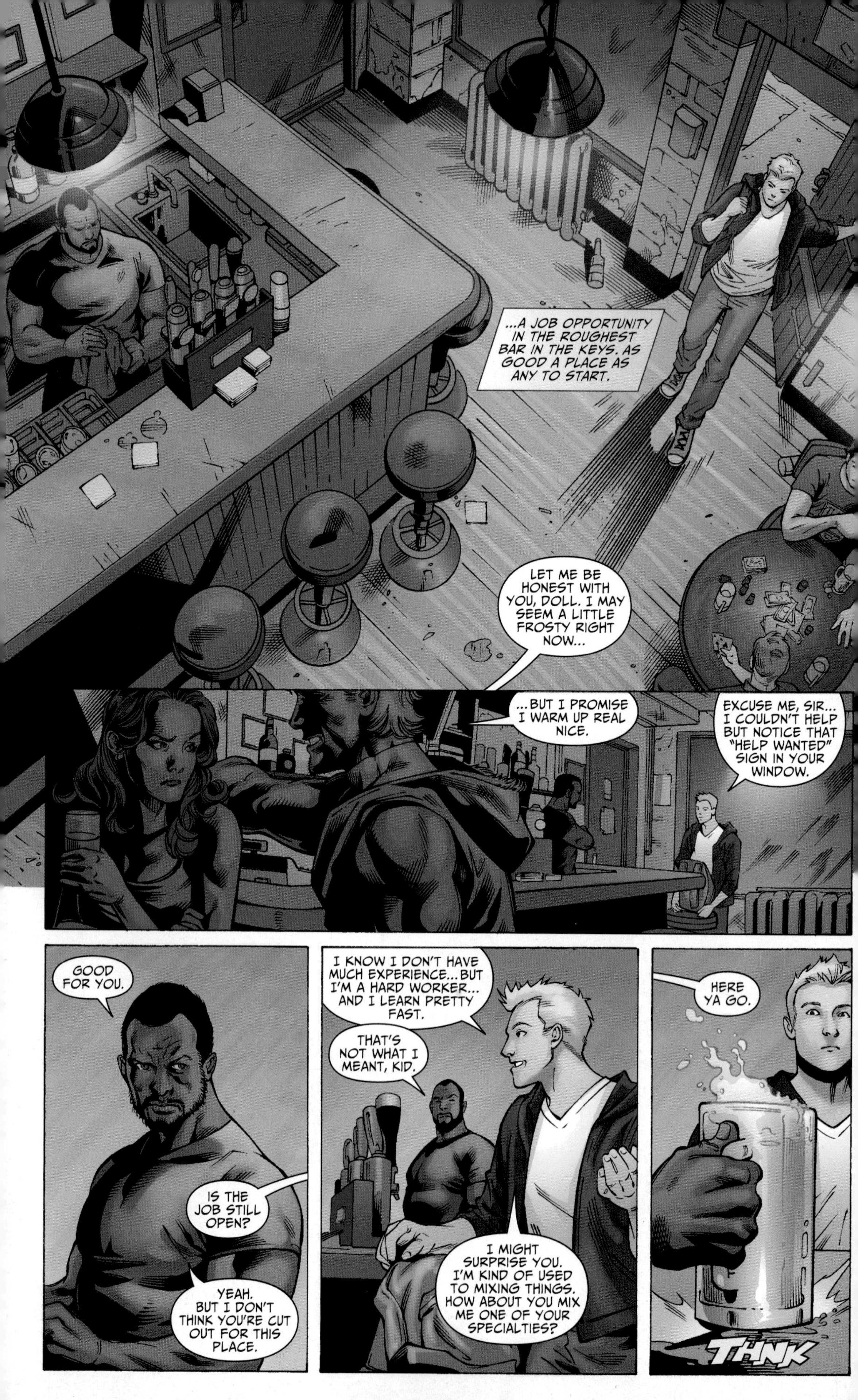
...A JOB OPPORTUNITY IN THE ROUGHEST BAR IN THE KEYS. AS GOOD A PLACE AS ANY TO START.
LET ME BE HONEST WITH YOU, DOLL. I MAY SEEM A LITTLE FROSTY RIGHT NOW...
...BUT I PROMISE I WARM UP REAL NICE.
EXCUSE ME, SIR... I COULDN'T HELP BUT NOTICE THAT "HELP WANTED" SIGN IN YOUR WINDOW.
GOOD FOR YOU.
IS THE JOB STILL OPEN?
YEAH. BUT I DON'T THINK YOU'RE CUT OUT FOR THIS PLACE.
I KNOW I DON'T HAVE MUCH EXPERIENCE... BUT I'M A HARD WORKER... AND I LEARN PRETTY FAST.
THAT'S NOT WHAT I MEANT, KID.
I MIGHT SURPRISE YOU. I'M KIND OF USED TO MIXING THINGS. HOW ABOUT YOU MIX ME ONE OF YOUR SPECIALTIES?
HERE YA GO.
THNK

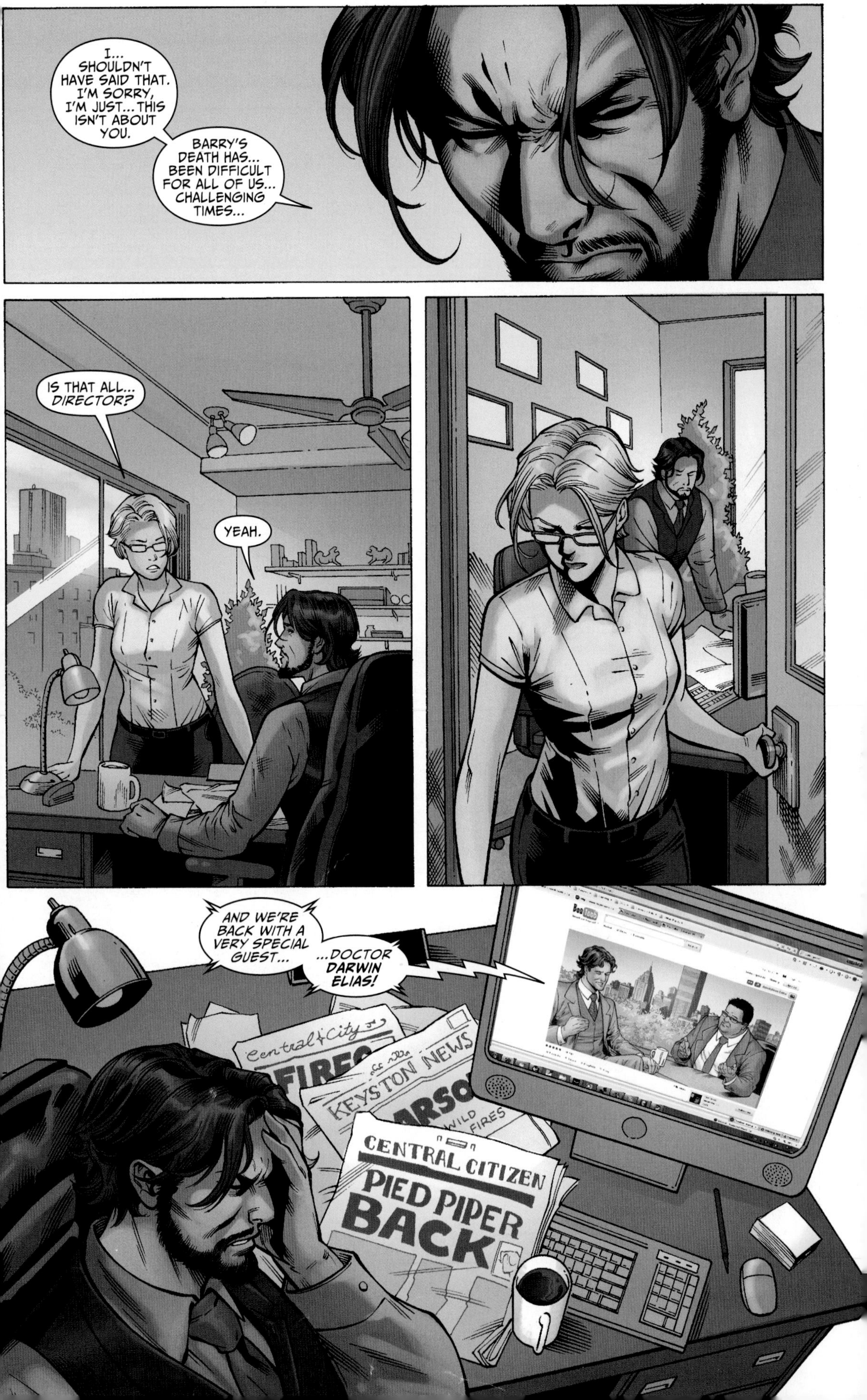
I... SHOULDN'T HAVE SAID THAT. I'M SORRY, I'M JUST...THIS ISN'T ABOUT YOU.
BARRY'S DEATH HAS... BEEN DIFFICULT FOR ALL OF US... CHALLENGING TIMES...
IS THAT ALL... DIRECTOR?
YEAH.
AND WE'RE BACK WITH A VERY SPECIAL GUEST...
...DOCTOR DARWIN ELIAS!
KEYSTON NEWS
WILD FIRES
CENTRAL CITIZEN
PIED PIPER BACK

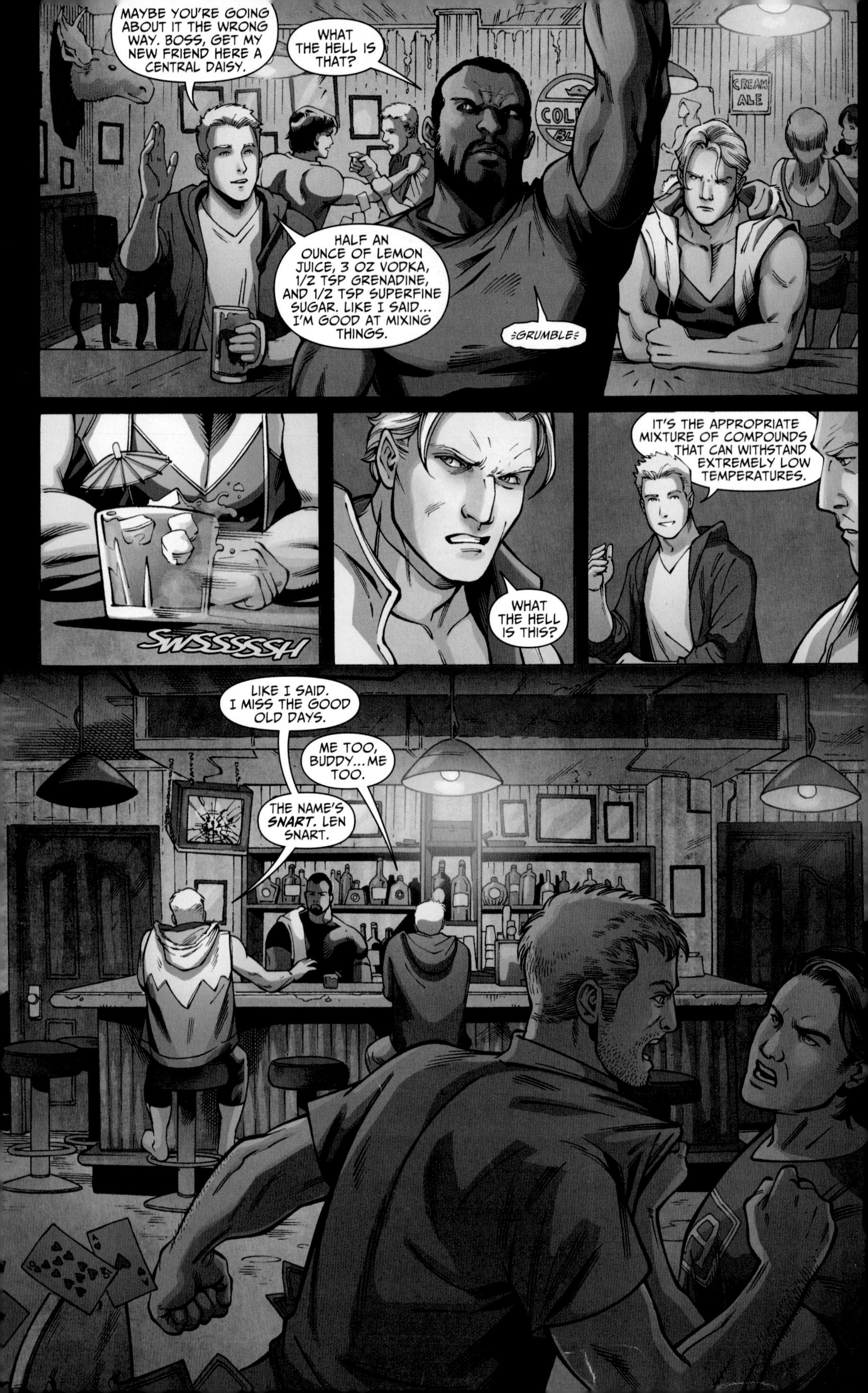
MAYBE YOU'RE GOING ABOUT IT THE WRONG WAY. BOSS, GET MY NEW FRIEND HERE A CENTRAL DAISY.
WHAT THE HELL IS THAT?
HALF AN OUNCE OF LEMON JUICE, 3 OZ VODKA, 1/2 TSP GRENADINE, AND 1/2 TSP SUPERFINE SUGAR. LIKE I SAID... I'M GOOD AT MIXING THINGS.
GRUMBLE
CREAM ALE
SWSSSSSH
WHAT THE HELL IS THIS?
IT'S THE APPROPRIATE MIXTURE OF COMPOUNDS THAT CAN WITHSTAND EXTREMELY LOW TEMPERATURES.
LIKE I SAID. I MISS THE GOOD OLD DAYS.
ME TOO, BUDDY... ME TOO.
THE NAME'S SNART. LEN SNART.

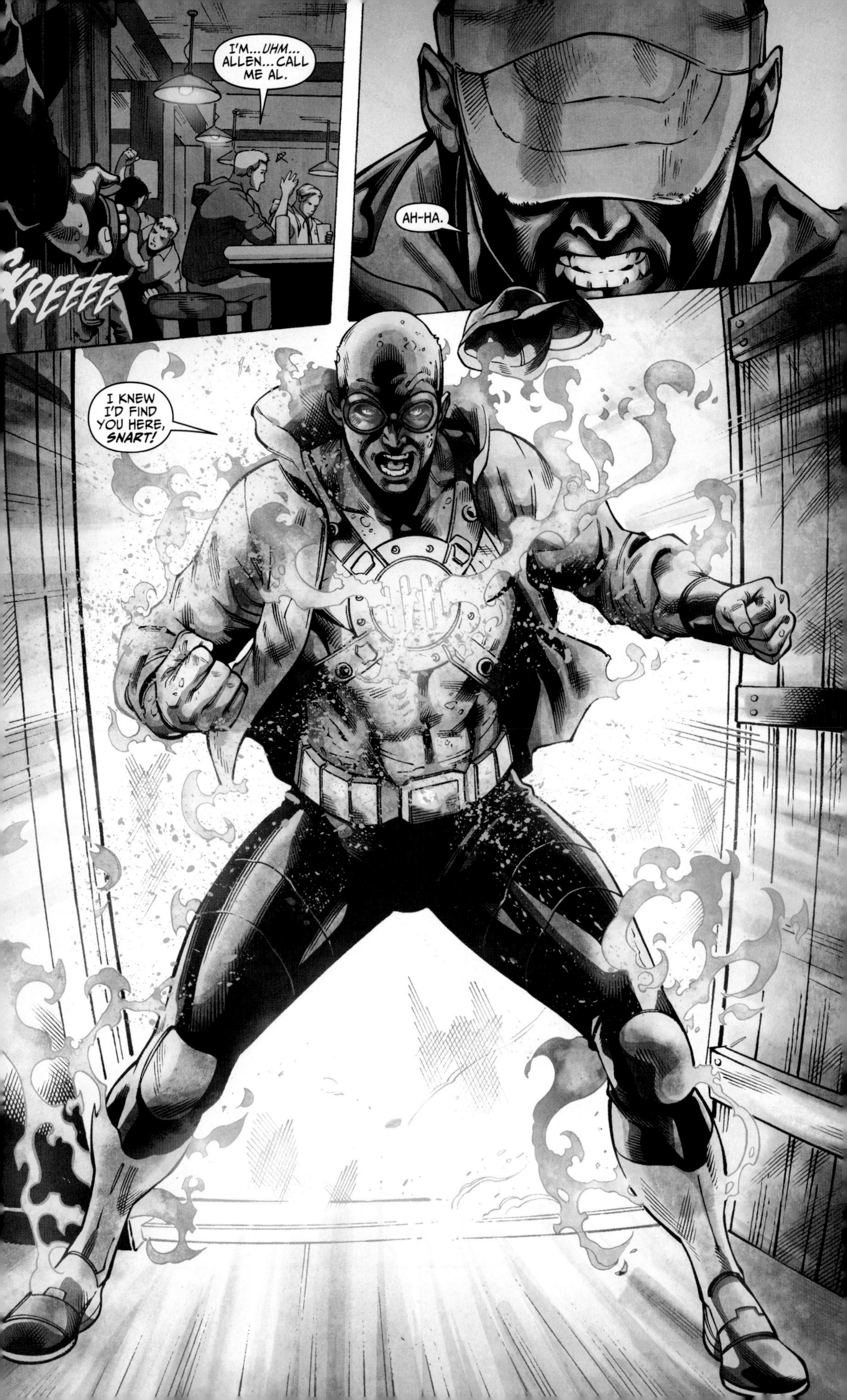
I'M...UHM... ALLEN...CALL ME AL.
SKREEEE
AH-HA.
I KNEW I'D FIND YOU HERE, SNART!

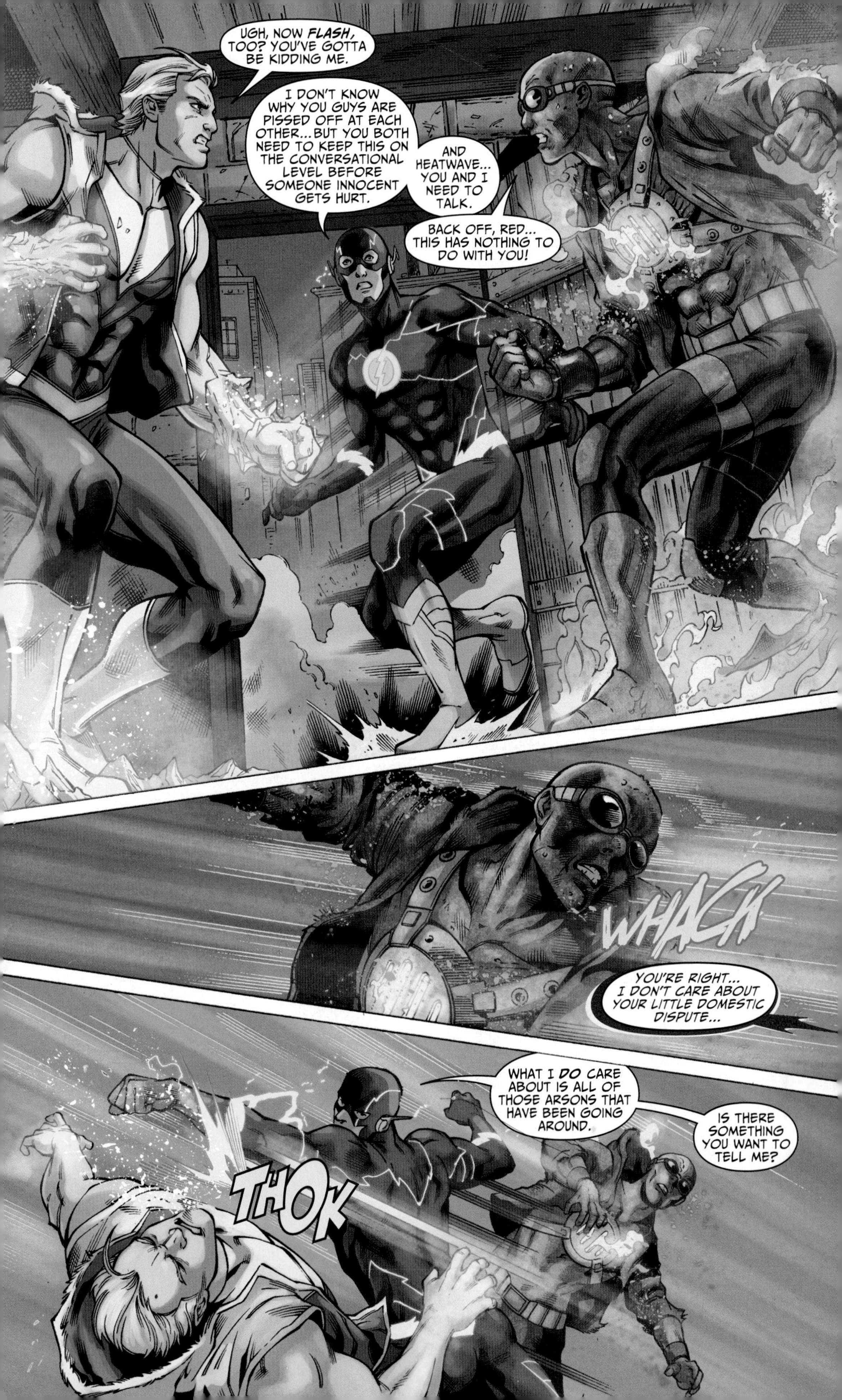

UGH, NOW FLASH, TOO? YOU'VE GOTTA BE KIDDING ME.
I DON'T KNOW WHY YOU GUYS ARE PISSED OFF AT EACH OTHER...BUT YOU BOTH NEED TO KEEP THIS ON THE CONVERSATIONAL LEVEL BEFORE SOMEONE INNOCENT GETS HURT.
AND HEATWAVE... YOU AND I NEED TO TALK.
BACK OFF, RED... THIS HAS NOTHING TO DO WITH YOU!
WHACK
YOU'RE RIGHT... I DON'T CARE ABOUT YOUR LITTLE DOMESTIC DISPUTE...
WHAT I DO CARE ABOUT IS ALL OF THOSE ARSONS THAT HAVE BEEN GOING AROUND.
IS THERE SOMETHING YOU WANT TO TELL ME?
THOK

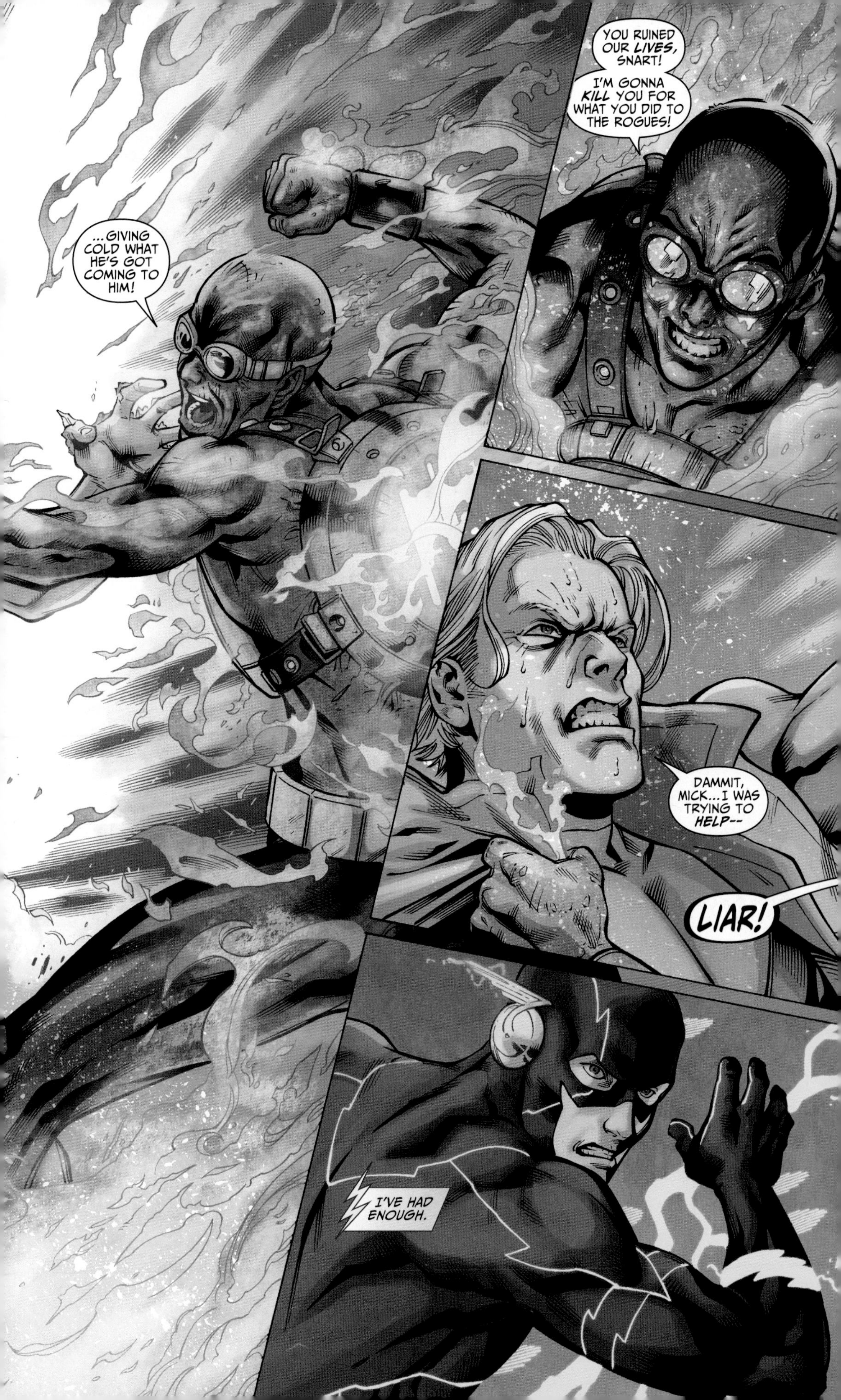
...GIVING COLD WHAT HE'S GOT COMING TO HIM!
YOU RUINED OUR LIVES, SNART!
I'M GONNA KILL YOU FOR WHAT YOU DID TO THE ROGUES!
DAMMIT, MICK...I WAS TRYING TO HELP--
LIAR!
I'VE HAD ENOUGH.

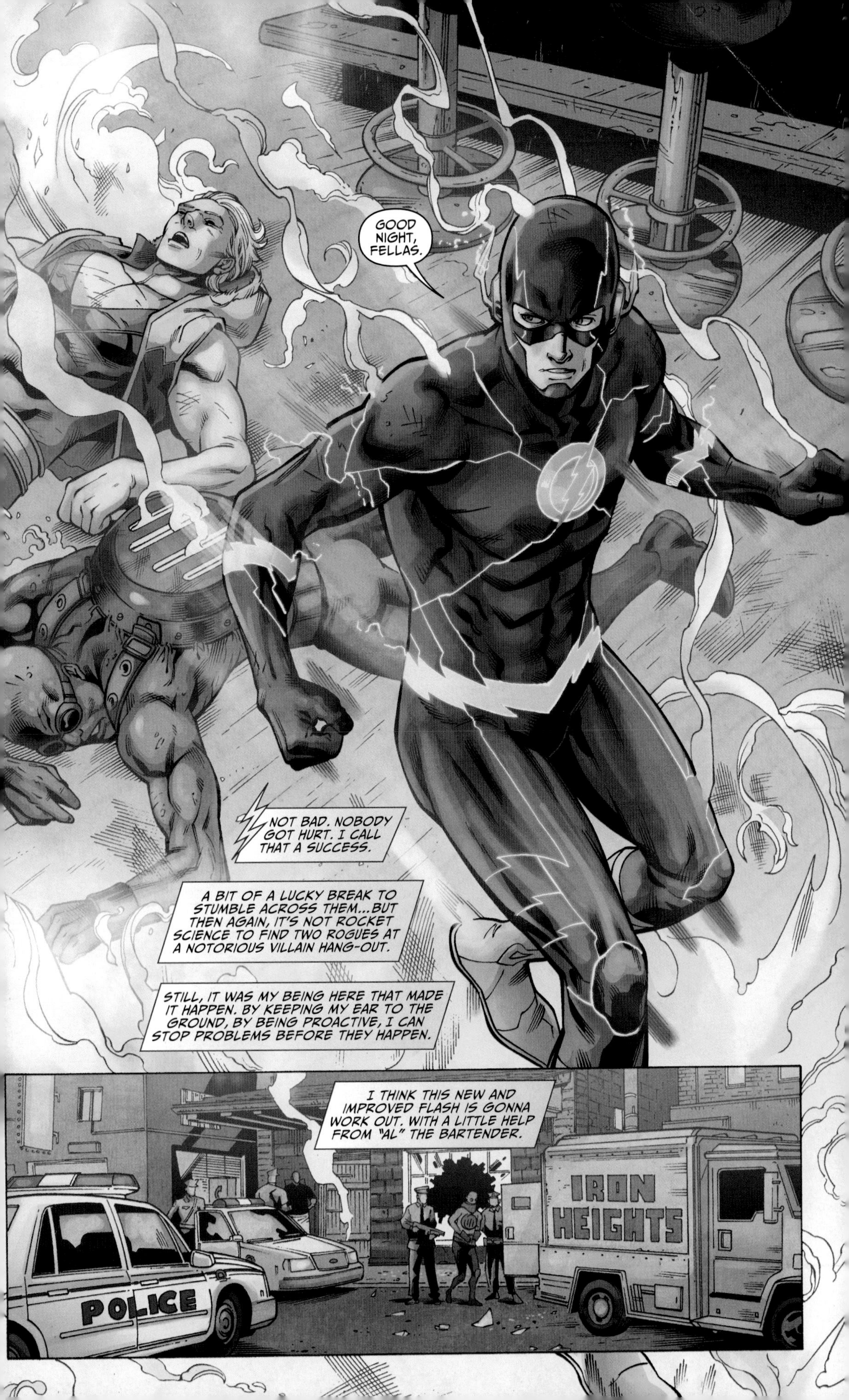
GOOD NIGHT, FELLAS.
NOT BAD. NOBODY GOT HURT. I CALL THAT A SUCCESS.
A BIT OF A LUCKY BREAK TO STUMBLE ACROSS THEM...BUT THEN AGAIN, IT'S NOT ROCKET SCIENCE TO FIND TWO ROGUES AT A NOTORIOUS VILLAIN HANG-OUT.
STILL, IT WAS MY BEING HERE THAT MADE IT HAPPEN. BY KEEPING MY EAR TO THE GROUND, BY BEING PROACTIVE, I CAN STOP PROBLEMS BEFORE THEY HAPPEN.
I THINK THIS NEW AND IMPROVED FLASH IS GONNA WORK OUT. WITH A LITTLE HELP FROM "AL" THE BARTENDER.
IRON HEIGHTS
POLICE

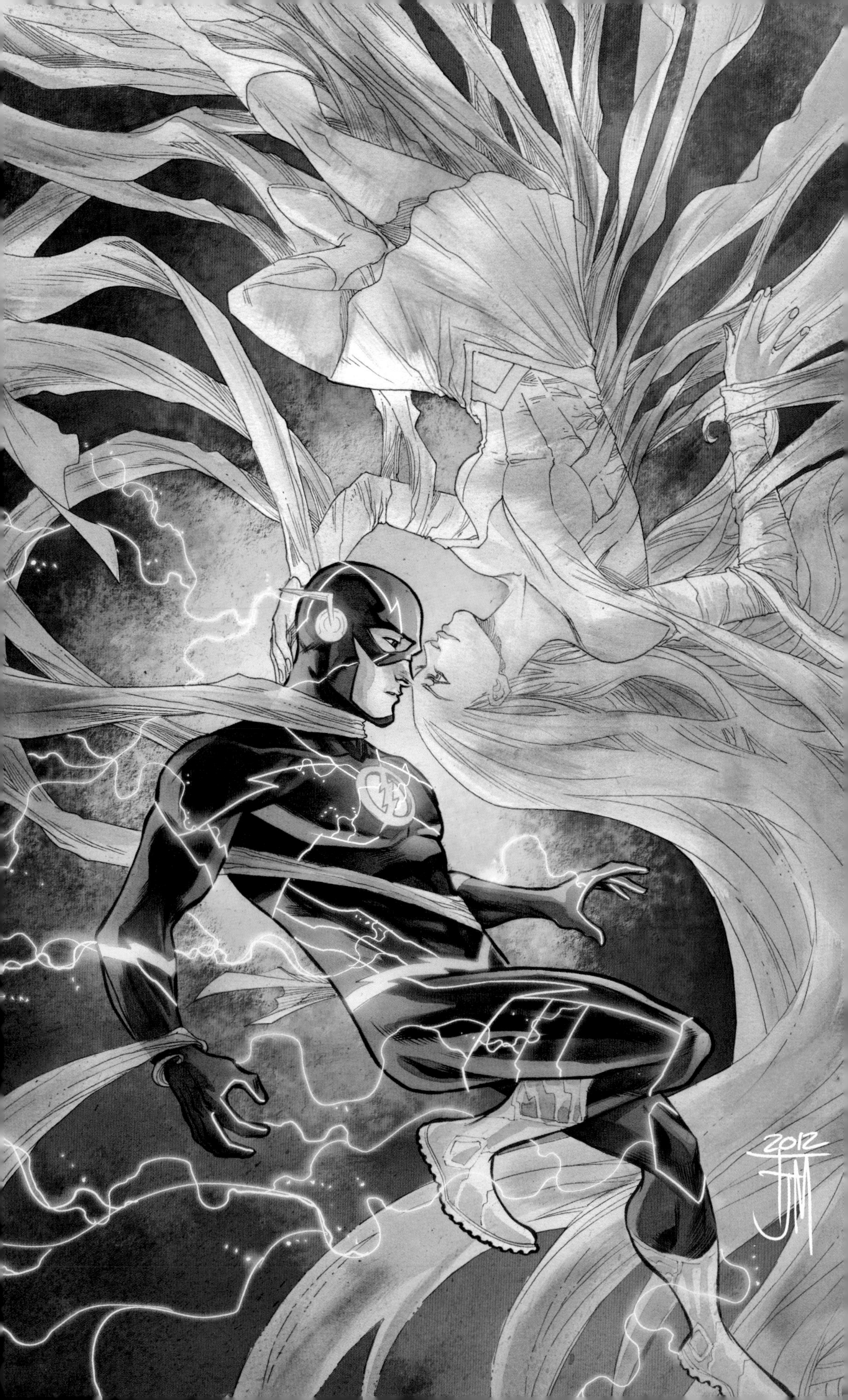
2012

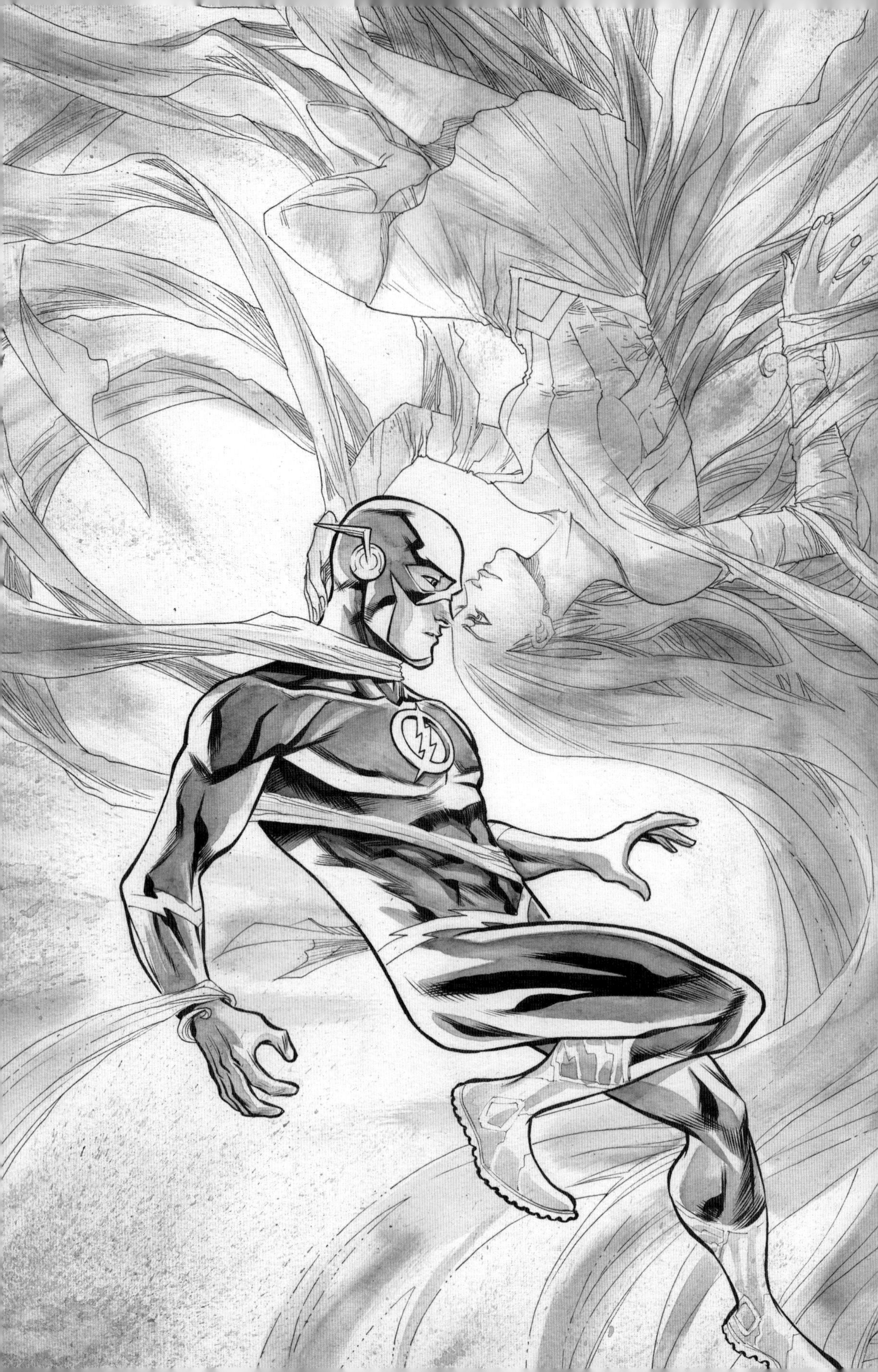

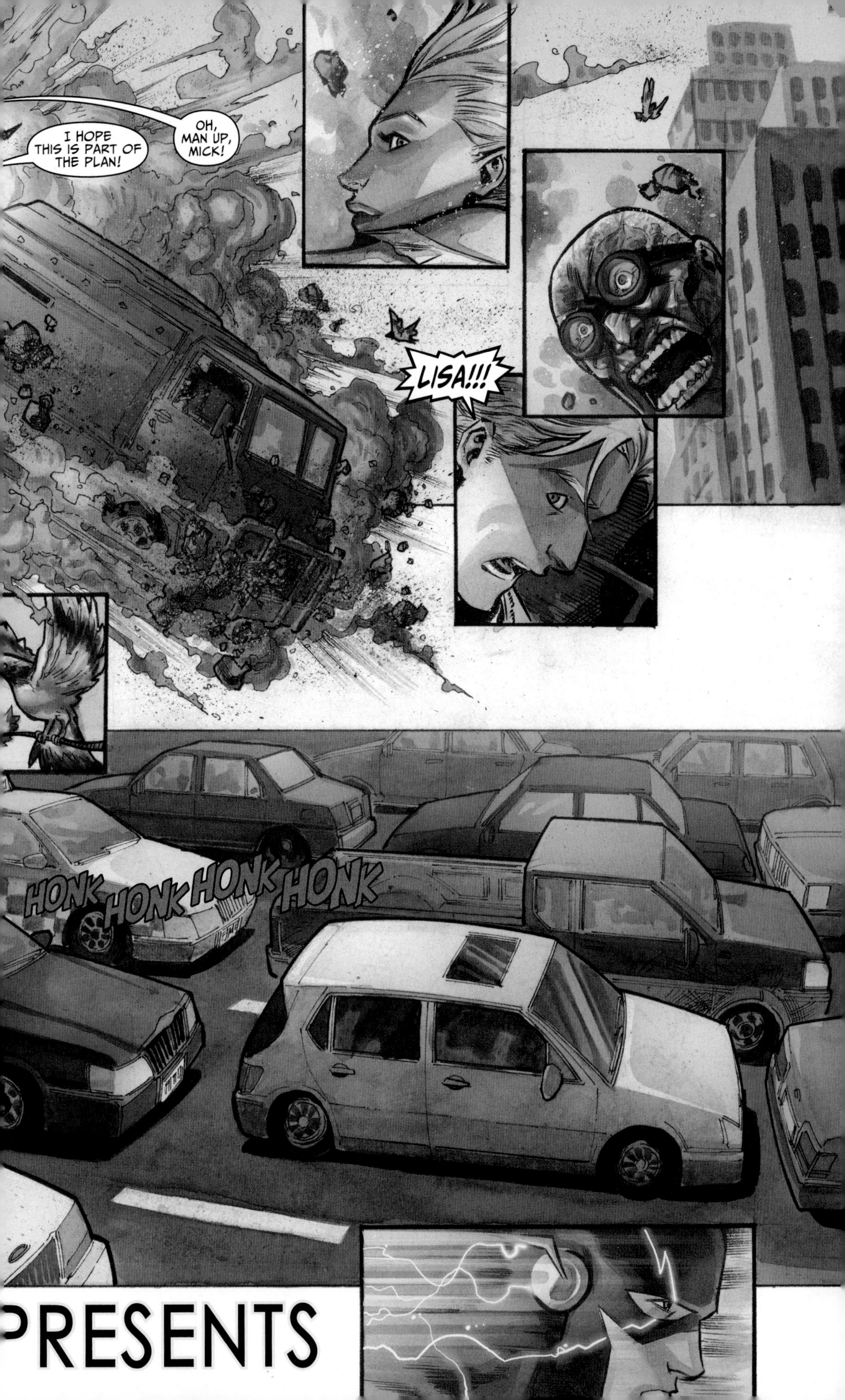
I HOPE THIS IS PART OF THE PLAN!
OH, MAN UP, MICK!
LISA!!!
HONK HONK HONK HONK
PRESENTS

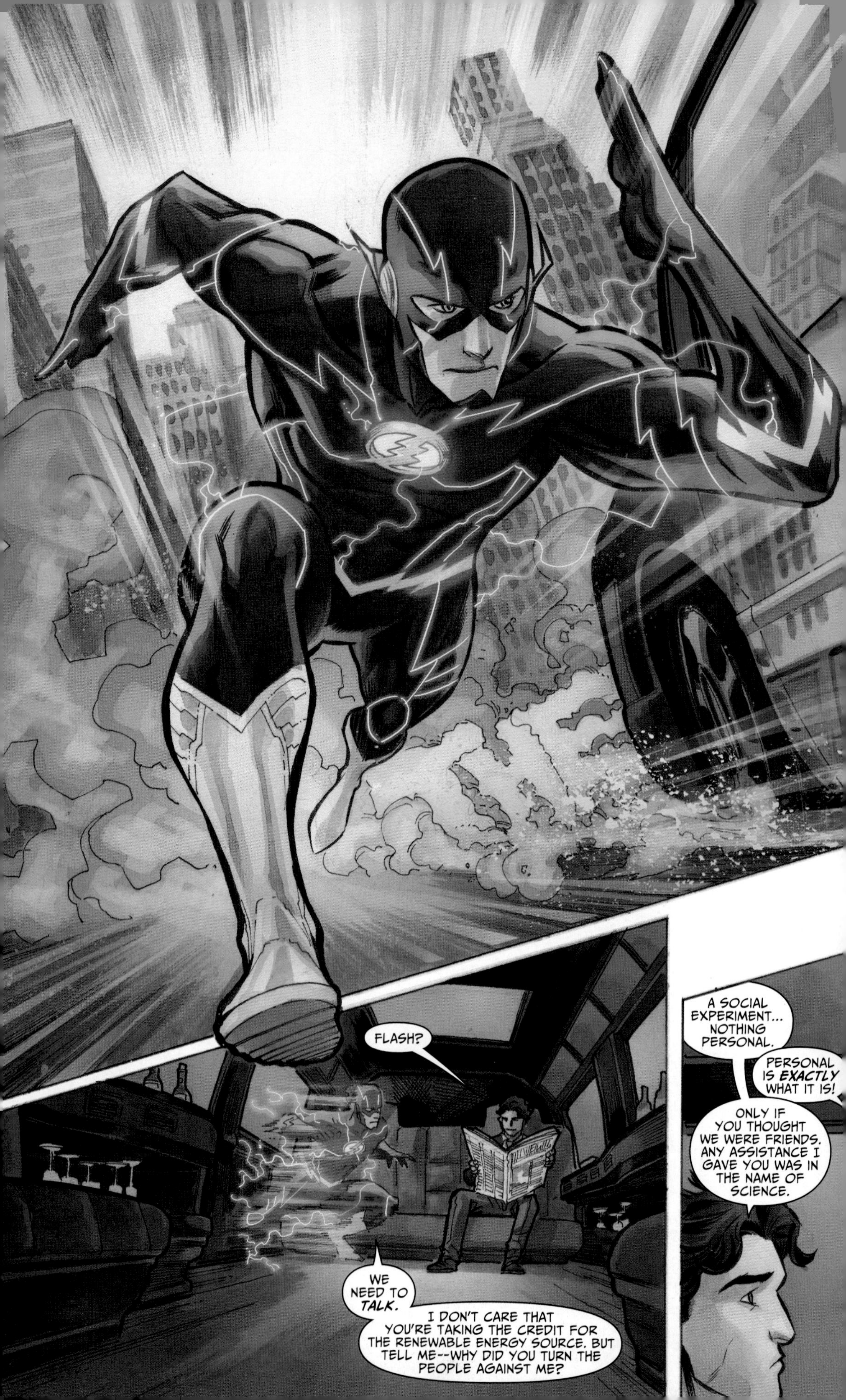
FLASH?
WE NEED TO *TALK*.
I DON'T CARE THAT YOU'RE TAKING THE CREDIT FOR THE RENEWABLE ENERGY SOURCE. BUT TELL ME--WHY DID YOU TURN THE PEOPLE AGAINST ME?
A SOCIAL EXPERIMENT... NOTHING PERSONAL.
PERSONAL IS *EXACTLY* WHAT IT IS!
ONLY IF YOU THOUGHT WE WERE FRIENDS. ANY ASSISTANCE I GAVE YOU WAS IN THE NAME OF SCIENCE.

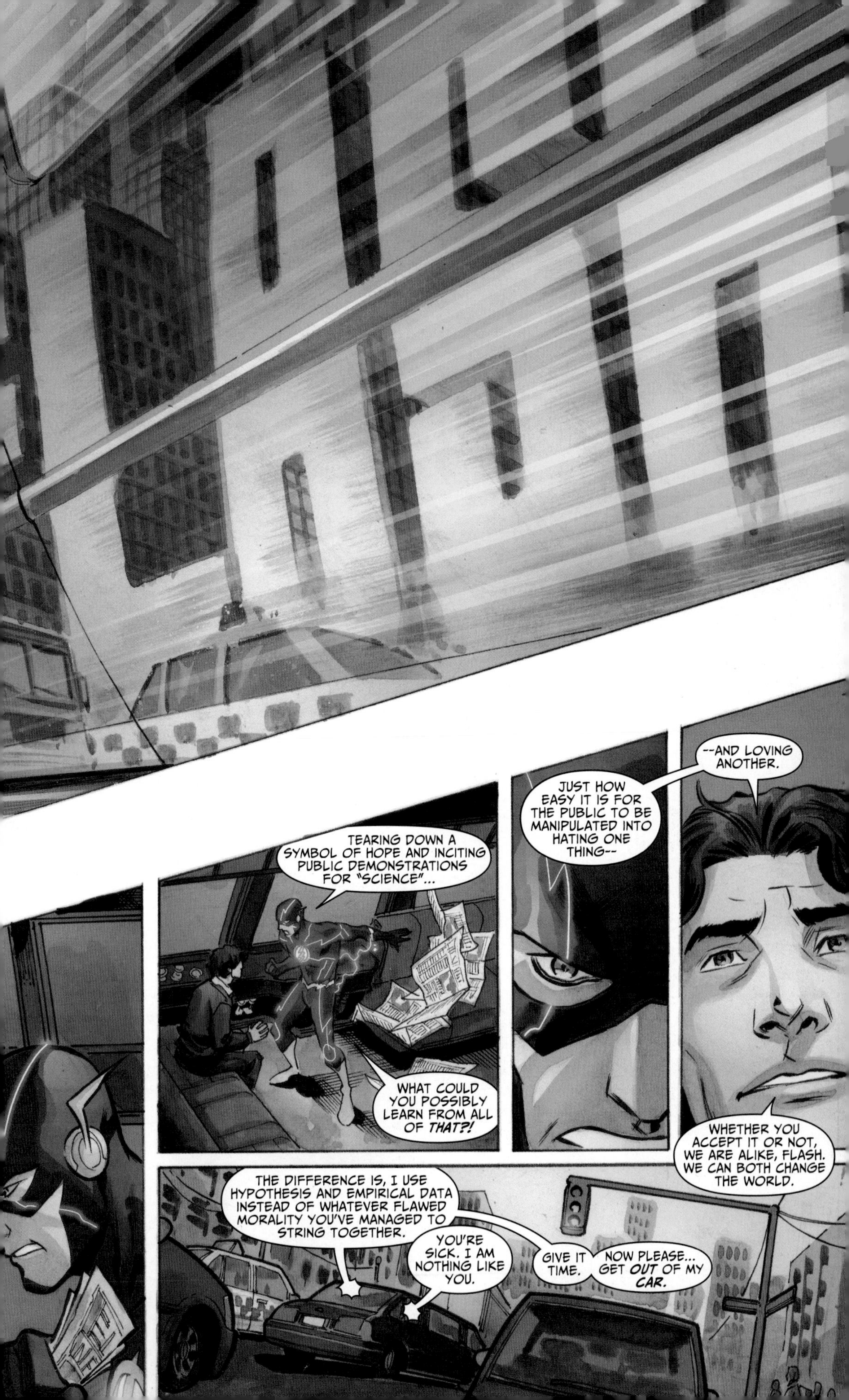
TEARING DOWN A SYMBOL OF HOPE AND INCITING PUBLIC DEMONSTRATIONS FOR "SCIENCE"...
WHAT COULD YOU POSSIBLY LEARN FROM ALL OF *THAT?!*
JUST HOW EASY IT IS FOR THE PUBLIC TO BE MANIPULATED INTO HATING ONE THING--
--AND LOVING ANOTHER.
WHETHER YOU ACCEPT IT OR NOT, WE ARE ALIKE, FLASH. WE CAN BOTH CHANGE THE WORLD.
THE DIFFERENCE IS, I USE HYPOTHESIS AND EMPIRICAL DATA INSTEAD OF WHATEVER FLAWED MORALITY YOU'VE MANAGED TO STRING TOGETHER.
YOU'RE SICK. I AM NOTHING LIKE YOU.
GIVE IT TIME.
NOW PLEASE... GET *OUT* OF MY *CAR.*

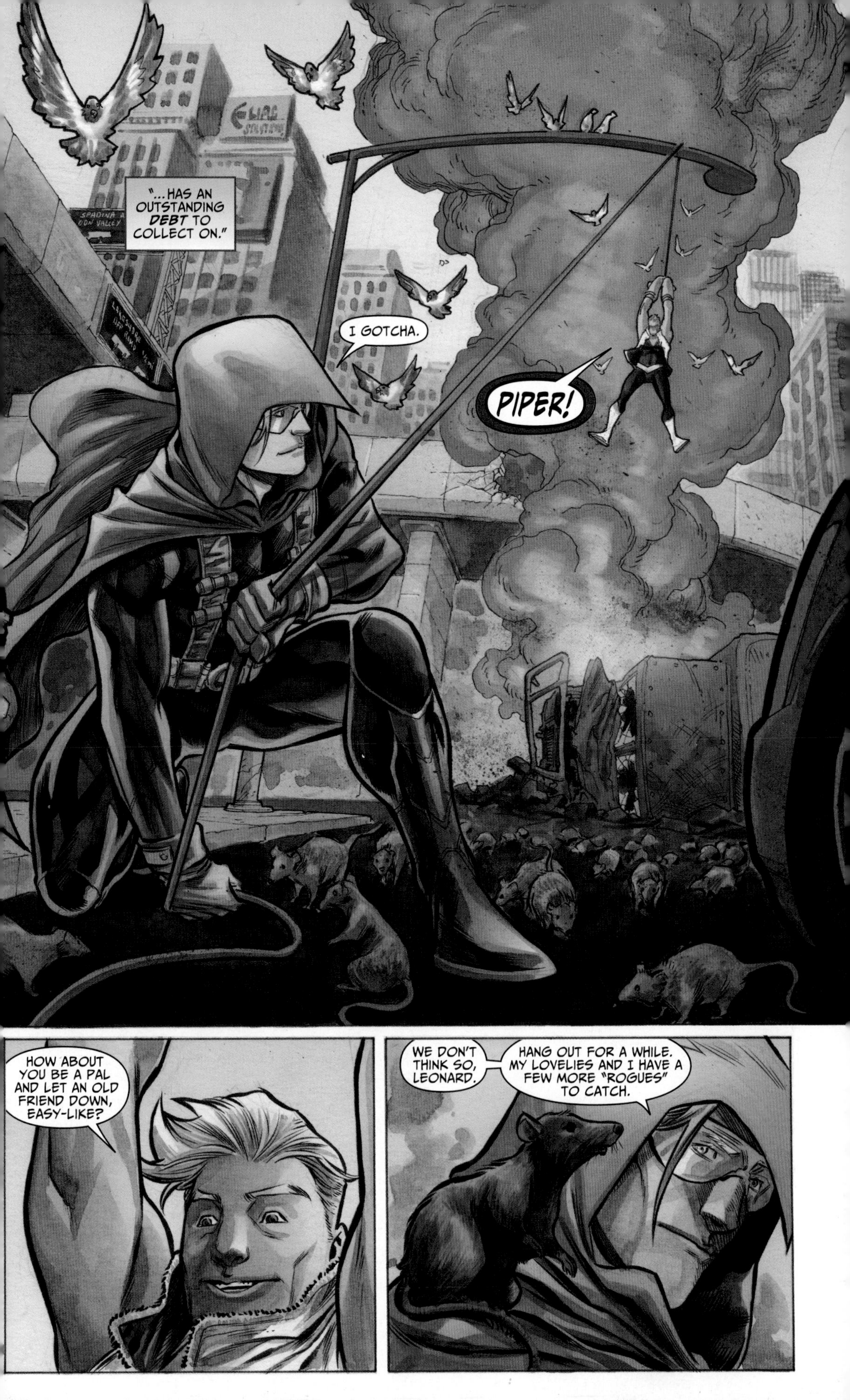
"...HAS AN OUTSTANDING DEBT TO COLLECT ON."
I GOTCHA.
PIPER!
HOW ABOUT YOU BE A PAL AND LET AN OLD FRIEND DOWN, EASY-LIKE?
WE DON'T THINK SO, LEONARD.
HANG OUT FOR A WHILE. MY LOVELIES AND I HAVE A FEW MORE "ROGUES" TO CATCH.

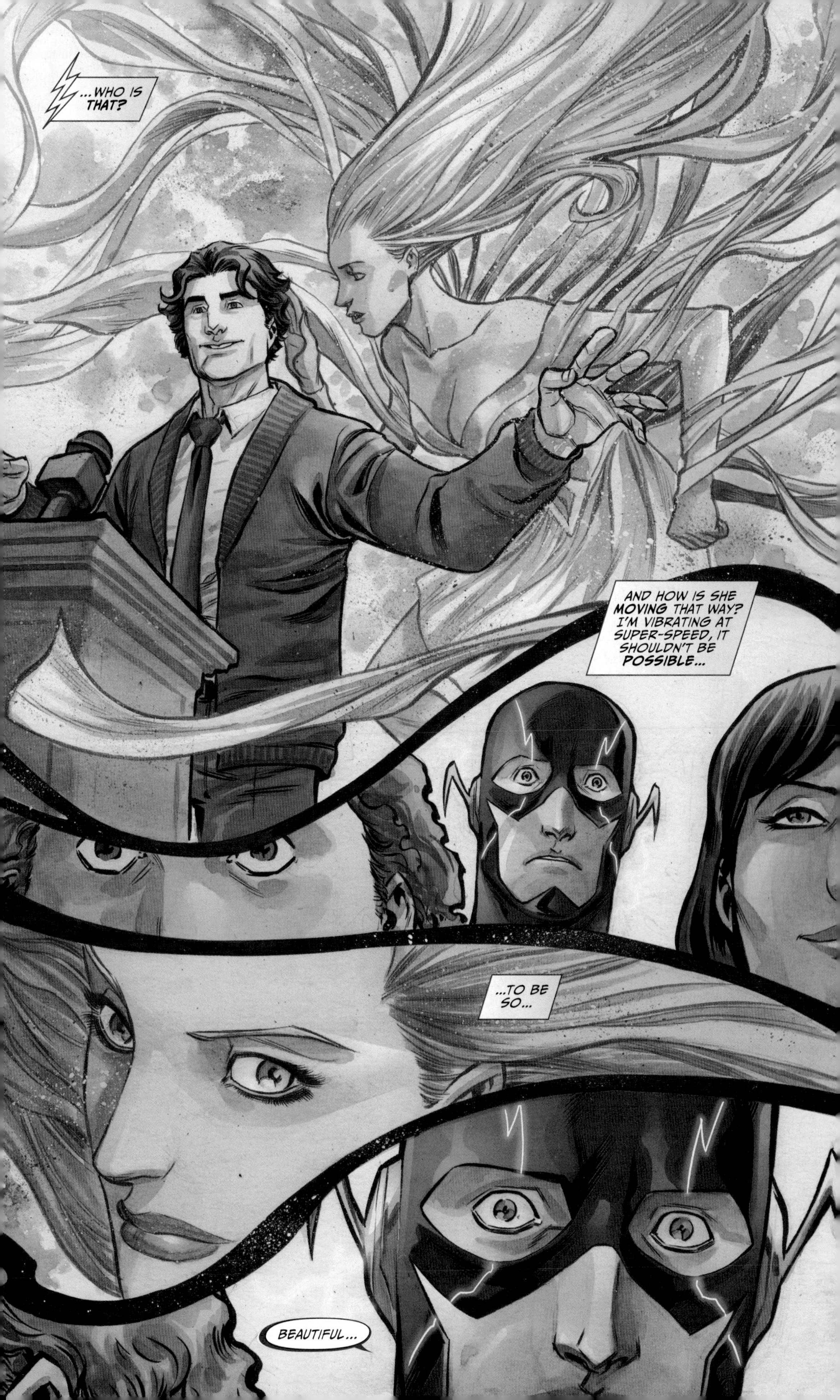
...WHO IS THAT?
AND HOW IS SHE MOVING THAT WAY? I'M VIBRATING AT SUPER-SPEED, IT SHOULDN'T BE POSSIBLE...
...TO BE SO...
BEAUTIFUL...

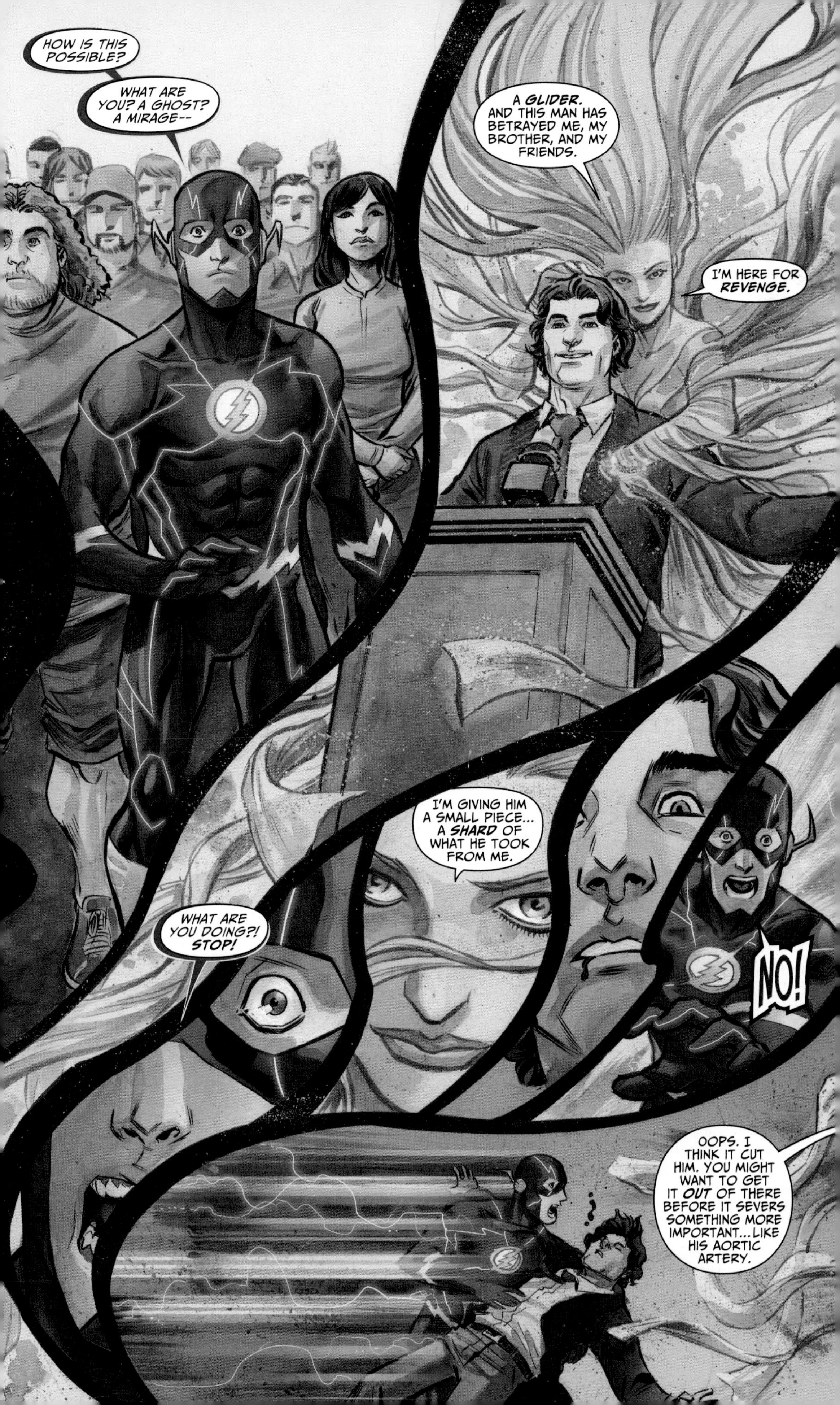
HOW IS THIS POSSIBLE?
WHAT ARE YOU? A GHOST? A MIRAGE--
A GLIDER. AND THIS MAN HAS BETRAYED ME, MY BROTHER, AND MY FRIENDS.
I'M HERE FOR REVENGE.
I'M GIVING HIM A SMALL PIECE... A SHARD OF WHAT HE TOOK FROM ME.
WHAT ARE YOU DOING?! STOP!
NO!
OOPS. I THINK IT CUT HIM. YOU MIGHT WANT TO GET IT OUT OF THERE BEFORE IT SEVERS SOMETHING MORE IMPORTANT...LIKE HIS AORTIC ARTERY.

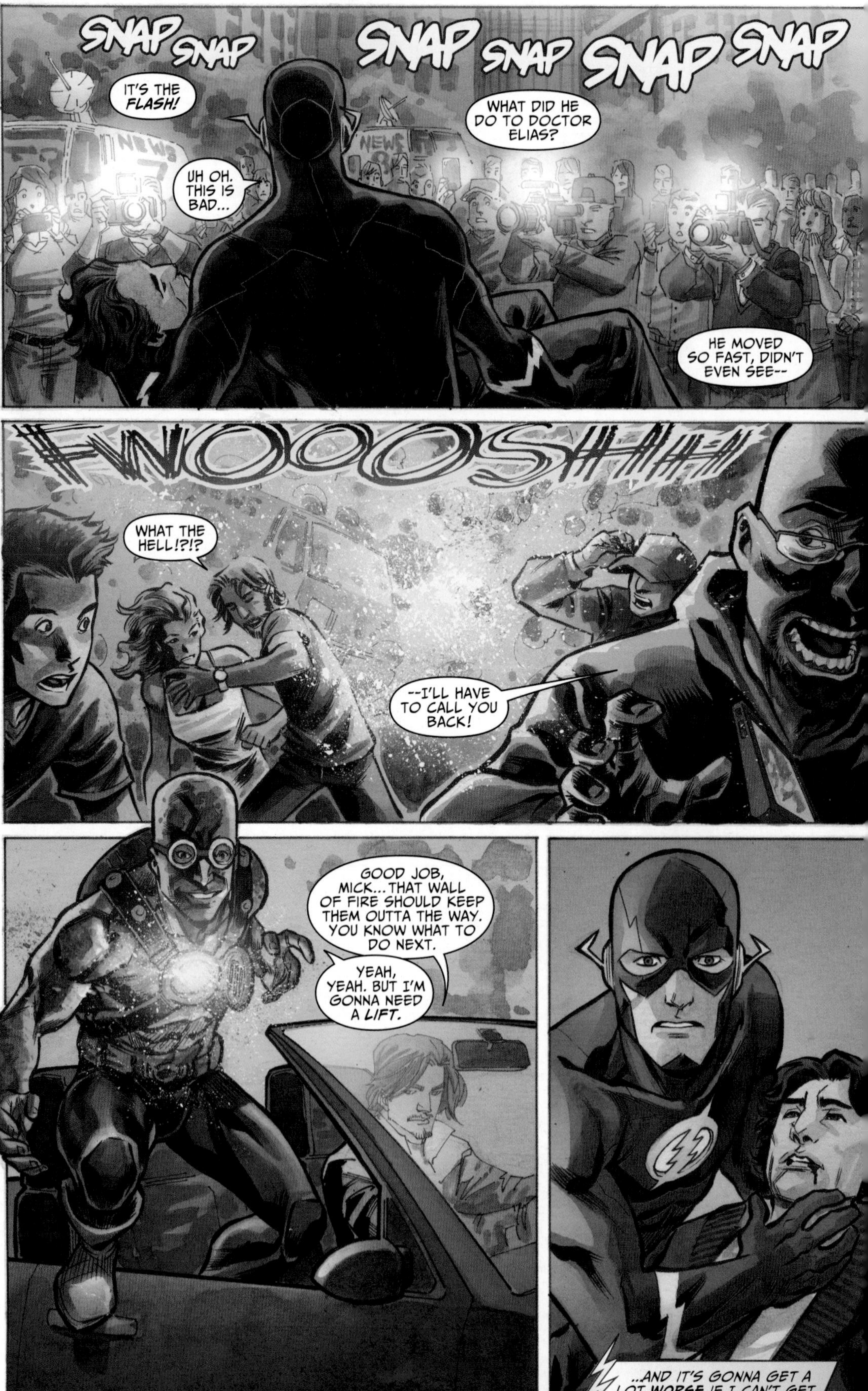
SNAP SNAP SNAP SNAP SNAP SNAP
IT'S THE FLASH!
WHAT DID HE DO TO DOCTOR ELIAS?
UH OH. THIS IS BAD...
HE MOVED SO FAST, DIDN'T EVEN SEE--
FWOOOSHHH
WHAT THE HELL!?!?
--I'LL HAVE TO CALL YOU BACK!
GOOD JOB, MICK...THAT WALL OF FIRE SHOULD KEEP THEM OUTTA THE WAY. YOU KNOW WHAT TO DO NEXT.
YEAH, YEAH. BUT I'M GONNA NEED A LIFT.
...AND IT'S GONNA GET A LOT WORSE IF I CAN'T GET THIS SHARD OUT OF ELIAS.

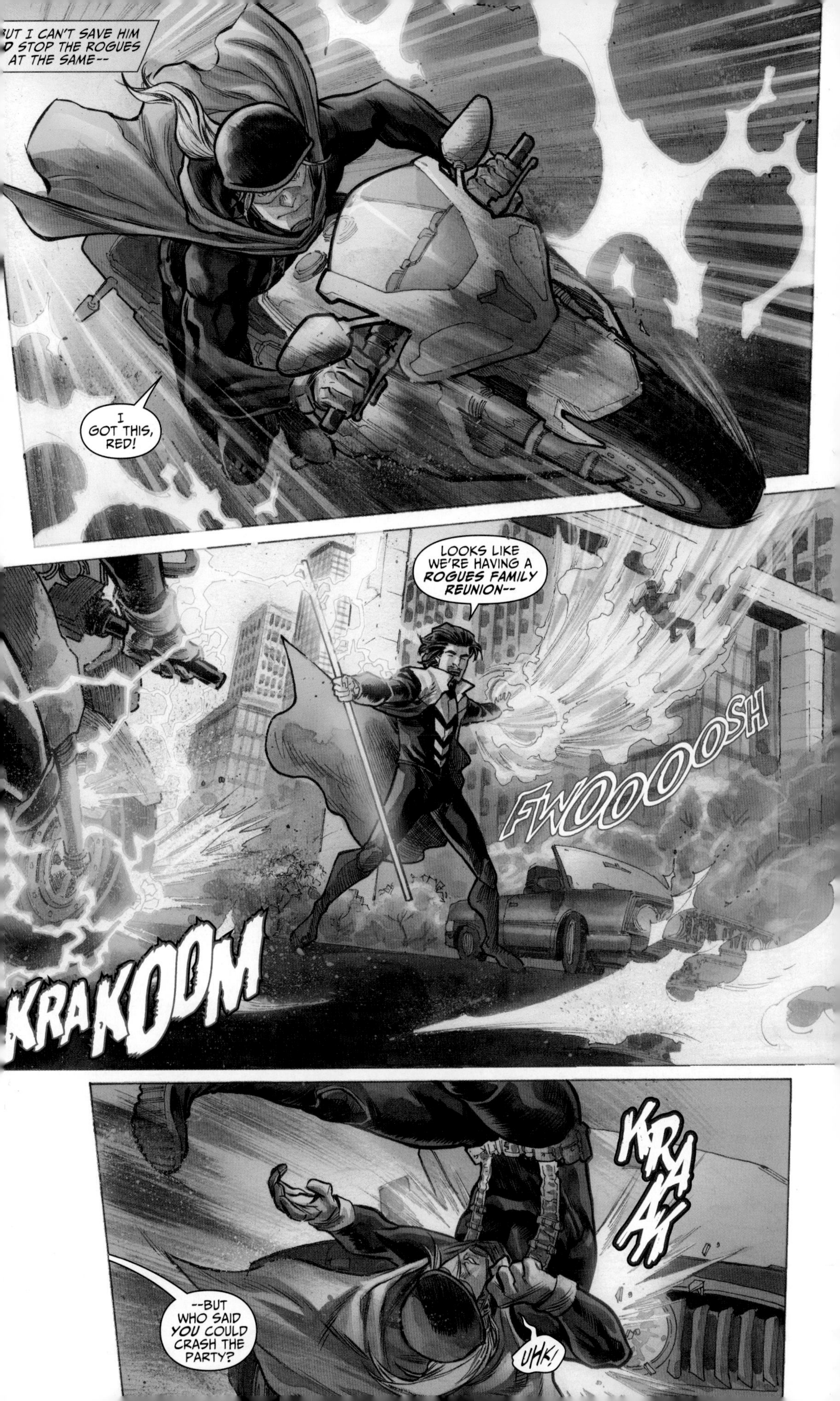

BUT I CAN'T SAVE HIM
D STOP THE ROGUES
AT THE SAME--
I GOT THIS, RED!
LOOKS LIKE WE'RE HAVING A ROGUES FAMILY REUNION--
FWOOOOOSH
KRAKOOM
KRAAK
--BUT WHO SAID YOU COULD CRASH THE PARTY?
UHK!

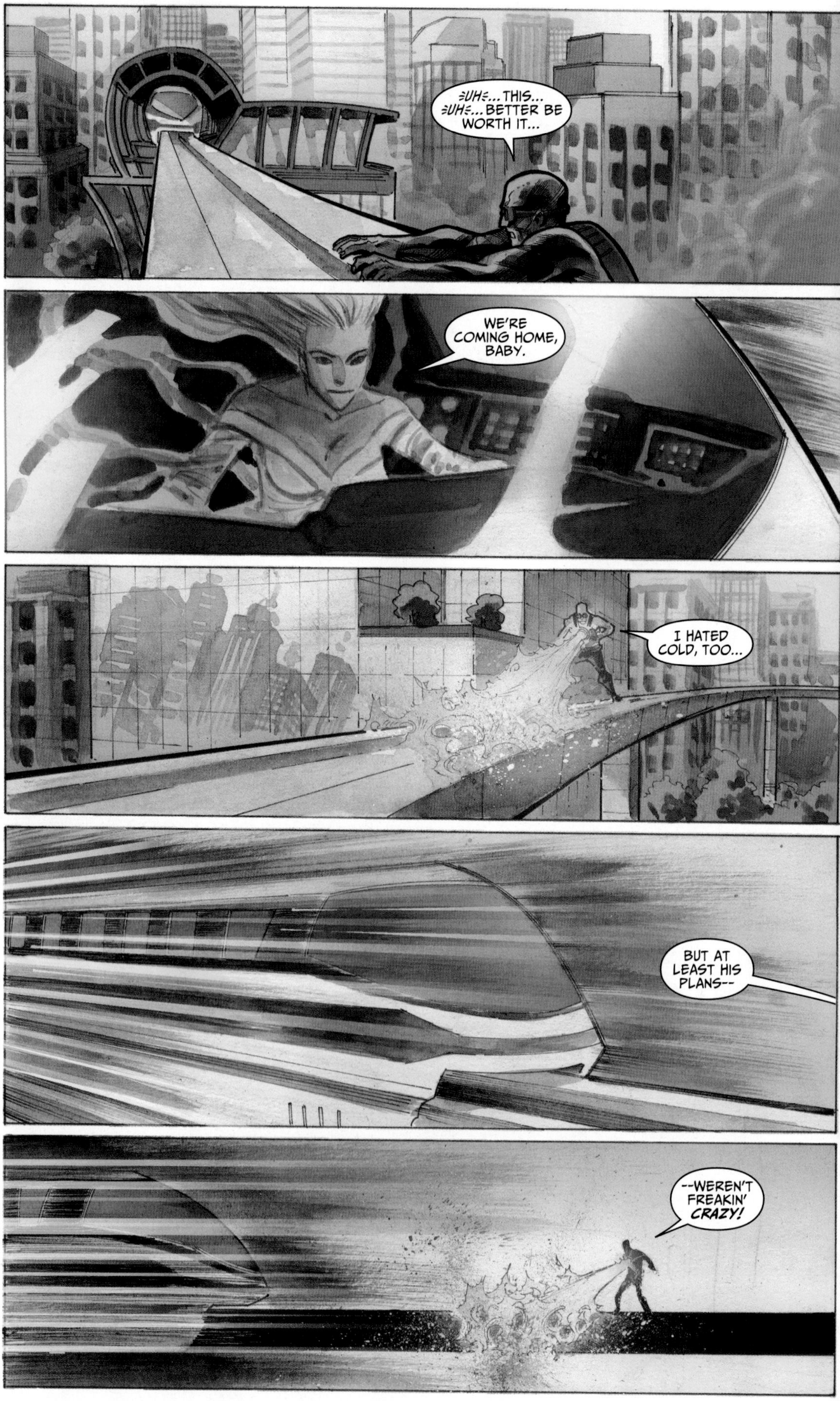

UHH... THIS... UHH... BETTER BE WORTH IT...
WE'RE COMING HOME, BABY.
I HATED COLD, TOO...
BUT AT LEAST HIS PLANS--
--WEREN'T FREAKIN' CRAZY!

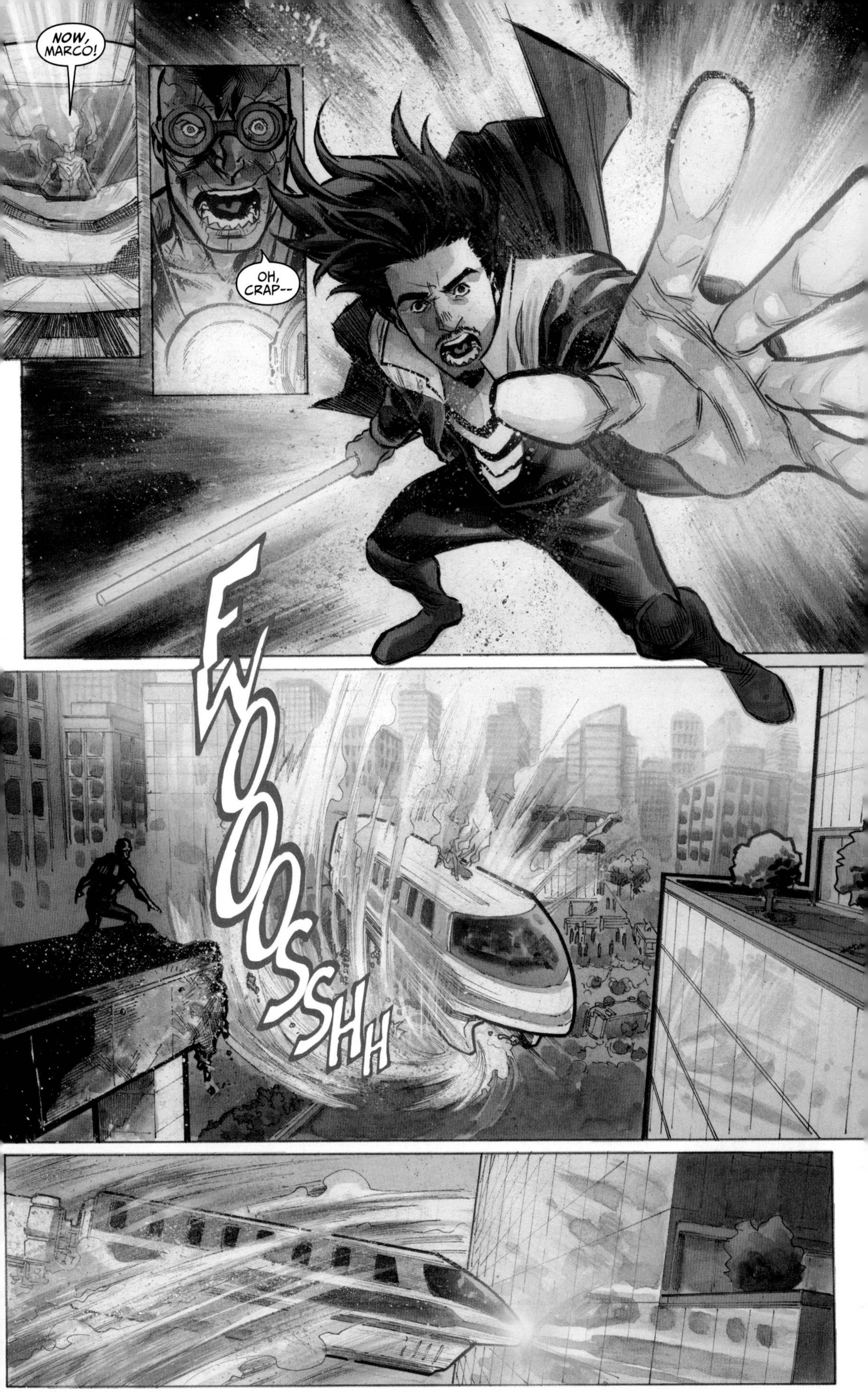
NOW, MARCO!
OH, CRAP--
FWOOOSSHH

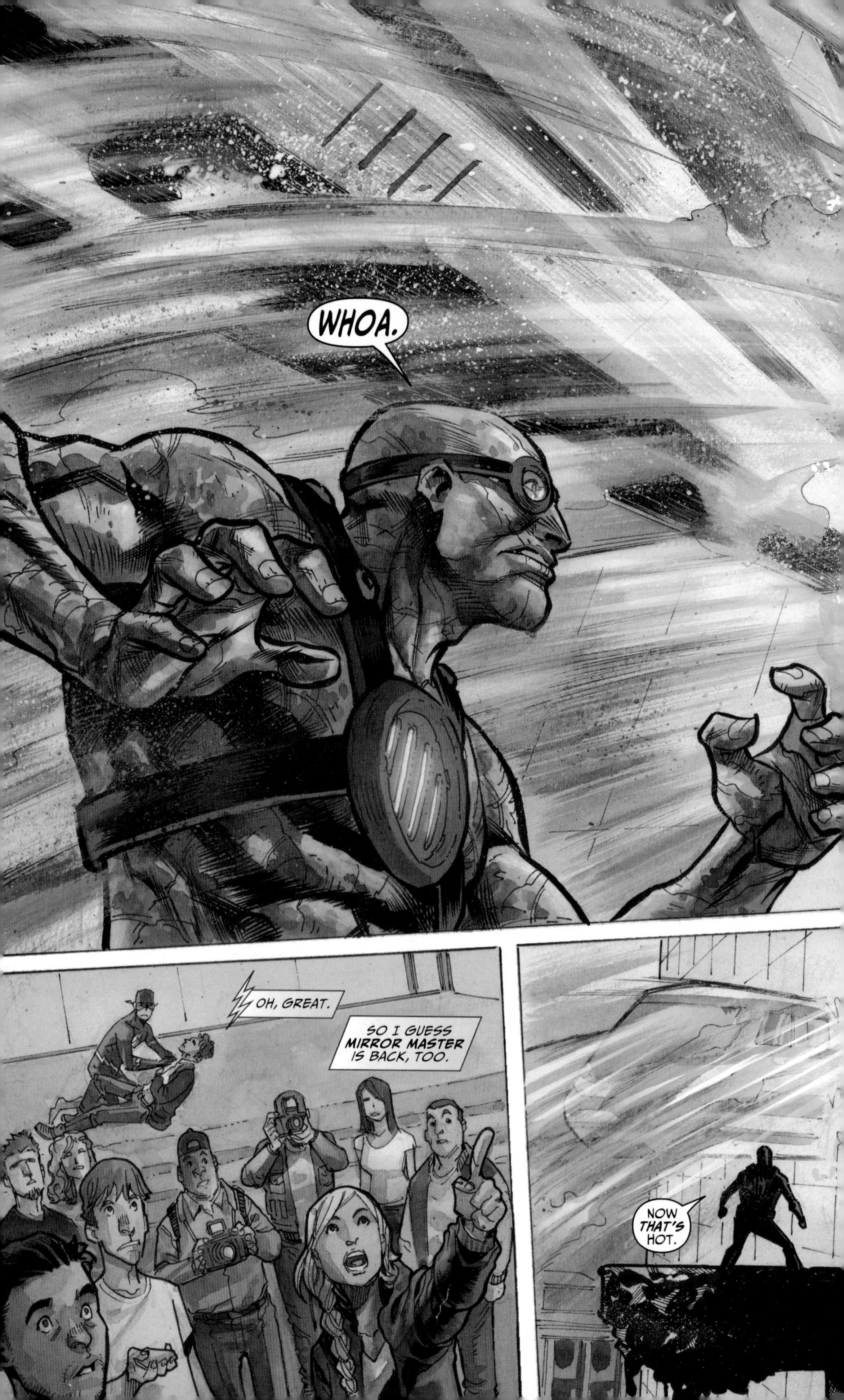
WHOA.
OH, GREAT.
SO I GUESS MIRROR MASTER IS BACK, TOO.
NOW THAT'S HOT.

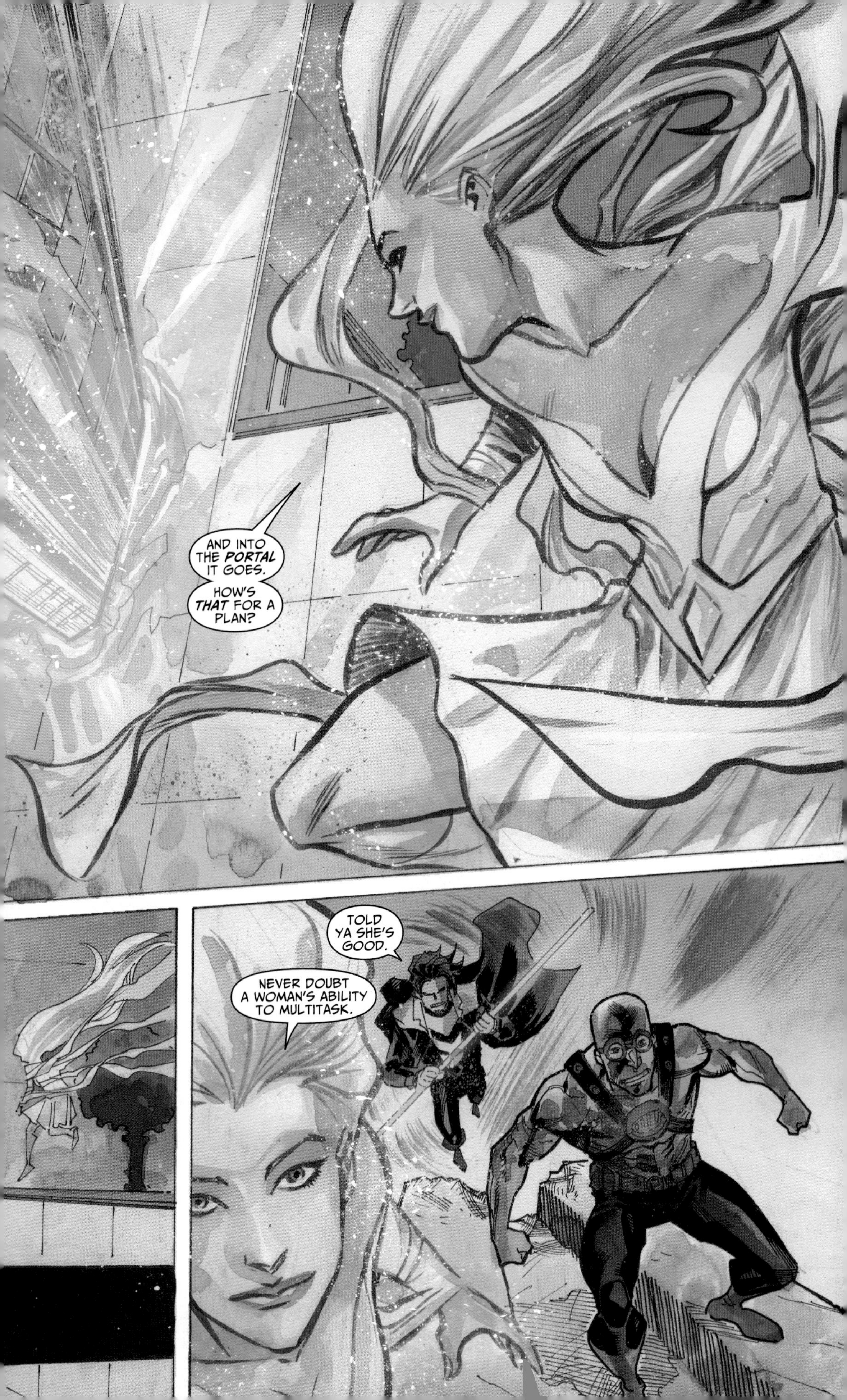
AND INTO THE PORTAL IT GOES.
HOW'S THAT FOR A PLAN?
TOLD YA SHE'S GOOD.
NEVER DOUBT A WOMAN'S ABILITY TO MULTITASK.

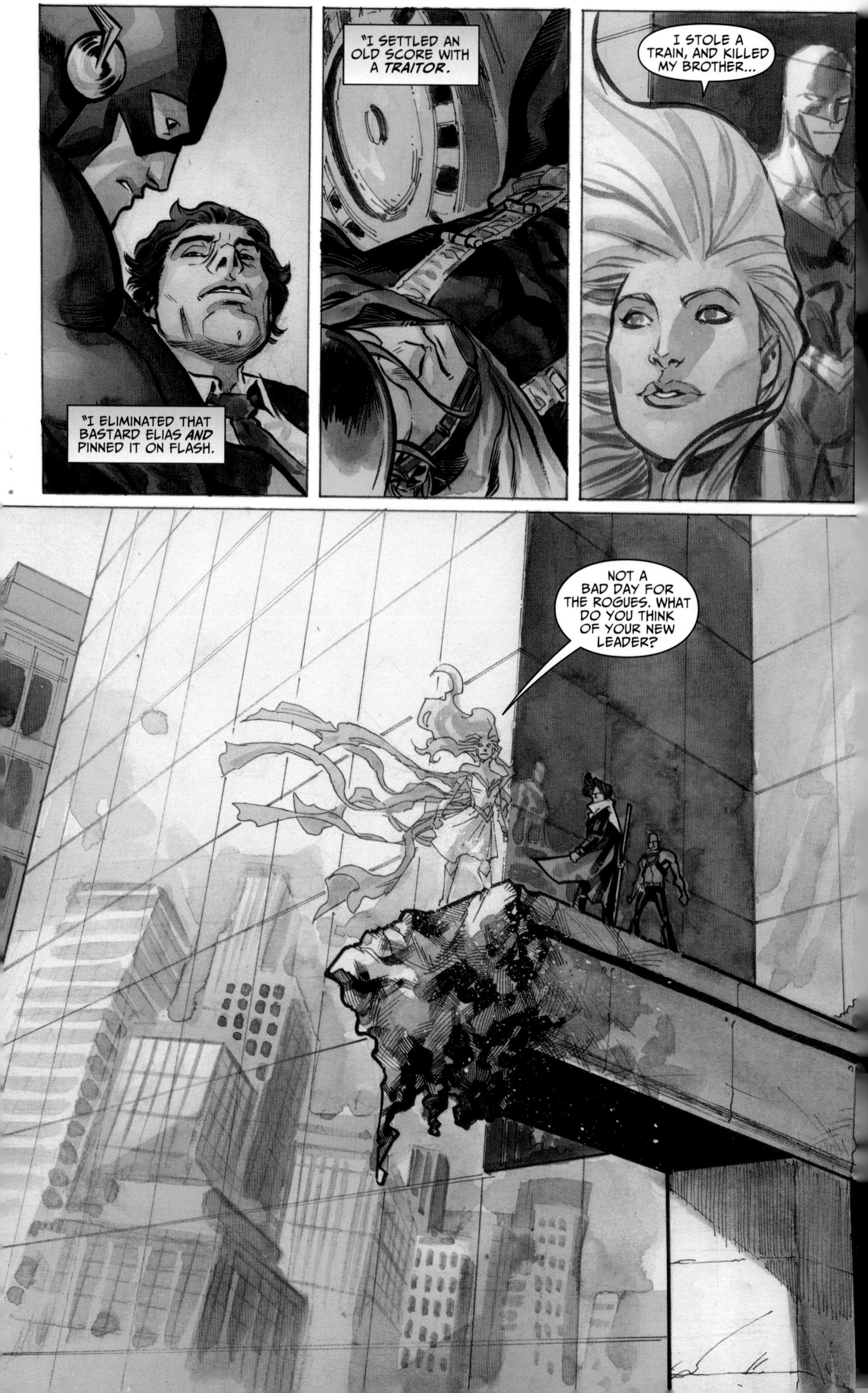
"I ELIMINATED THAT BASTARD ELIAS AND PINNED IT ON FLASH.
"I SETTLED AN OLD SCORE WITH A TRAITOR.
I STOLE A TRAIN, AND KILLED MY BROTHER...
NOT A BAD DAY FOR THE ROGUES. WHAT DO YOU THINK OF YOUR NEW LEADER?

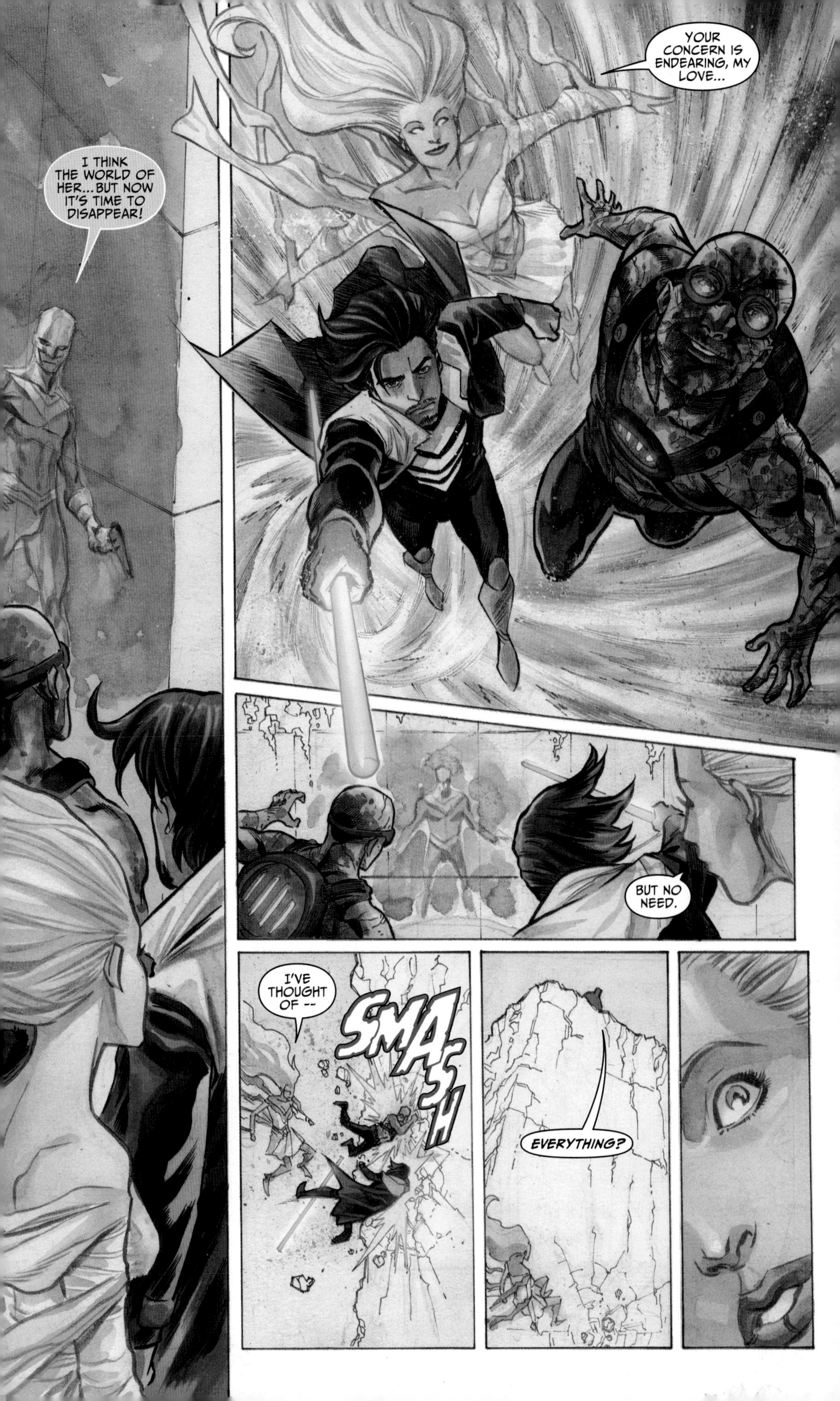

I THINK THE WORLD OF HER...BUT NOW IT'S TIME TO DISAPPEAR!
YOUR CONCERN IS ENDEARING, MY LOVE...
BUT NO NEED.
I'VE THOUGHT OF --
SMASH
EVERYTHING?

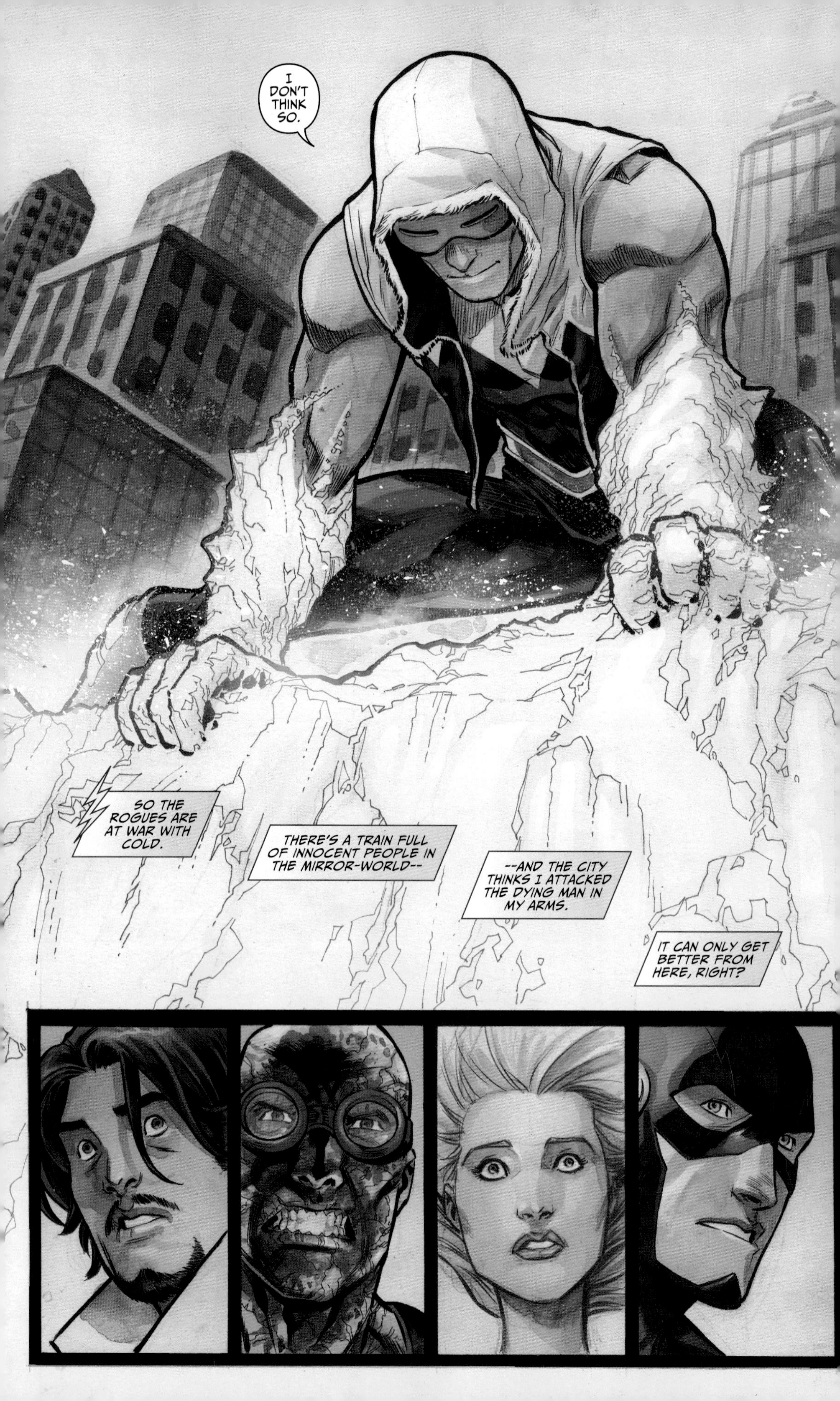

I DON'T THINK SO.
SO THE ROGUES ARE AT WAR WITH COLD.
THERE'S A TRAIN FULL OF INNOCENT PEOPLE IN THE MIRROR-WORLD--
--AND THE CITY THINKS I ATTACKED THE DYING MAN IN MY ARMS.
IT CAN ONLY GET BETTER FROM HERE, RIGHT?

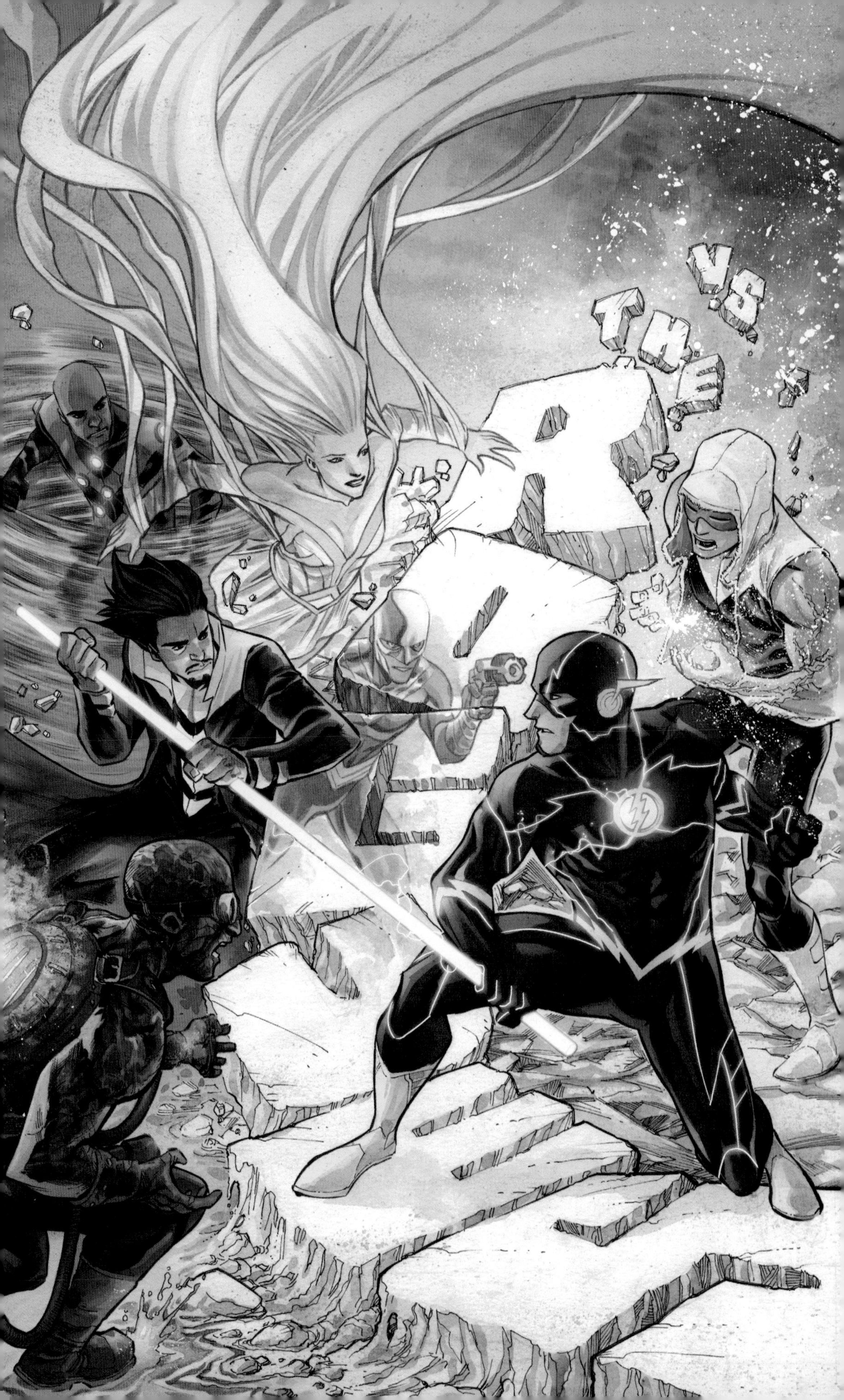
T.H.E.
V.S

FRANCIS MANAPUL & BRIAN BUCCELLATO writers FRANCIS MANAPUL breakdowns MARCUS TO & RAY McCARTHY artists – chapter one
SCOTT KOLINS artist – chapter two DIOGENES NEVES & OCLAIR ALBERT artists – chapter three
MARCIO TAKARA artist – chapter four WES CRAIG artist – chapter five

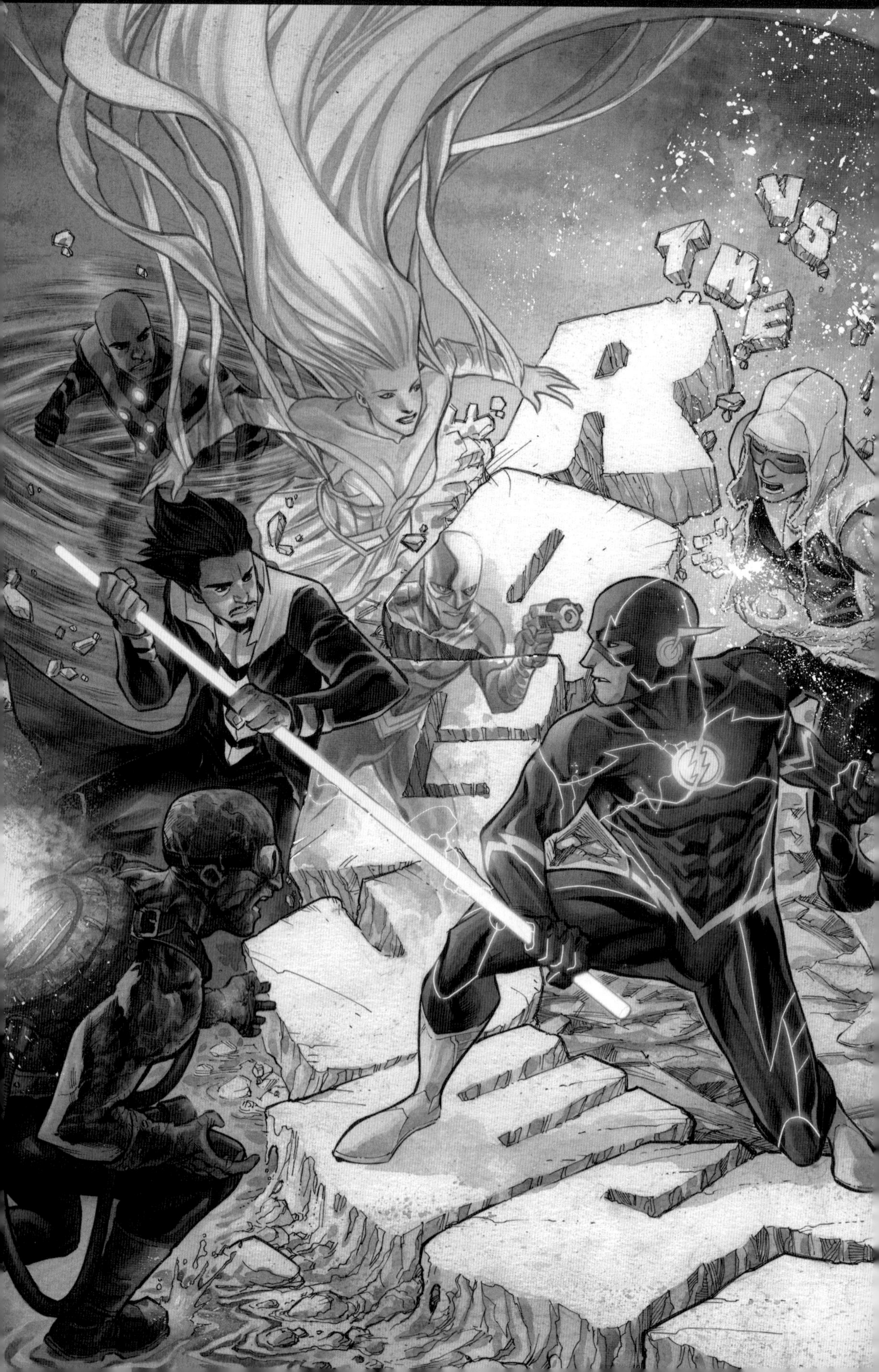
VS
THE

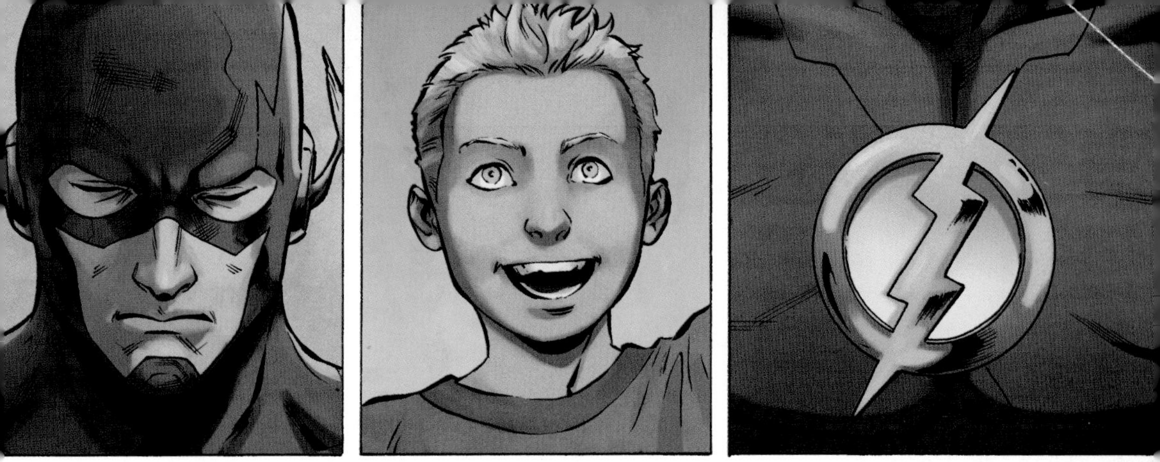

UNITED THEY FALL
CHAPTER 1: THE FLATS

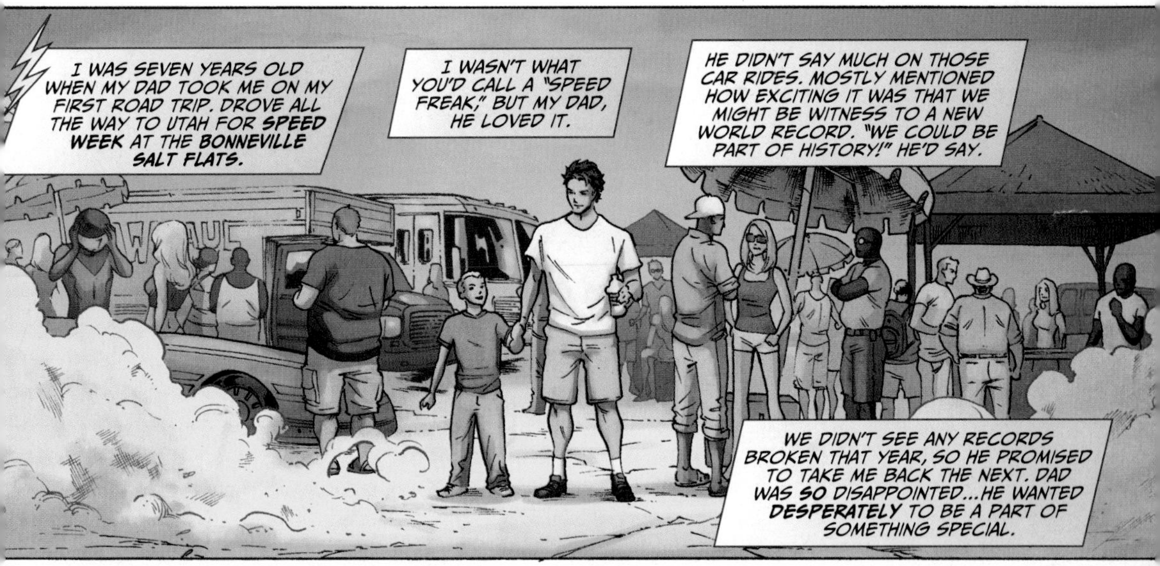

I WAS SEVEN YEARS OLD WHEN MY DAD TOOK ME ON MY FIRST ROAD TRIP. DROVE ALL THE WAY TO UTAH FOR SPEED WEEK AT THE BONNEVILLE SALT FLATS.
I WASN'T WHAT YOU'D CALL A "SPEED FREAK," BUT MY DAD, HE LOVED IT.
HE DIDN'T SAY MUCH ON THOSE CAR RIDES. MOSTLY MENTIONED HOW EXCITING IT WAS THAT WE MIGHT BE WITNESS TO A NEW WORLD RECORD. "WE COULD BE PART OF HISTORY!" HE'D SAY.
WE DIDN'T SEE ANY RECORDS BROKEN THAT YEAR, SO HE PROMISED TO TAKE ME BACK THE NEXT. DAD WAS SO DISAPPOINTED...HE WANTED DESPERATELY TO BE A PART OF SOMETHING SPECIAL.

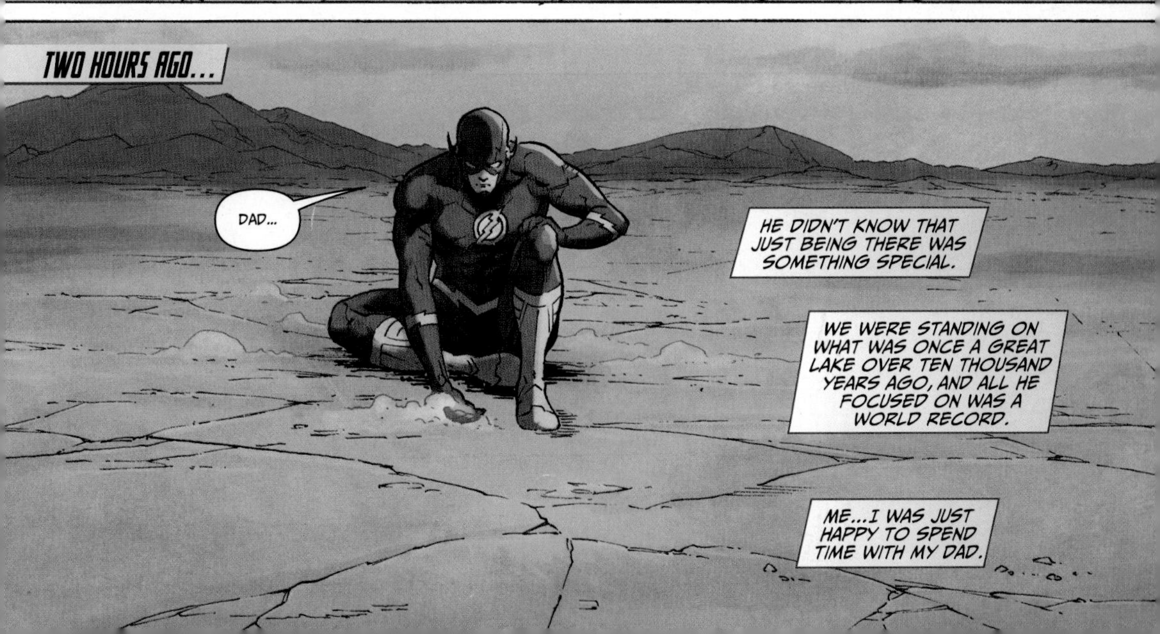

TWO HOURS AGO...
DAD...
HE DIDN'T KNOW THAT JUST BEING THERE WAS SOMETHING SPECIAL.
WE WERE STANDING ON WHAT WAS ONCE A GREAT LAKE OVER TEN THOUSAND YEARS AGO, AND ALL HE FOCUSED ON WAS A WORLD RECORD.
ME...I WAS JUST HAPPY TO SPEND TIME WITH MY DAD.

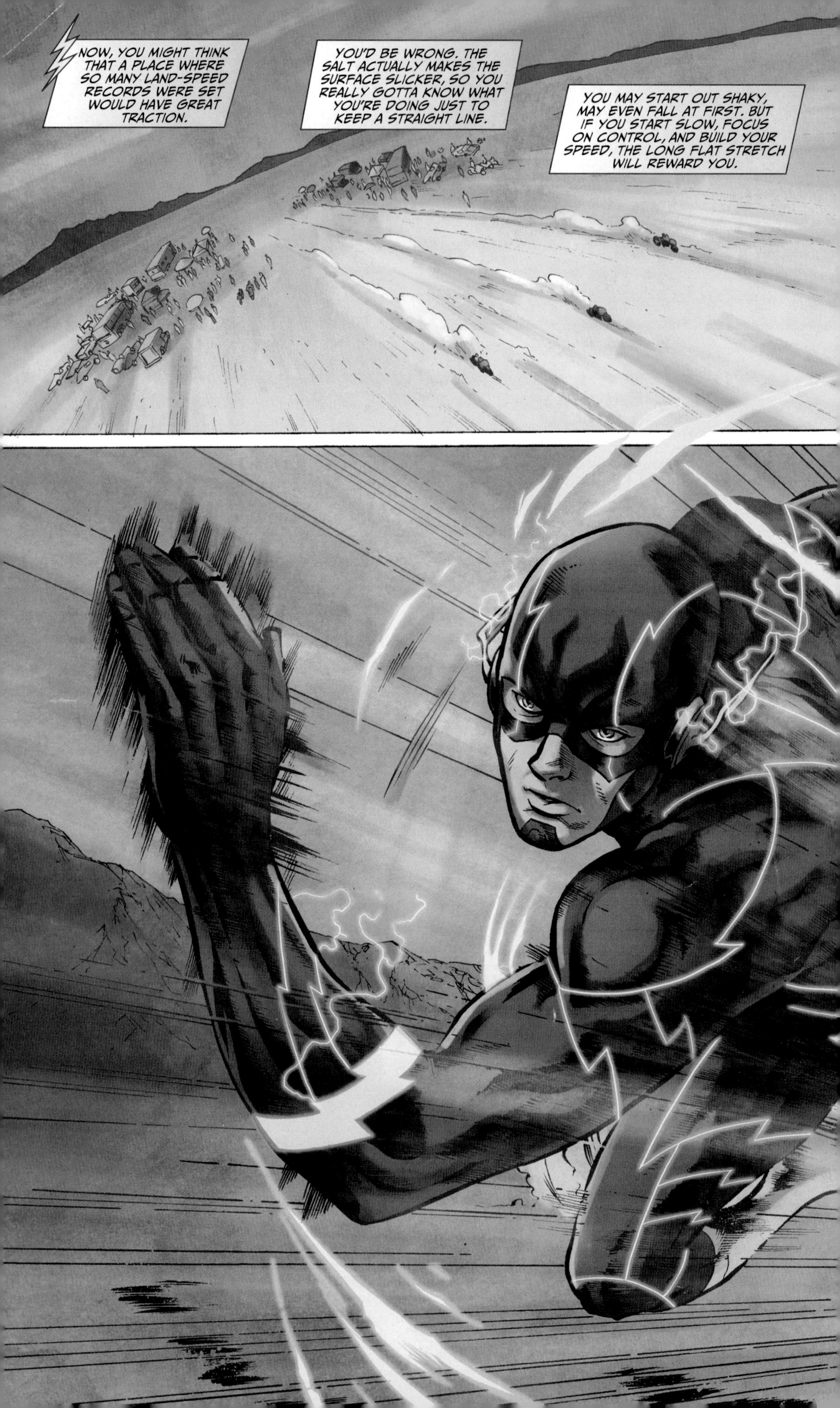
NOW, YOU MIGHT THINK THAT A PLACE WHERE SO MANY LAND-SPEED RECORDS WERE SET WOULD HAVE GREAT TRACTION.
YOU'D BE WRONG. THE SALT ACTUALLY MAKES THE SURFACE SLICKER, SO YOU REALLY GOTTA KNOW WHAT YOU'RE DOING JUST TO KEEP A STRAIGHT LINE.
YOU MAY START OUT SHAKY, MAY EVEN FALL AT FIRST. BUT IF YOU START SLOW, FOCUS ON CONTROL, AND BUILD YOUR SPEED, THE LONG FLAT STRETCH WILL REWARD YOU.

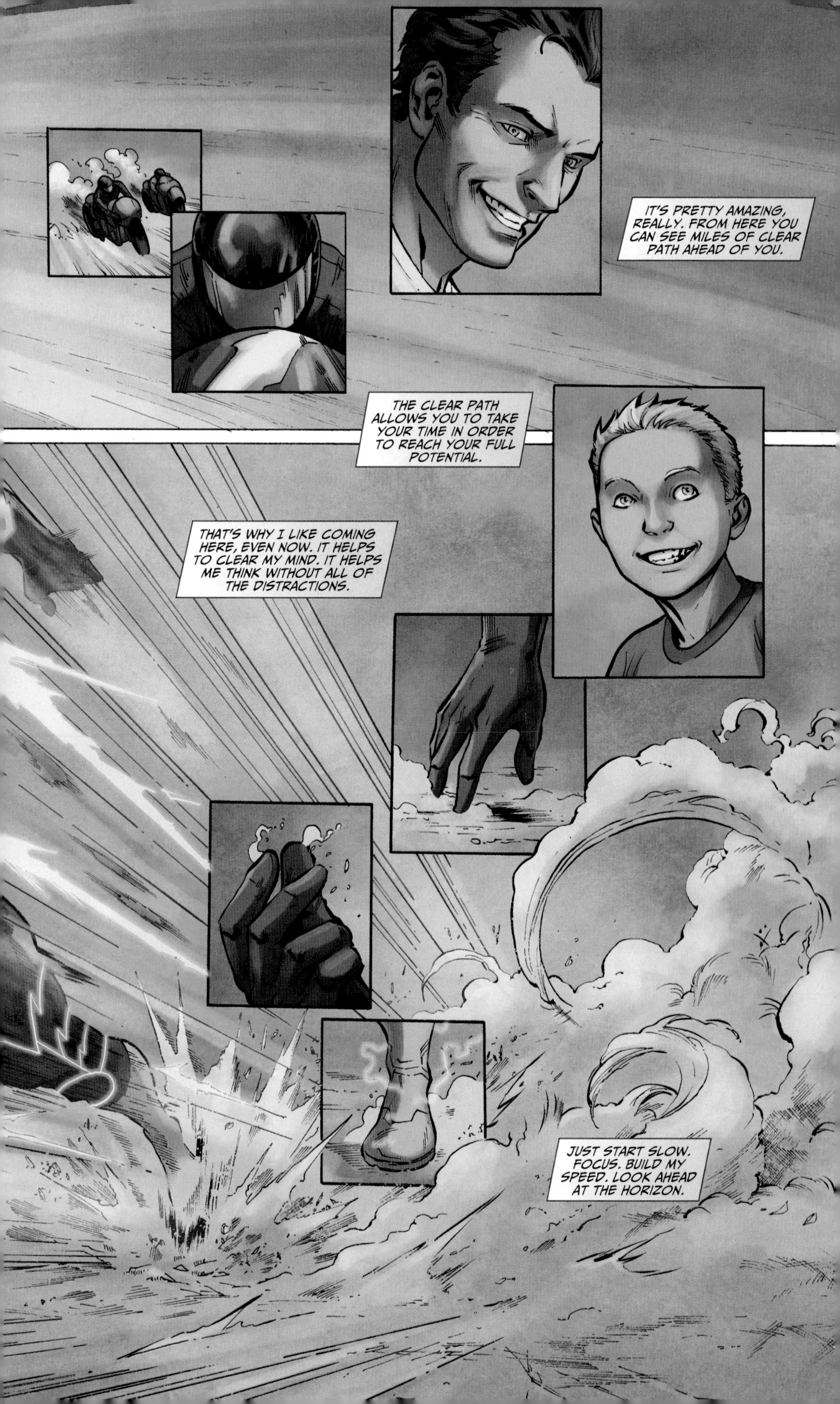
IT'S PRETTY AMAZING, REALLY. FROM HERE YOU CAN SEE MILES OF CLEAR PATH AHEAD OF YOU.
THE CLEAR PATH ALLOWS YOU TO TAKE YOUR TIME IN ORDER TO REACH YOUR FULL POTENTIAL.
THAT'S WHY I LIKE COMING HERE, EVEN NOW. IT HELPS TO CLEAR MY MIND. IT HELPS ME THINK WITHOUT ALL OF THE DISTRACTIONS.
JUST START SLOW. FOCUS. BUILD MY SPEED. LOOK AHEAD AT THE HORIZON.

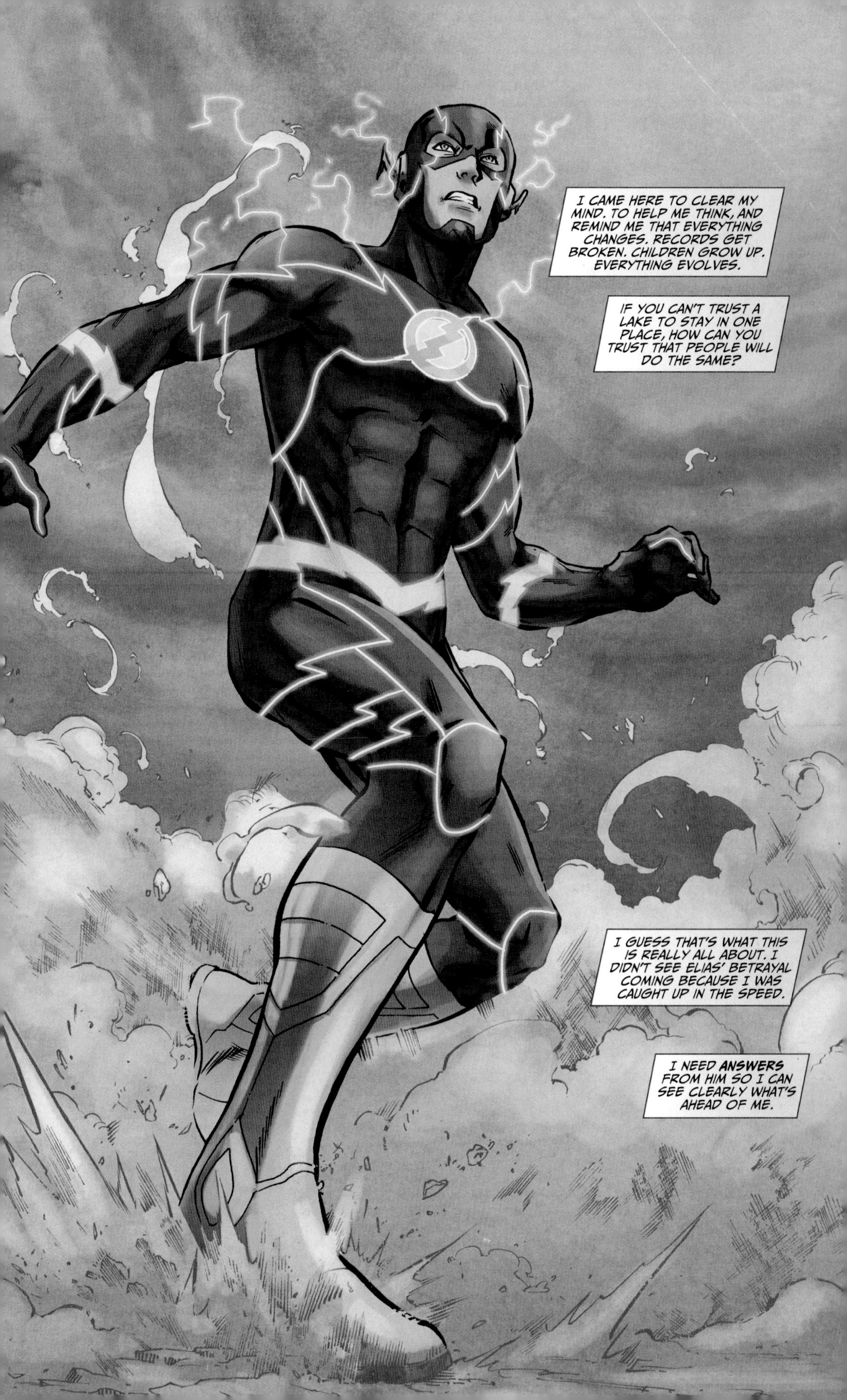
I CAME HERE TO CLEAR MY MIND. TO HELP ME THINK, AND REMIND ME THAT EVERYTHING CHANGES. RECORDS GET BROKEN. CHILDREN GROW UP. EVERYTHING EVOLVES.
IF YOU CAN'T TRUST A LAKE TO STAY IN ONE PLACE, HOW CAN YOU TRUST THAT PEOPLE WILL DO THE SAME?
I GUESS THAT'S WHAT THIS IS REALLY ALL ABOUT. I DIDN'T SEE ELIAS' BETRAYAL COMING BECAUSE I WAS CAUGHT UP IN THE SPEED.
I NEED **ANSWERS** FROM HIM SO I CAN SEE CLEARLY WHAT'S AHEAD OF ME.

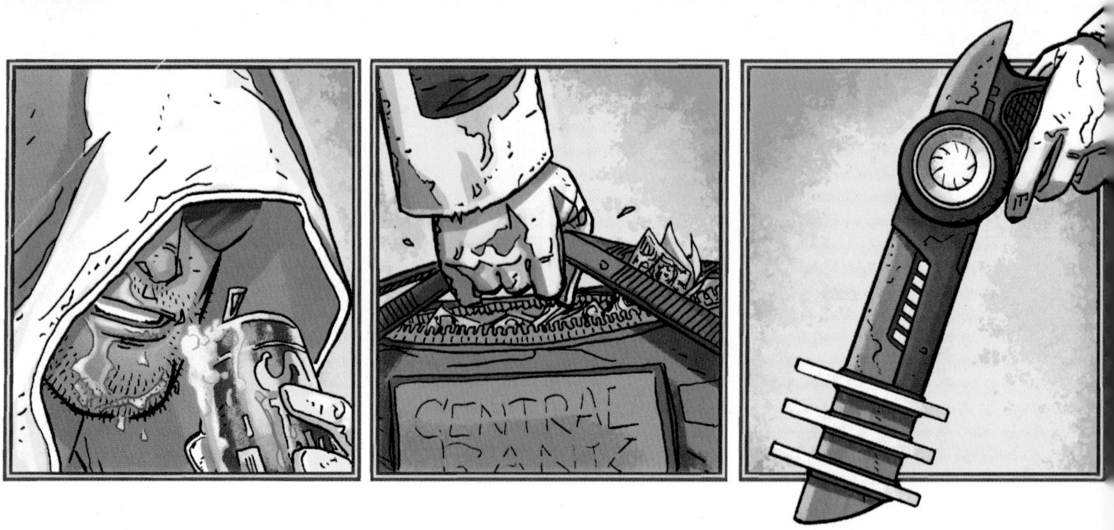
CENTRAL

CHAPTER 2: THE OPPORTUNITY

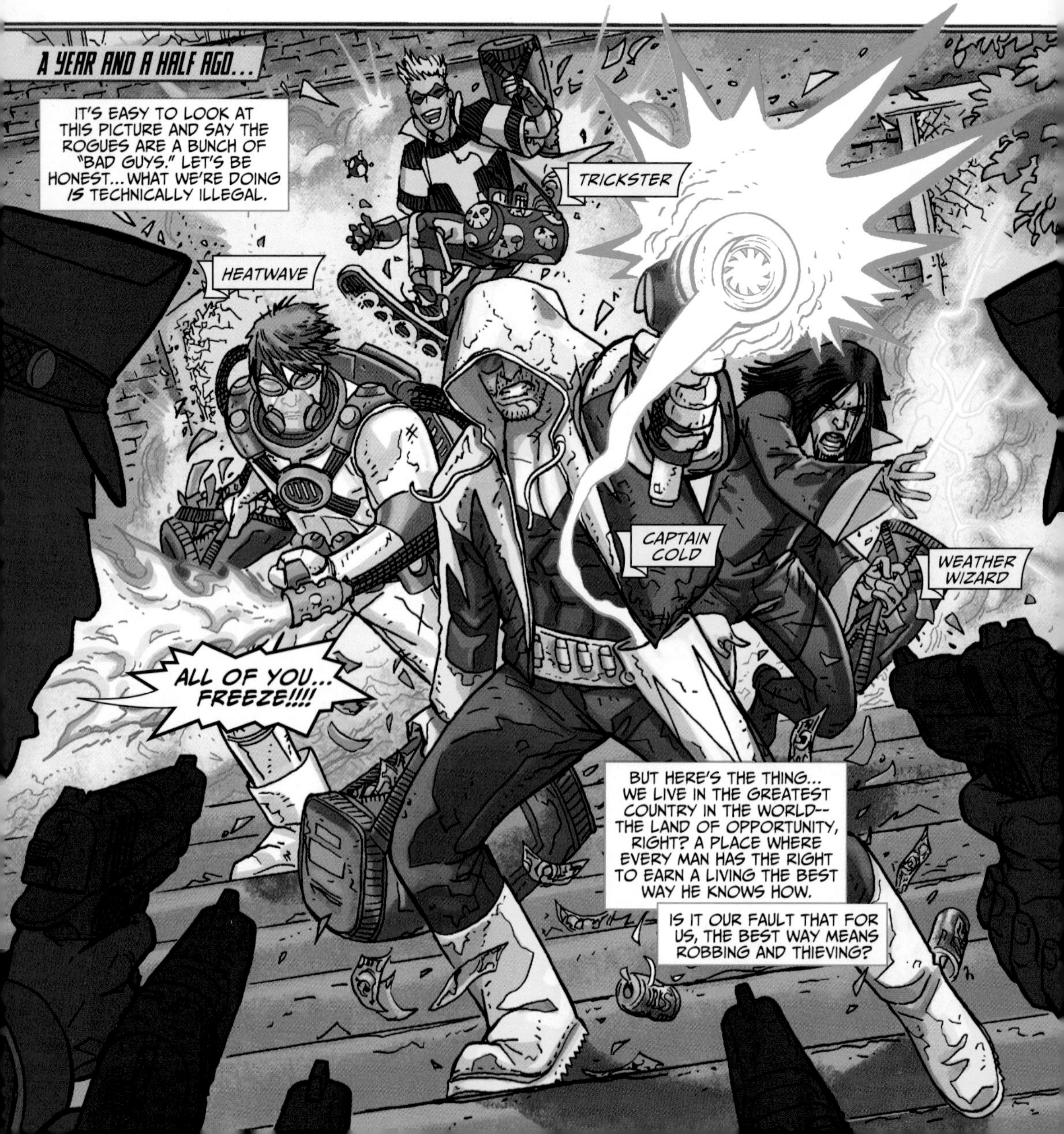
A YEAR AND A HALF AGO...
IT'S EASY TO LOOK AT THIS PICTURE AND SAY THE ROGUES ARE A BUNCH OF "BAD GUYS." LET'S BE HONEST...WHAT WE'RE DOING *IS* TECHNICALLY ILLEGAL.
TRICKSTER
HEATWAVE
CAPTAIN COLD
WEATHER WIZARD
ALL OF YOU... FREEZE!!!!
BUT HERE'S THE THING... WE LIVE IN THE GREATEST COUNTRY IN THE WORLD-- THE LAND OF OPPORTUNITY, RIGHT? A PLACE WHERE EVERY MAN HAS THE RIGHT TO EARN A LIVING THE BEST WAY HE KNOWS HOW.
IS IT OUR FAULT THAT FOR US, THE BEST WAY MEANS ROBBING AND THIEVING?

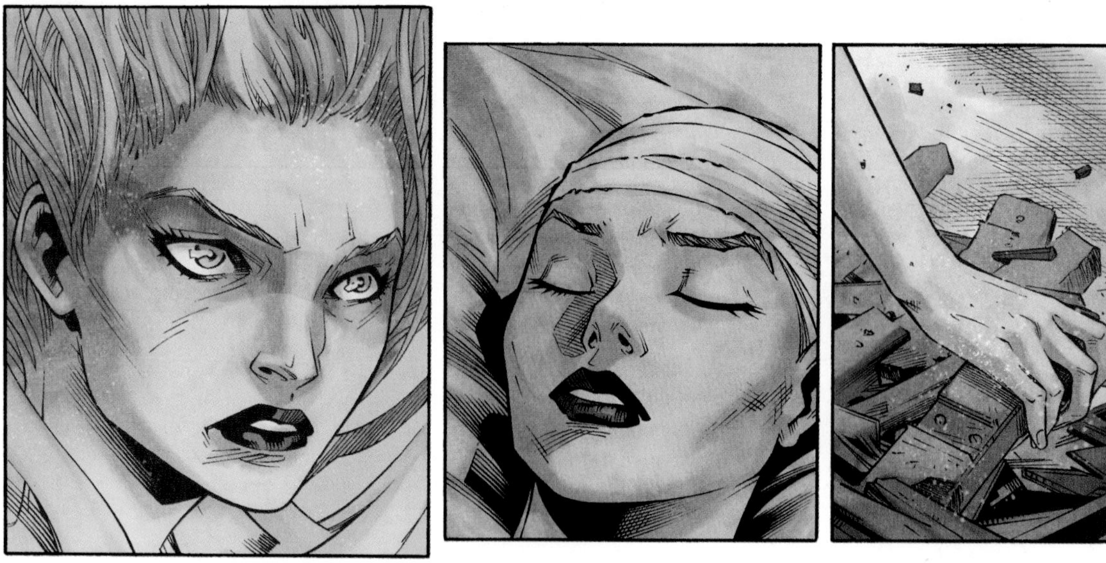

CHAPTER 3: THE PRICE

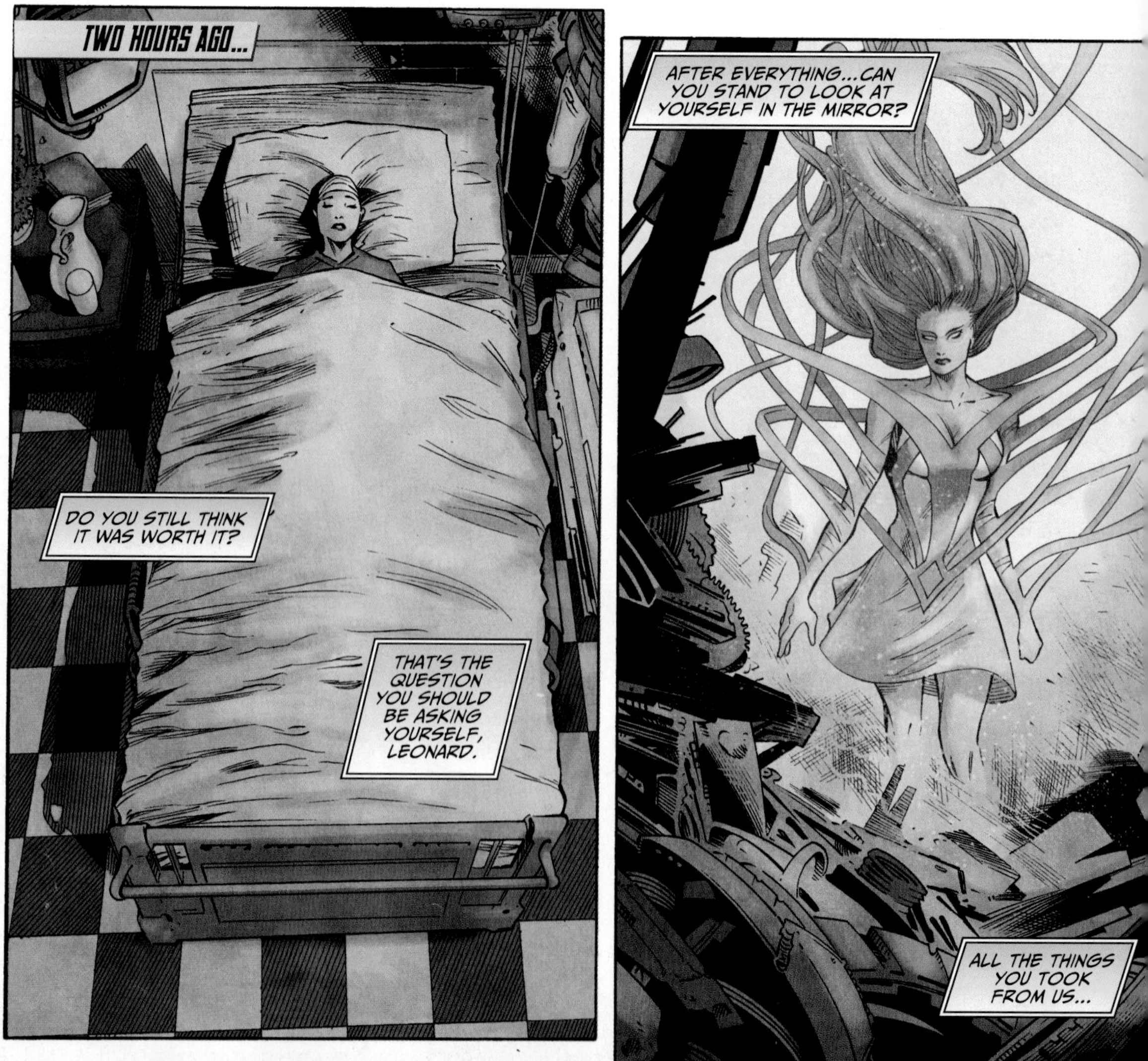
TWO HOURS AGO...
DO YOU STILL THINK IT WAS WORTH IT?
THAT'S THE QUESTION YOU SHOULD BE ASKING YOURSELF, LEONARD.
AFTER EVERYTHING...CAN YOU STAND TO LOOK AT YOURSELF IN THE MIRROR?
ALL THE THINGS YOU TOOK FROM US...

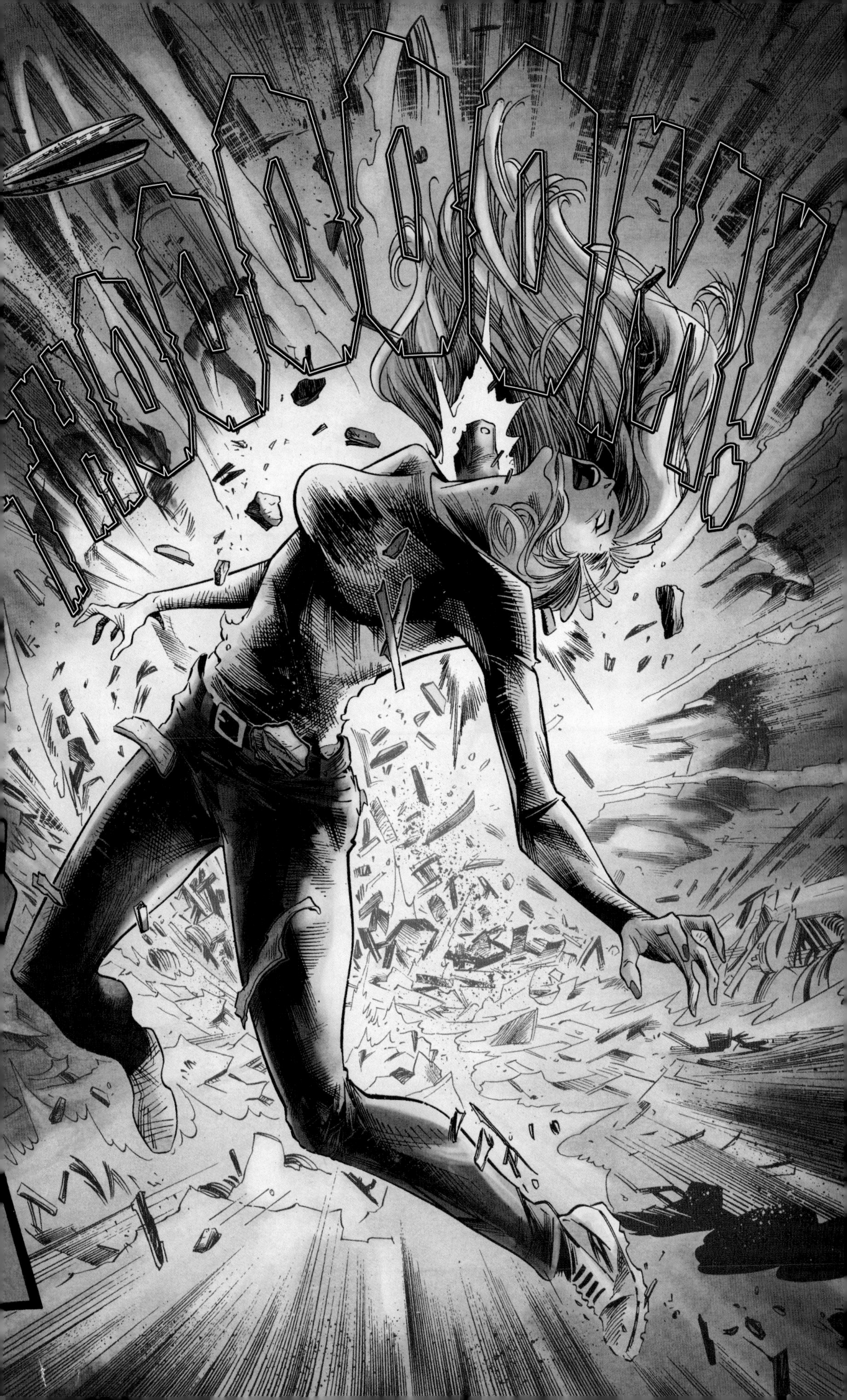

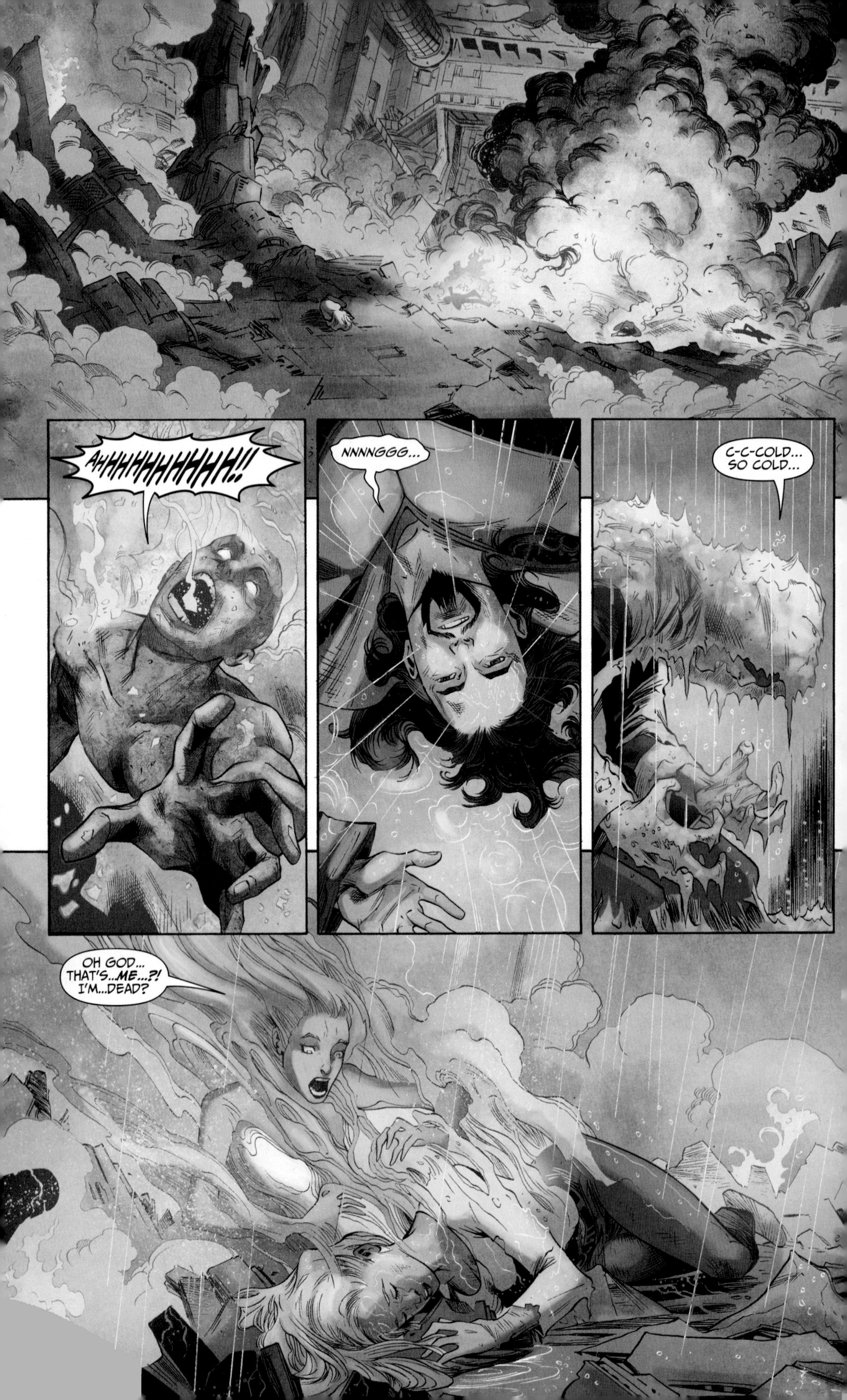
AHHHHHHHHHH!!
NNNNGGG...
C-C-COLD... SO COLD...
OH GOD... THAT'S...ME...?! I'M...DEAD?

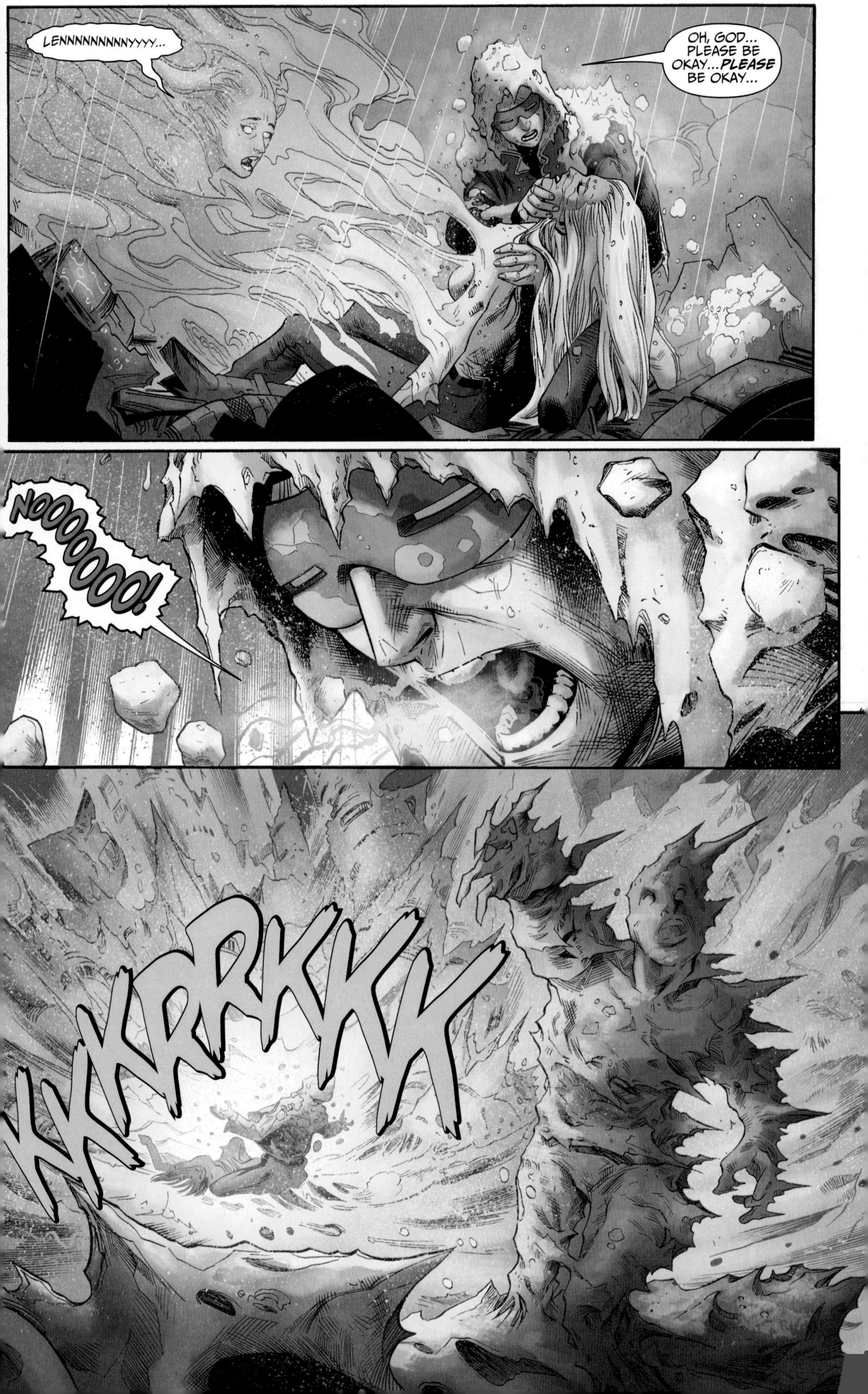
LENNNNNNNNNYYYY...
OH, GOD... PLEASE BE OKAY...PLEASE BE OKAY...
NOOOOOOOO!
KKKRKKK

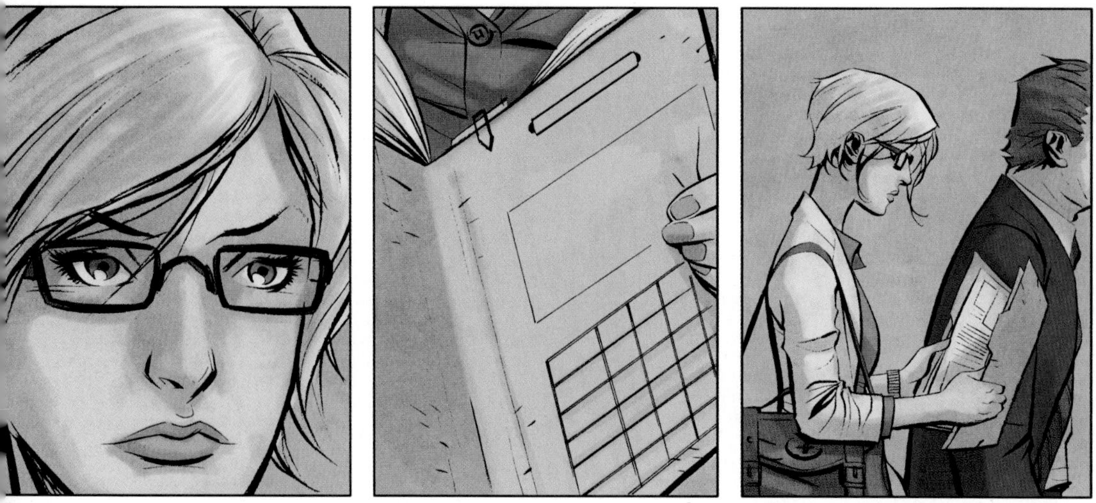

CHAPTER 4: THE SECRET

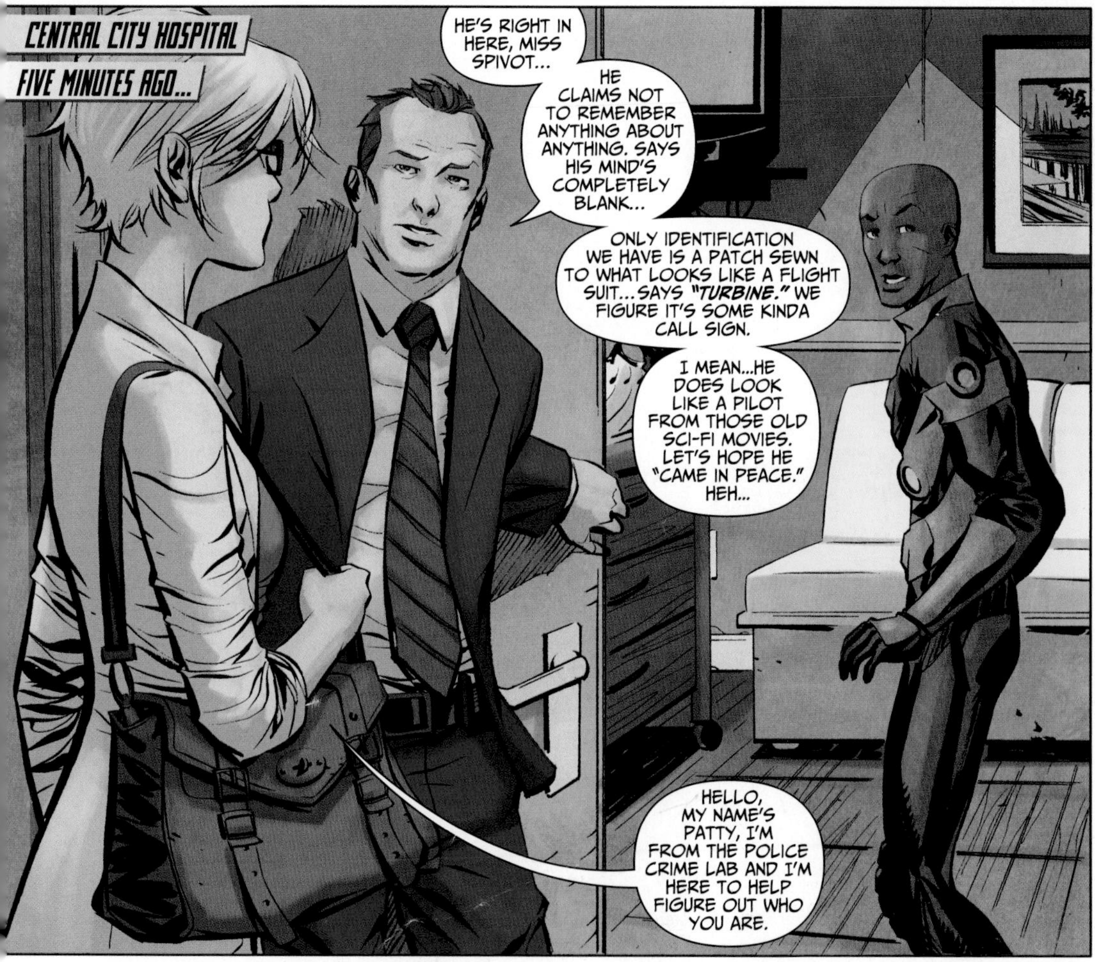

CENTRAL CITY HOSPITAL
FIVE MINUTES AGO...
HE'S RIGHT IN HERE, MISS SPIVOT...
HE CLAIMS NOT TO REMEMBER ANYTHING ABOUT ANYTHING. SAYS HIS MIND'S COMPLETELY BLANK...
ONLY IDENTIFICATION WE HAVE IS A PATCH SEWN TO WHAT LOOKS LIKE A FLIGHT SUIT...SAYS "TURBINE." WE FIGURE IT'S SOME KINDA CALL SIGN.
I MEAN...HE DOES LOOK LIKE A PILOT FROM THOSE OLD SCI-FI MOVIES. LET'S HOPE HE "CAME IN PEACE." HEH...
HELLO, MY NAME'S PATTY, I'M FROM THE POLICE CRIME LAB AND I'M HERE TO HELP FIGURE OUT WHO YOU ARE.

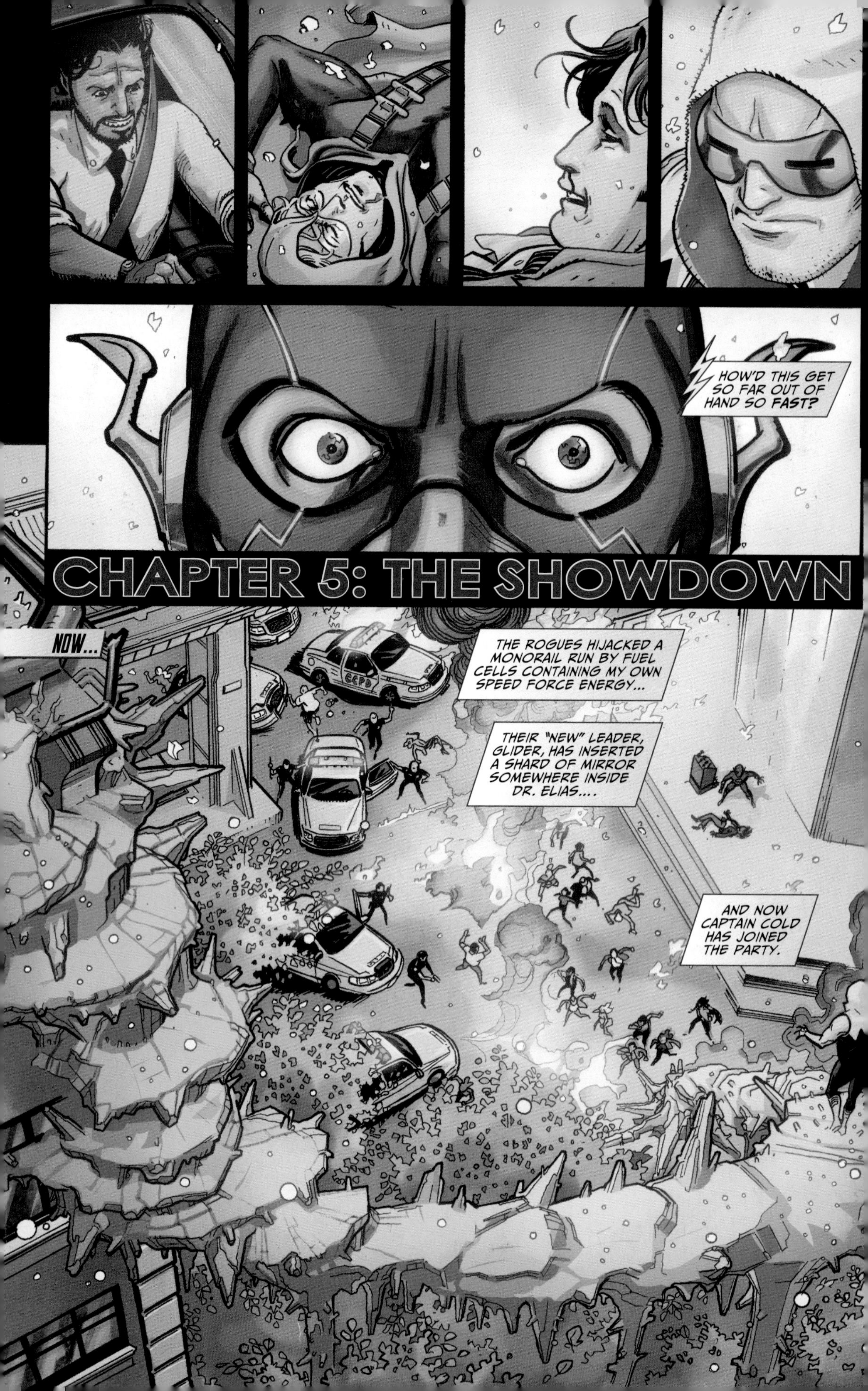
HOW'D THIS GET SO FAR OUT OF HAND SO FAST?
CHAPTER 5: THE SHOWDOWN
NOW...
THE ROGUES HIJACKED A MONORAIL RUN BY FUEL CELLS CONTAINING MY OWN SPEED FORCE ENERGY...
THEIR "NEW" LEADER, GLIDER, HAS INSERTED A SHARD OF MIRROR SOMEWHERE INSIDE DR. ELIAS....
AND NOW CAPTAIN COLD HAS JOINED THE PARTY.

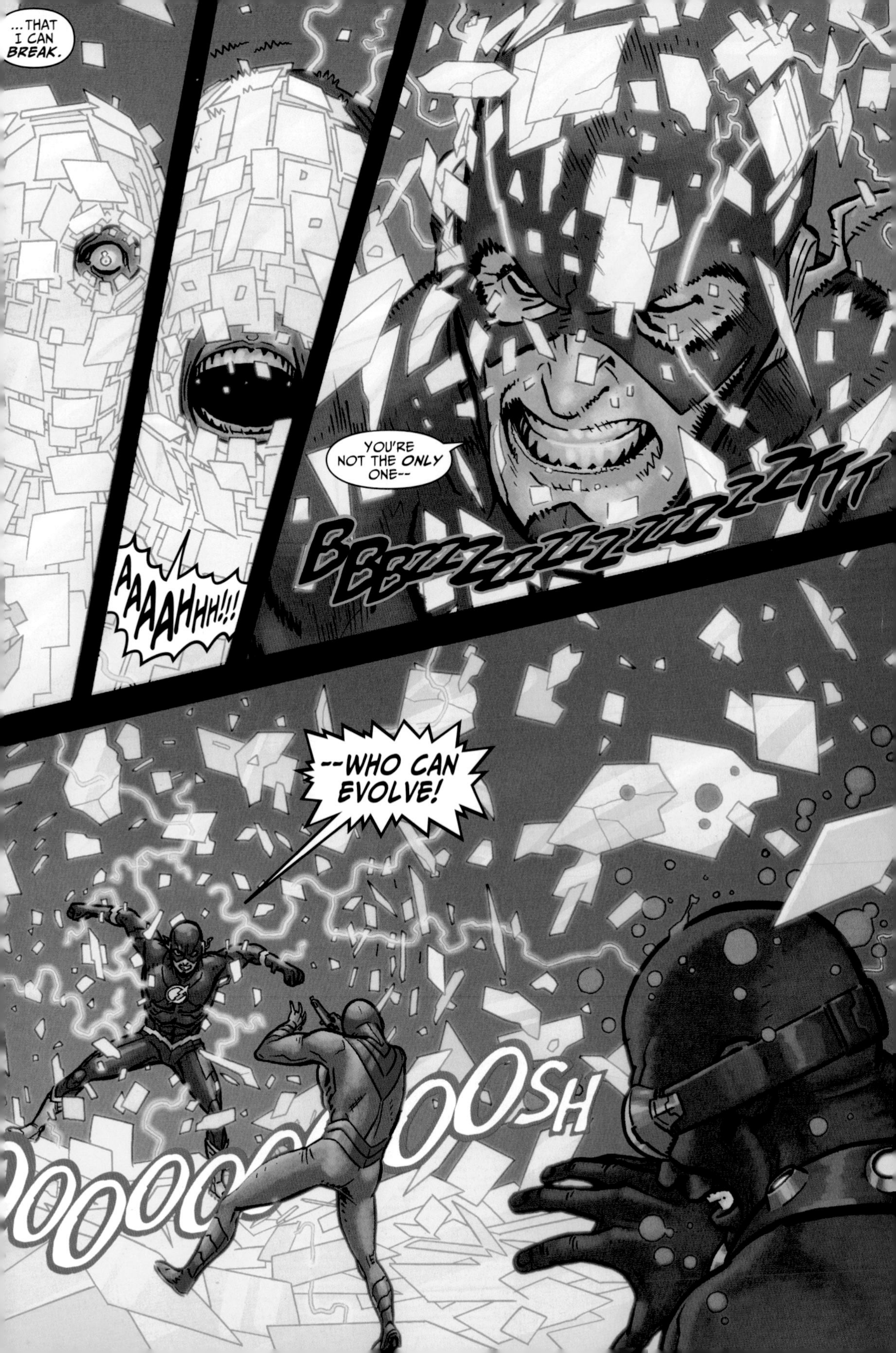
...THAT I CAN BREAK.
YOU'RE NOT THE ONLY ONE--
AAAAHHH!!!
BBBZZZZZZZZZZZZZZZZTTT
--WHO CAN EVOLVE!
OOOOOOOOOSH

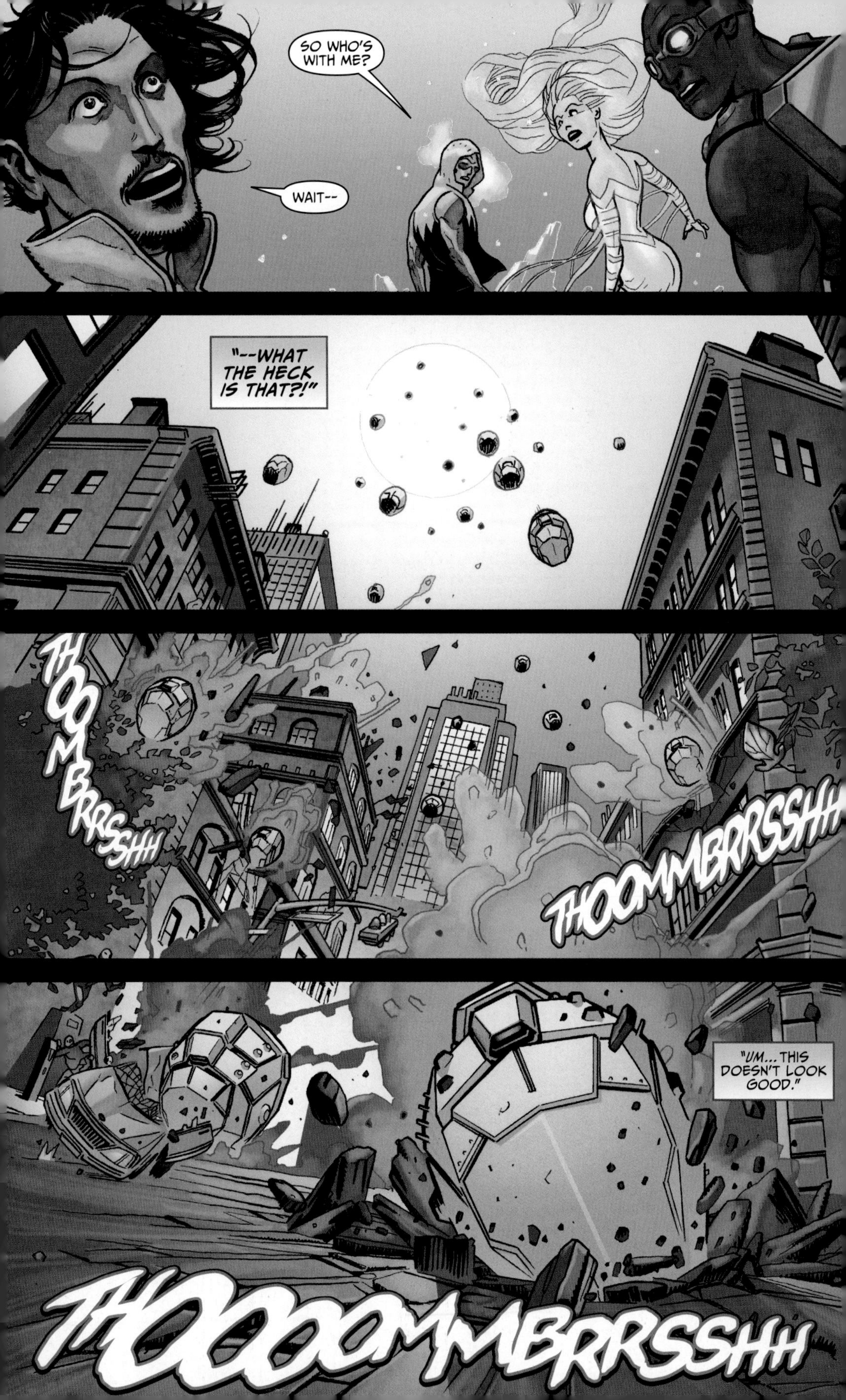
SO WHO'S WITH ME?
WAIT--
"--WHAT THE HECK IS THAT?!"
THOOMBRRSSHH
THOOMMBRRSSHH
"UM... THIS DOESN'T LOOK GOOD."
THOOOOMMBRRSSHH

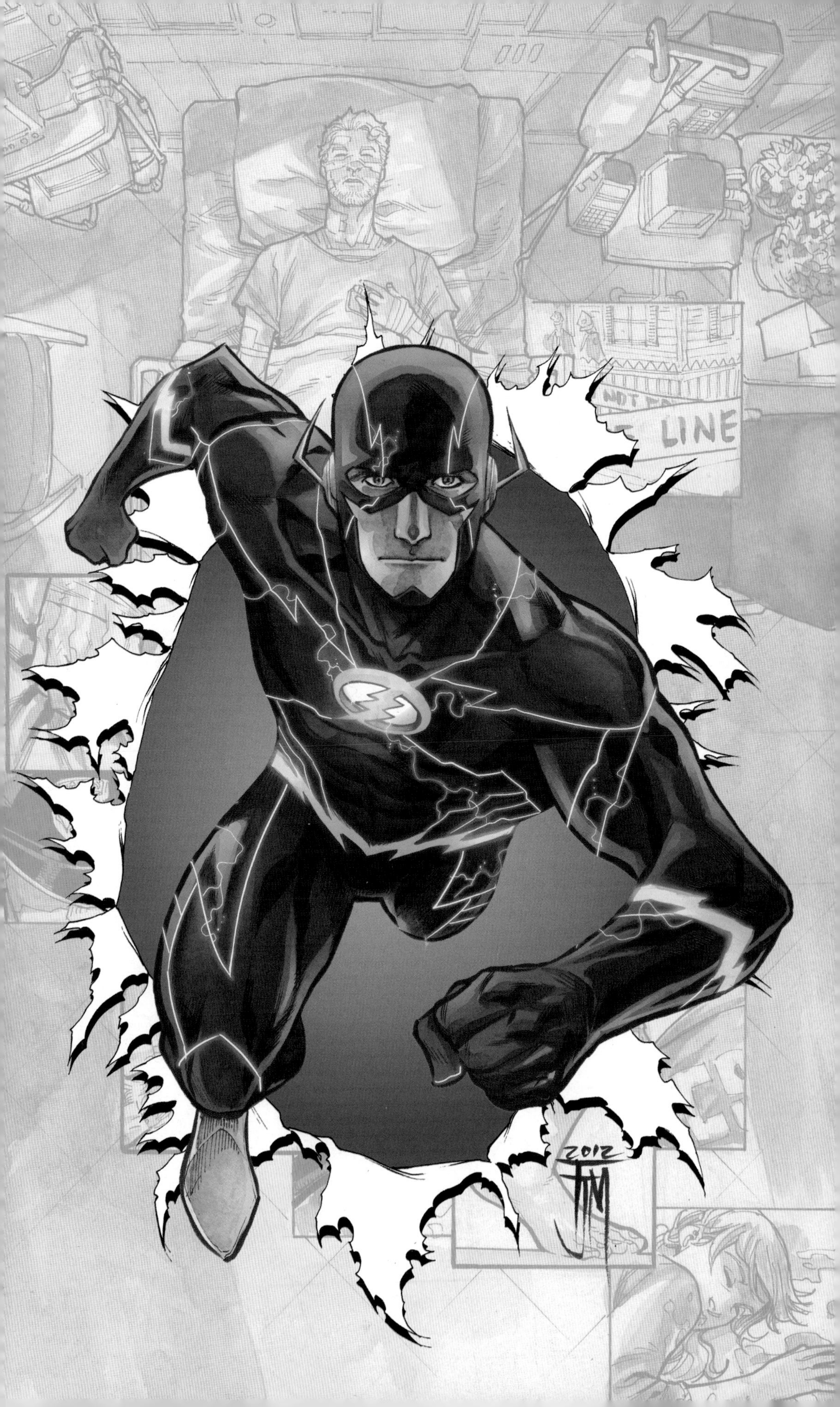
LINE
2012

JL artist

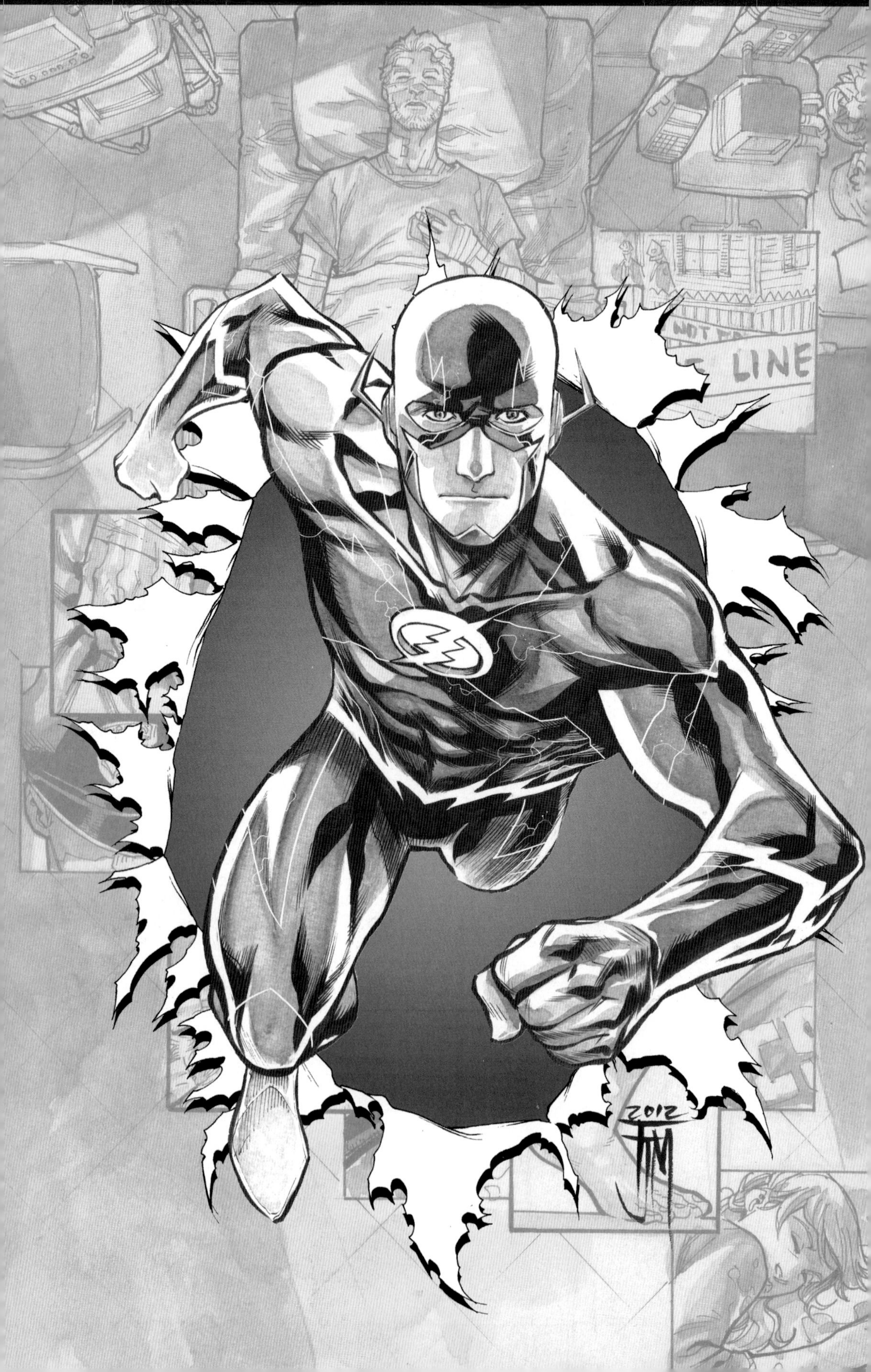

LINE
2012

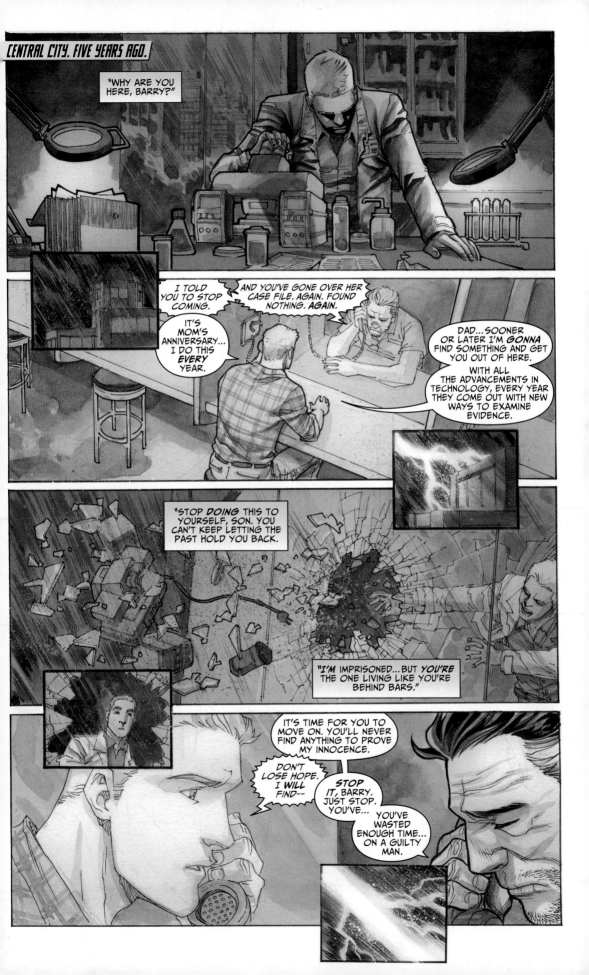

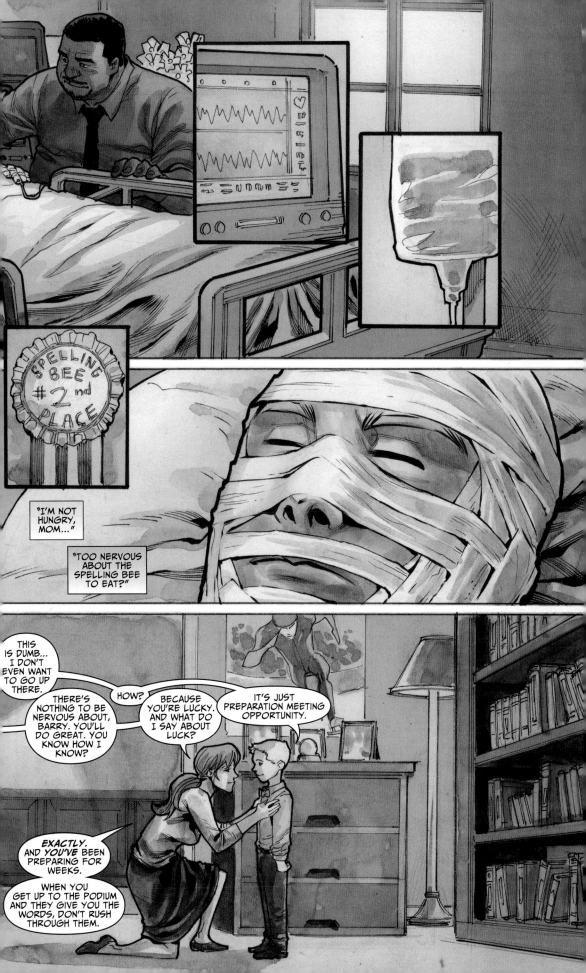

SPELLING BEE #2nd PLACE

"I'M NOT HUNGRY, MOM..."

"TOO NERVOUS ABOUT THE SPELLING BEE TO EAT?"

THIS IS DUMB... I DON'T EVEN WANT TO GO UP THERE.

THERE'S NOTHING TO BE NERVOUS ABOUT, BARRY. YOU'LL DO GREAT. YOU KNOW HOW I KNOW?

HOW?

BECAUSE YOU'RE LUCKY. AND WHAT DO I SAY ABOUT LUCK?

IT'S JUST PREPARATION MEETING OPPORTUNITY.

EXACTLY. AND YOU'VE BEEN PREPARING FOR WEEKS. WHEN YOU GET UP TO THE PODIUM AND THEY GIVE YOU THE WORDS, DON'T RUSH THROUGH THEM.

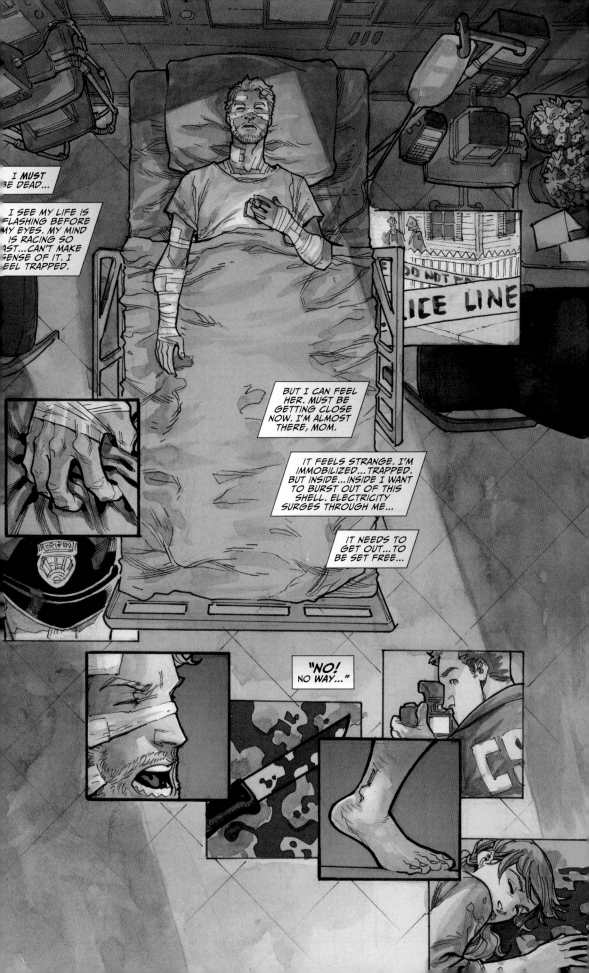

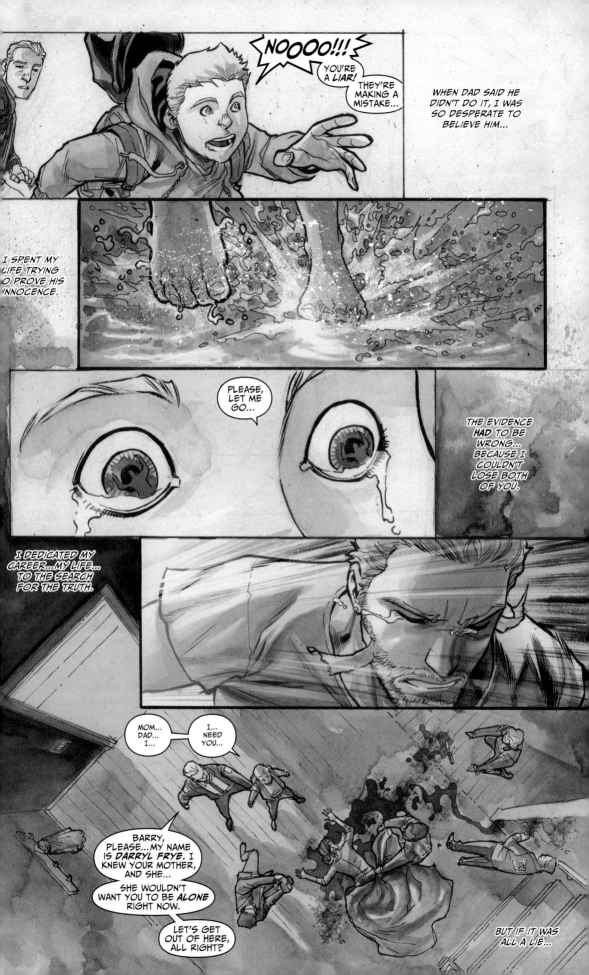

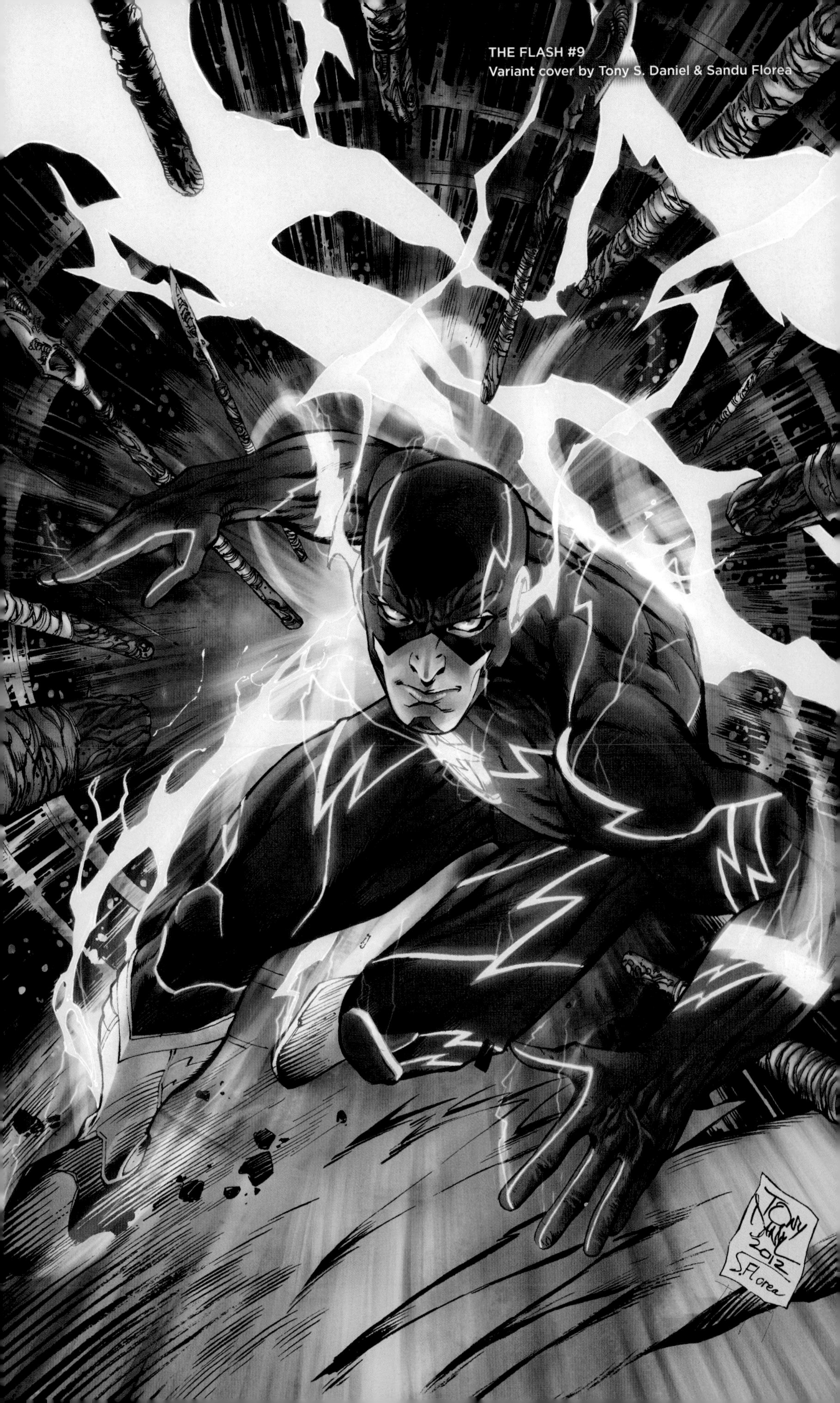

THE FLASH #9
Variant cover by Tony S. Daniel & Sandu Florea

THE FLASH #9 cover pencils

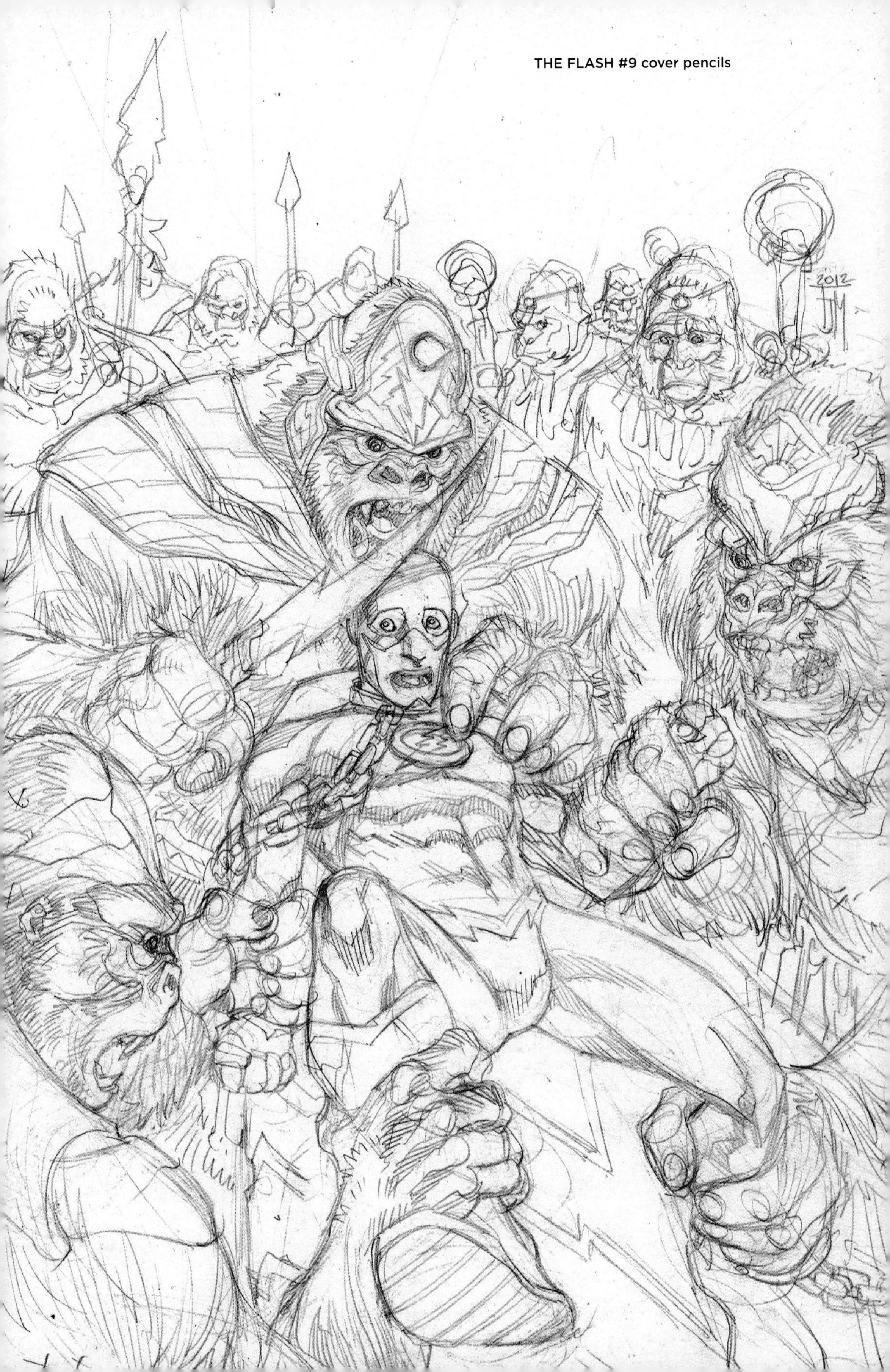
2012

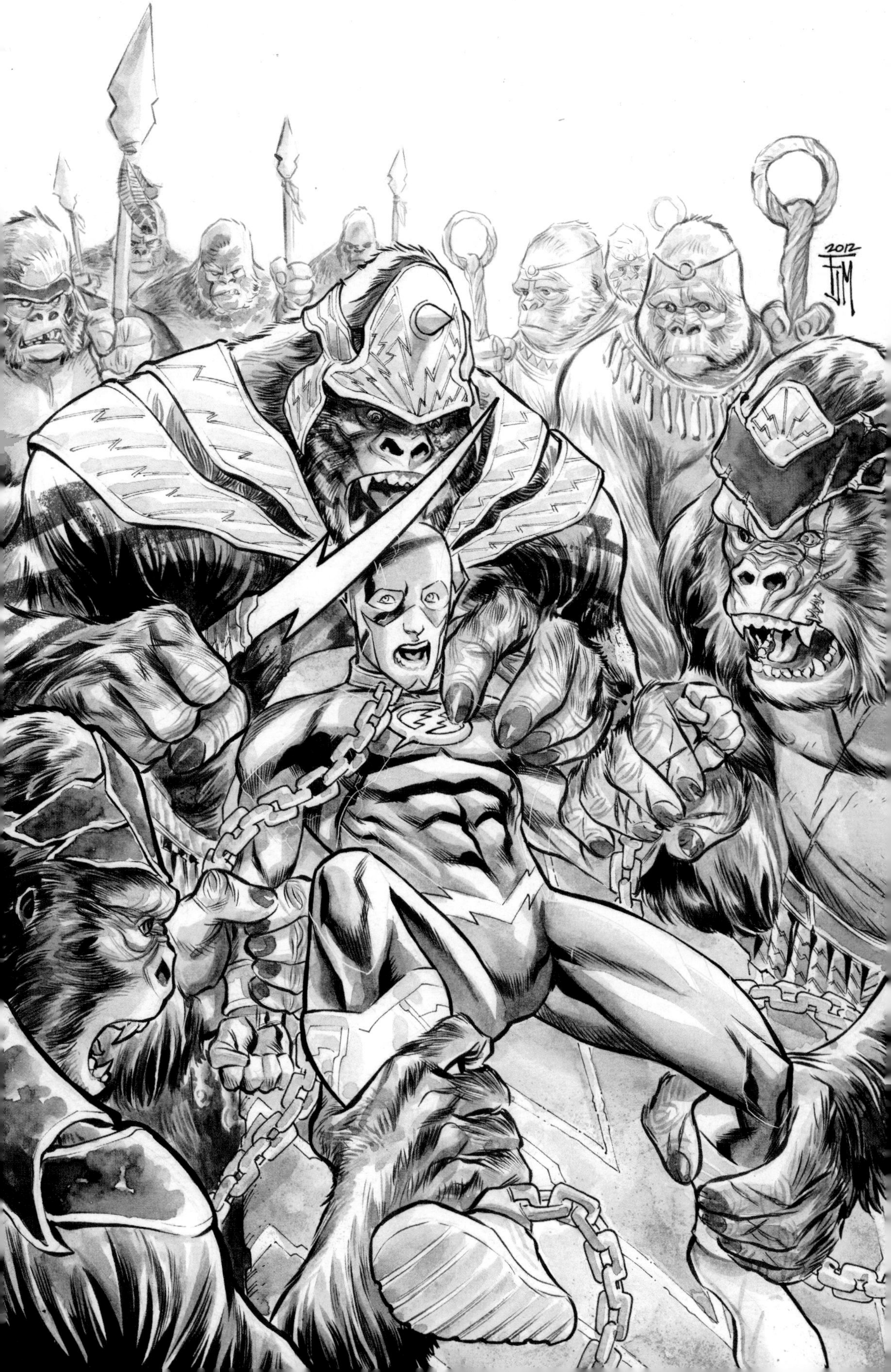

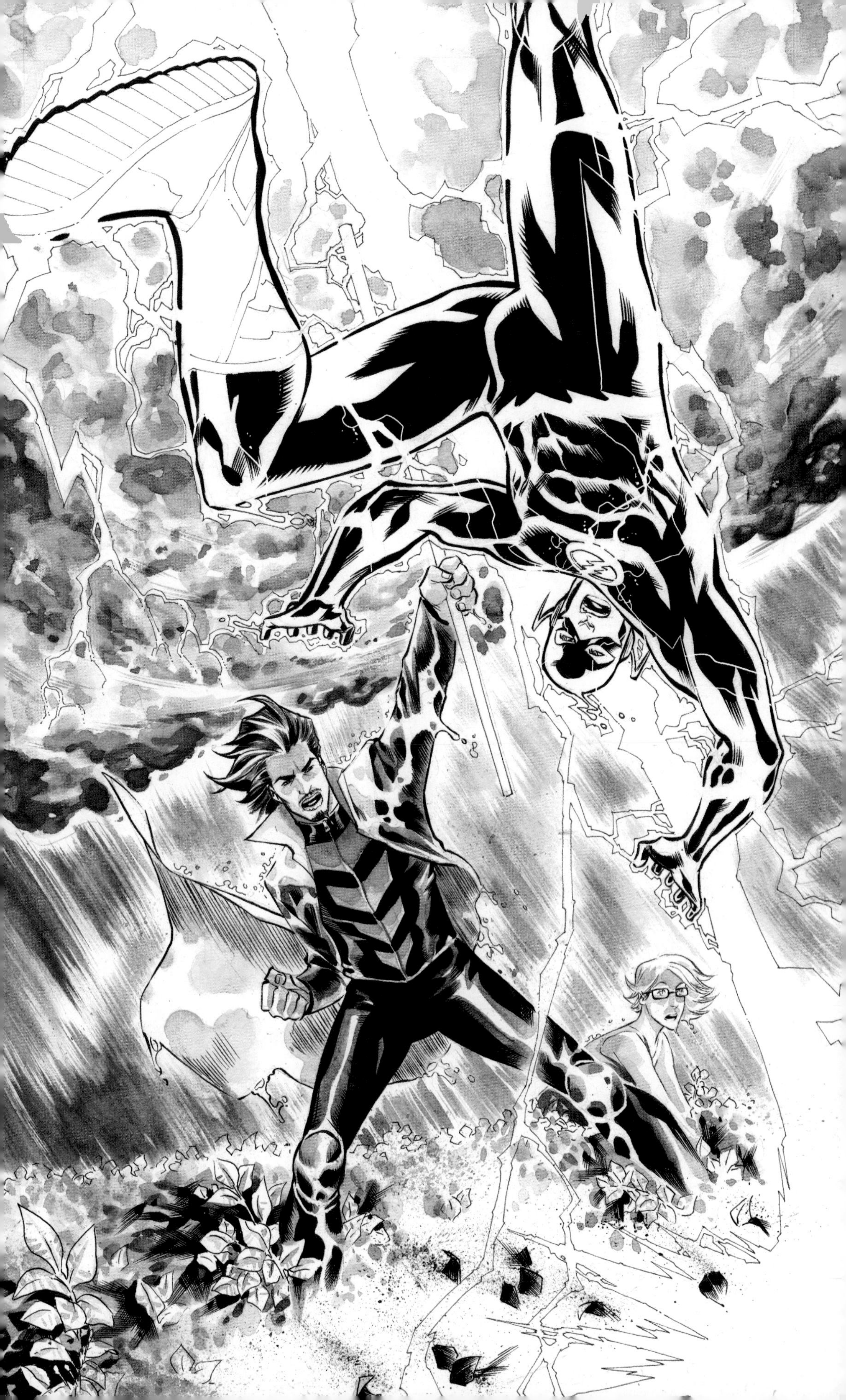

THE FLASH #11 cover sketches and final inked cover

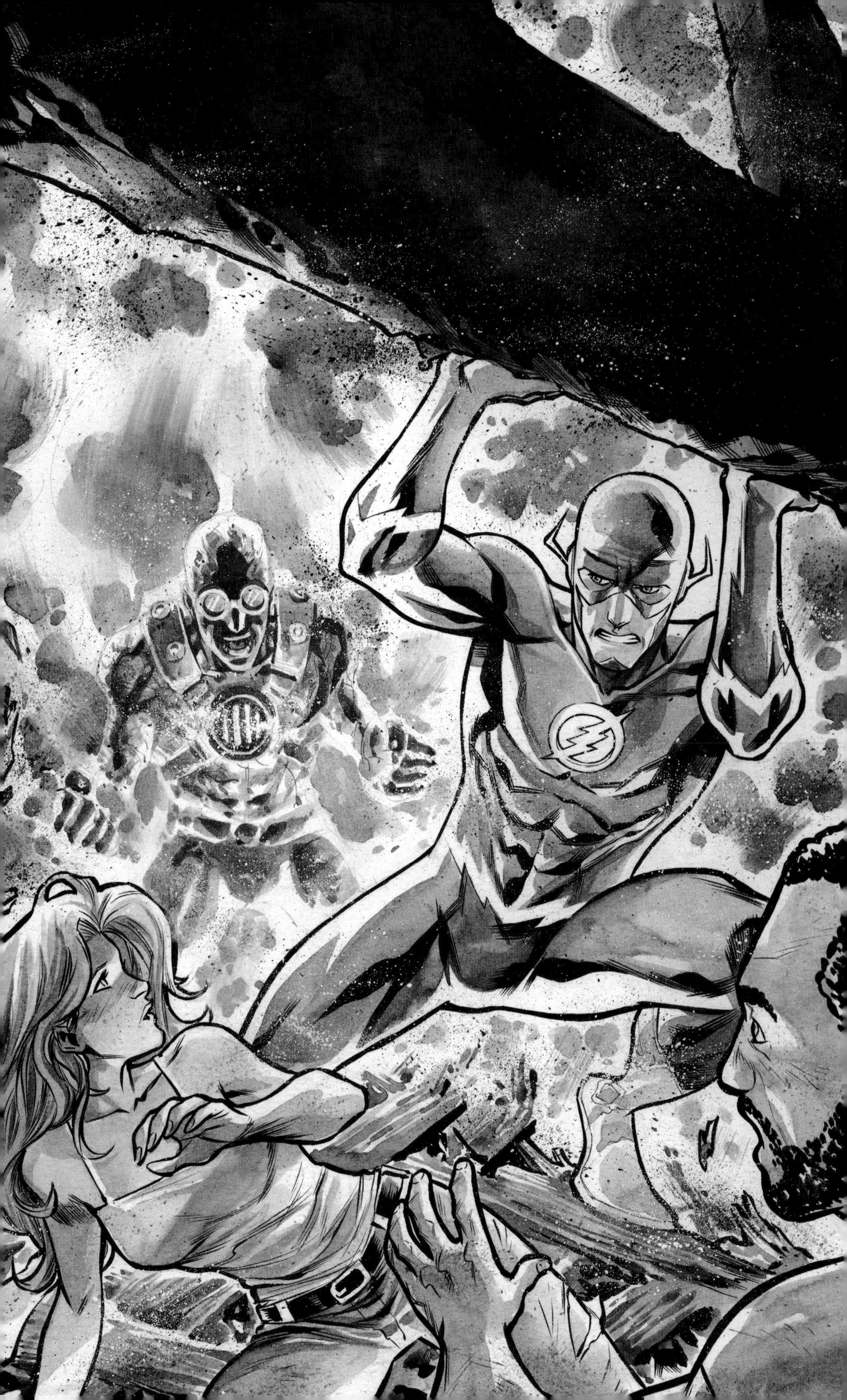

THE FLASH #12 cover inks

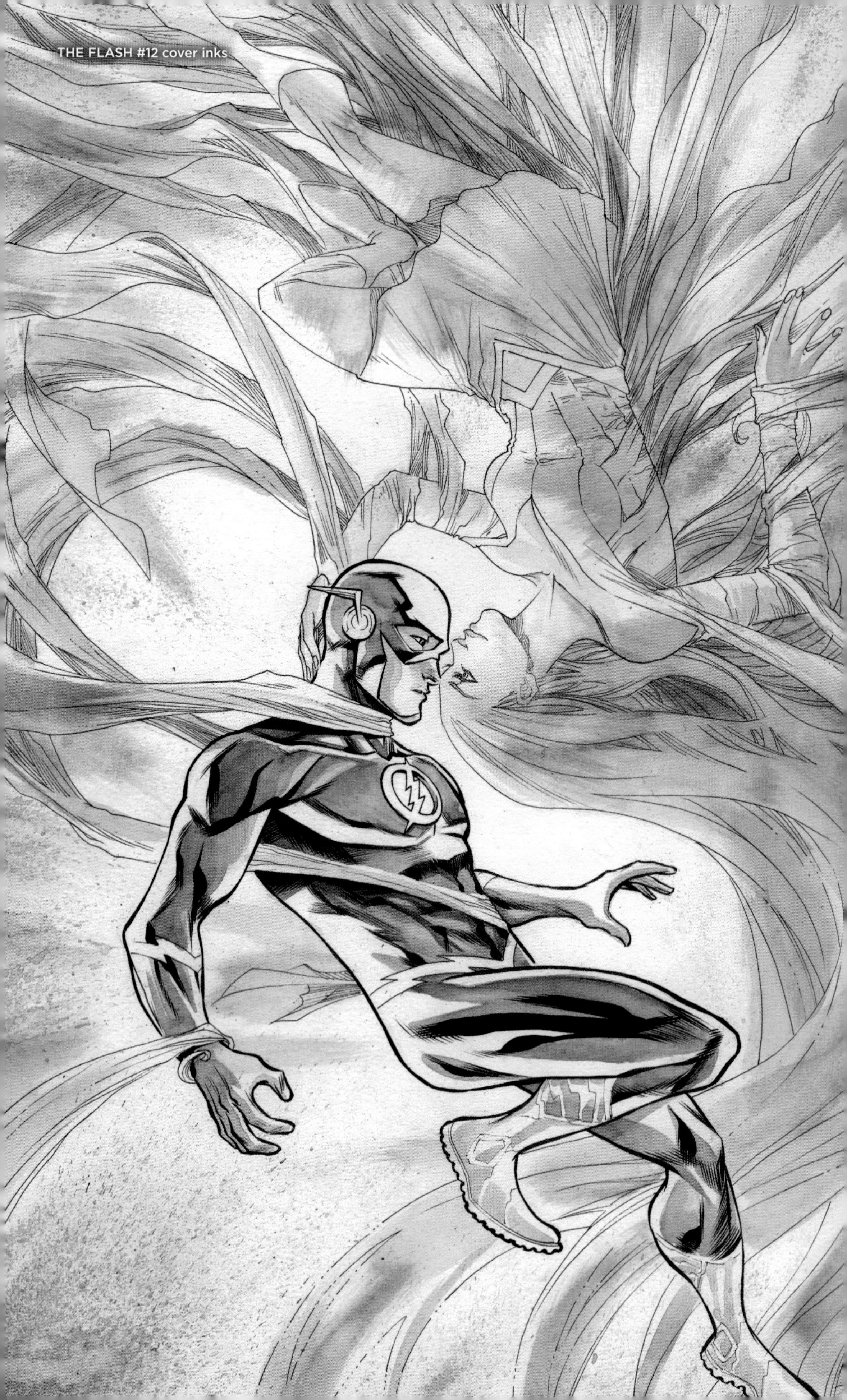

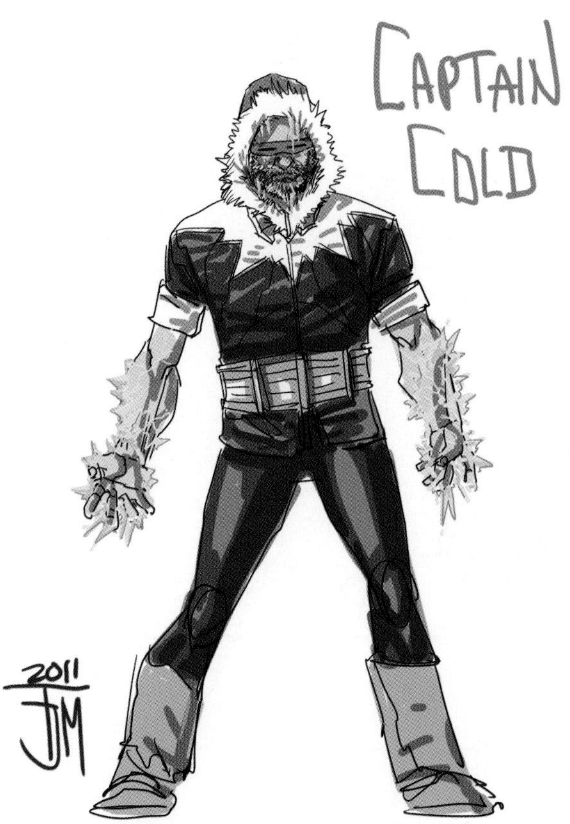
CAPTAIN COLD
2011
JJM

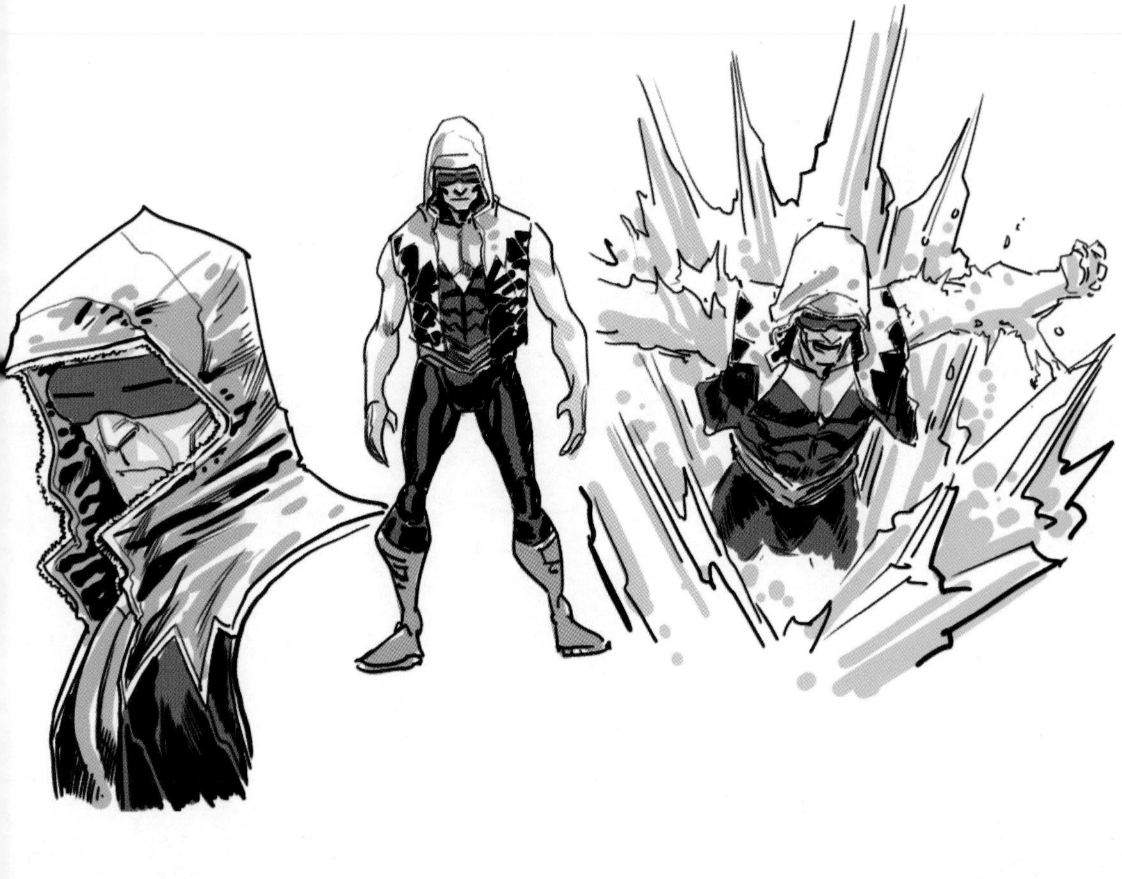

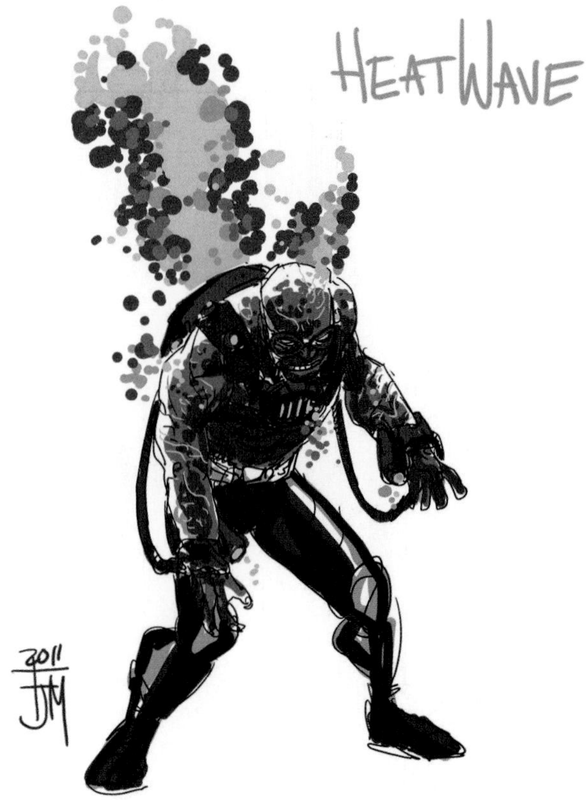
HEATWAVE
2011
FJM

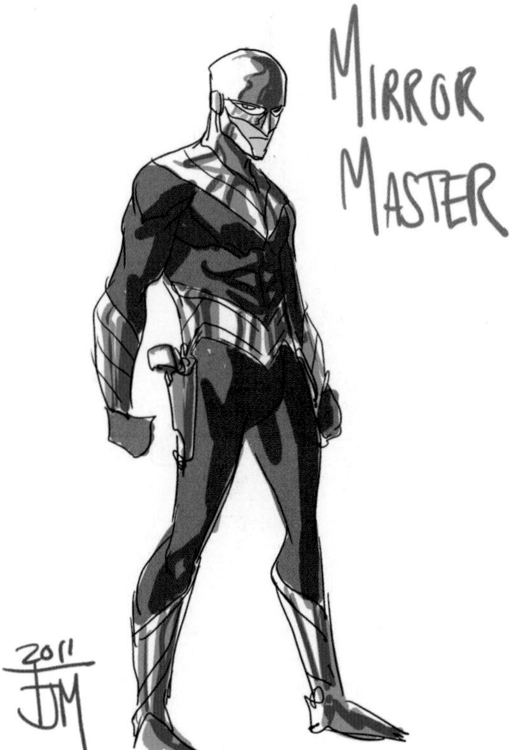
MIRROR
MASTER
2011
FJM

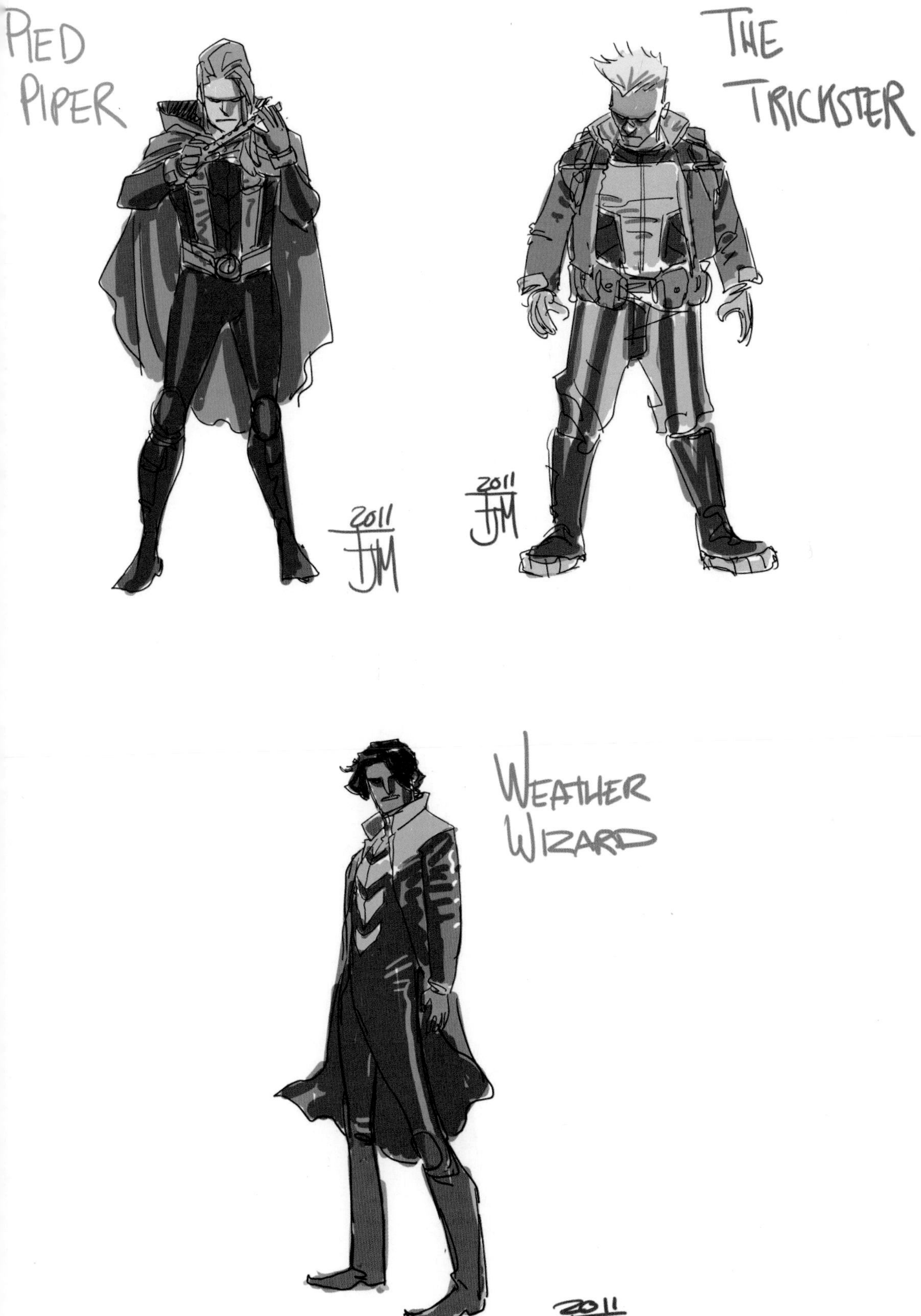
PIED PIPER
THE TRICKSTER
WEATHER WIZARD
2011
2011
2011

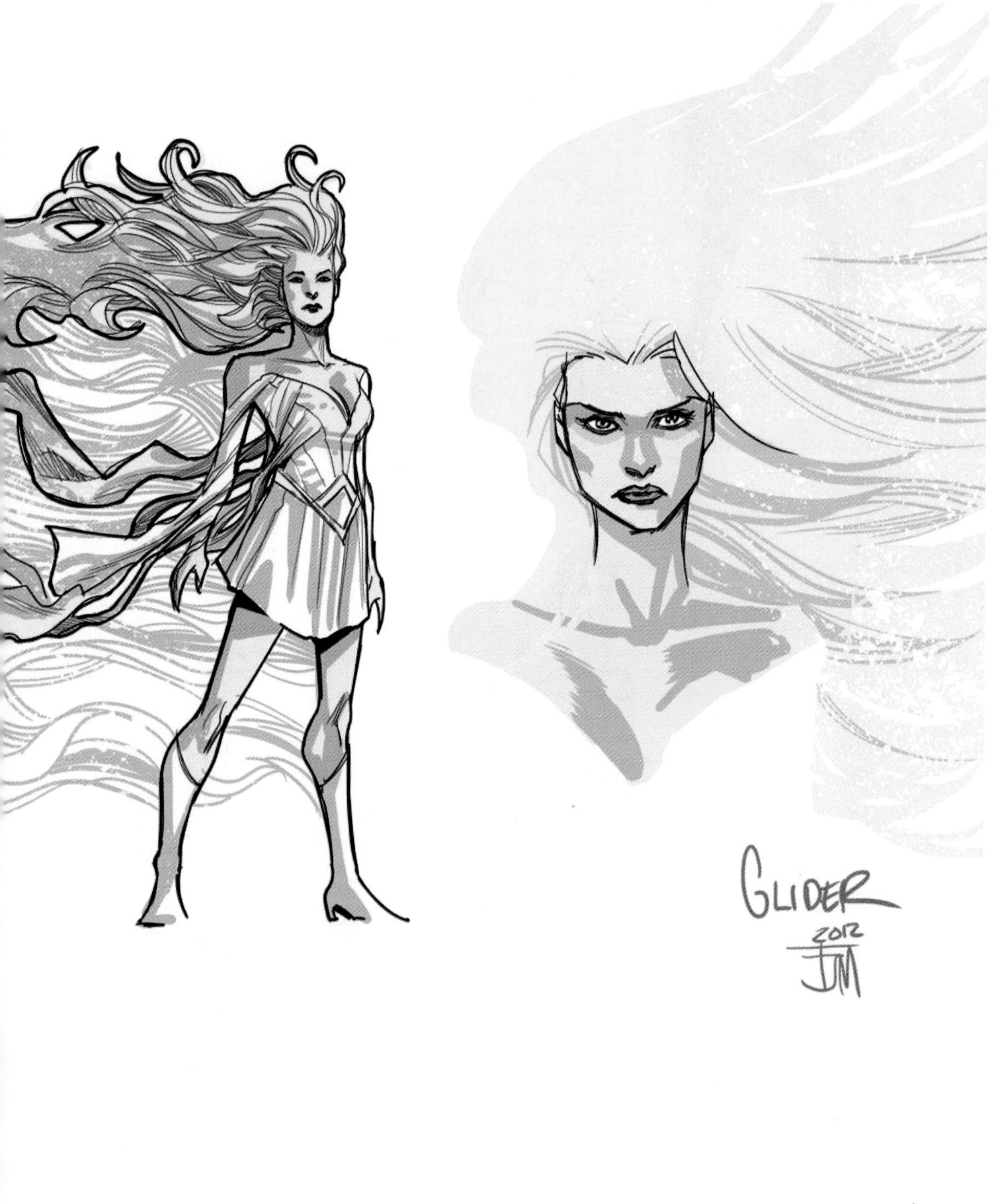
GLIDER
2012
JM

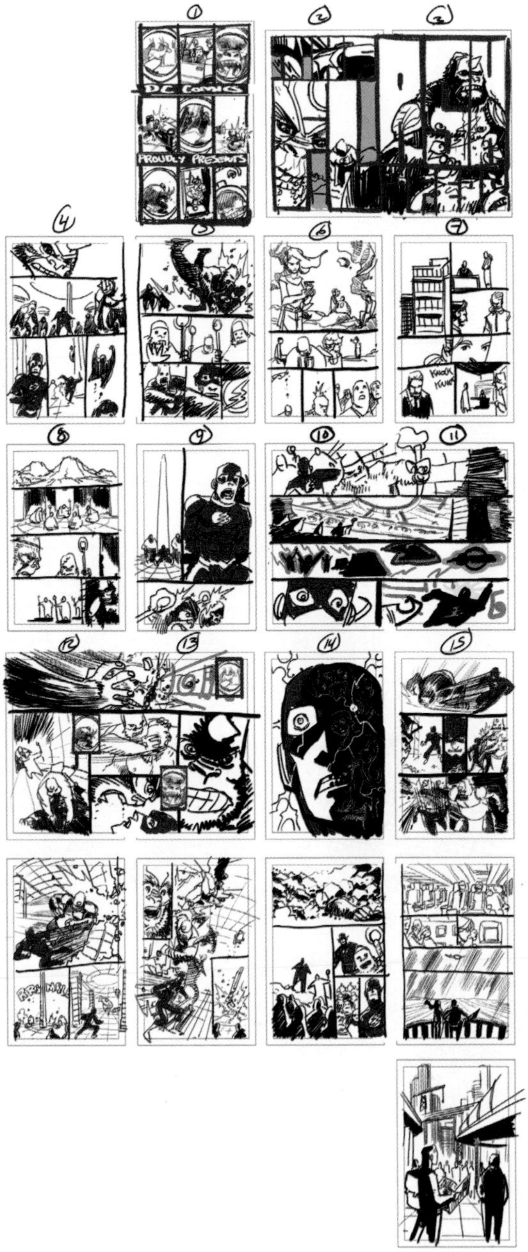
DC COMICS
PROUDLY PRESENTS

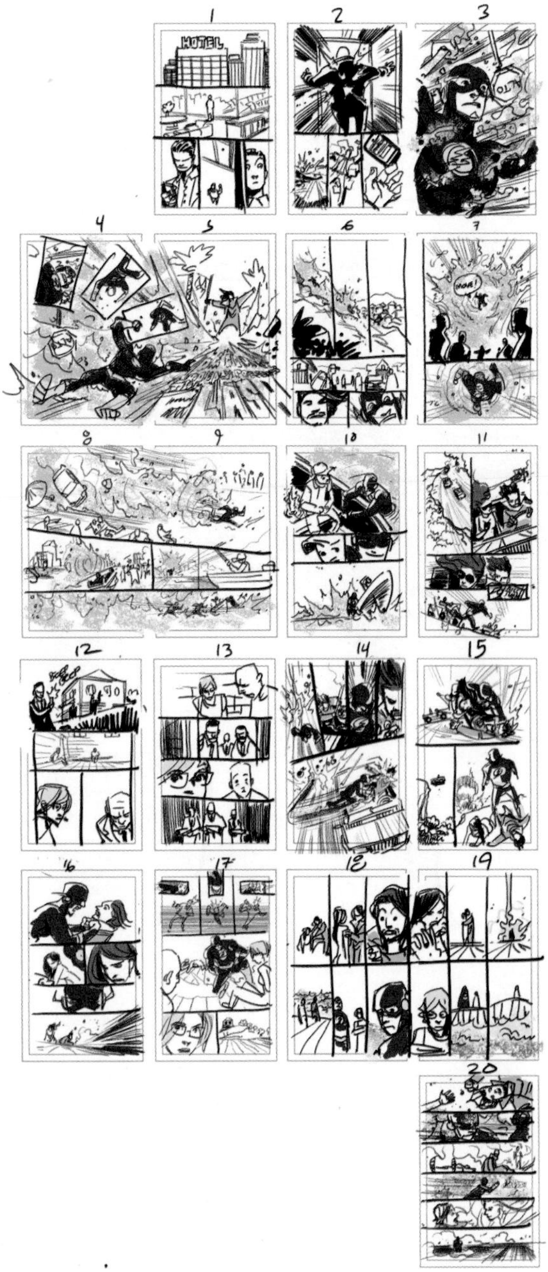
HOTEL

THE FLASH #11 & 12 rough layouts

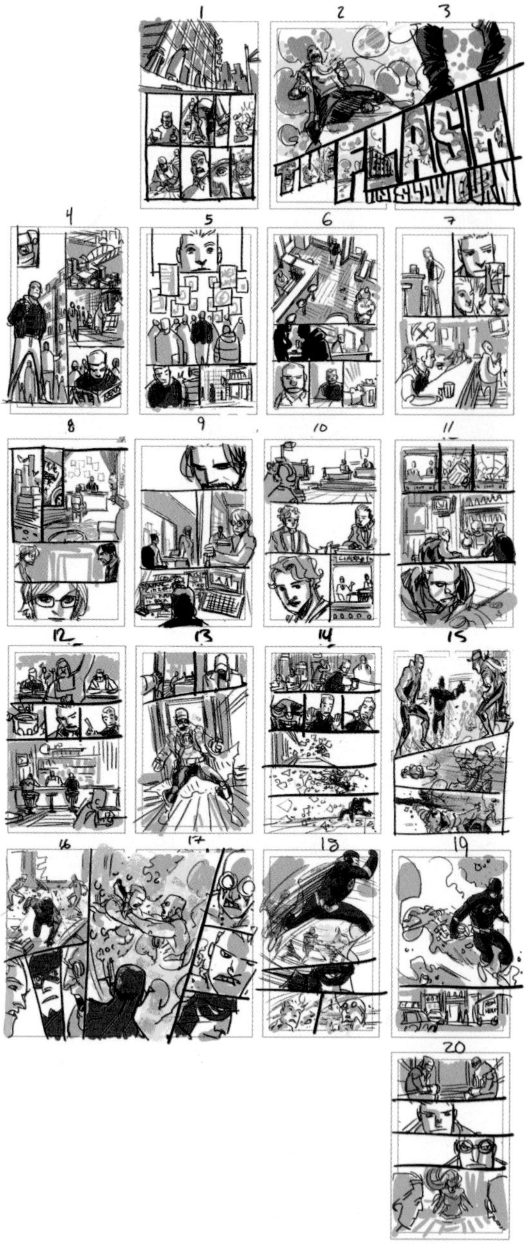
THE FLASH

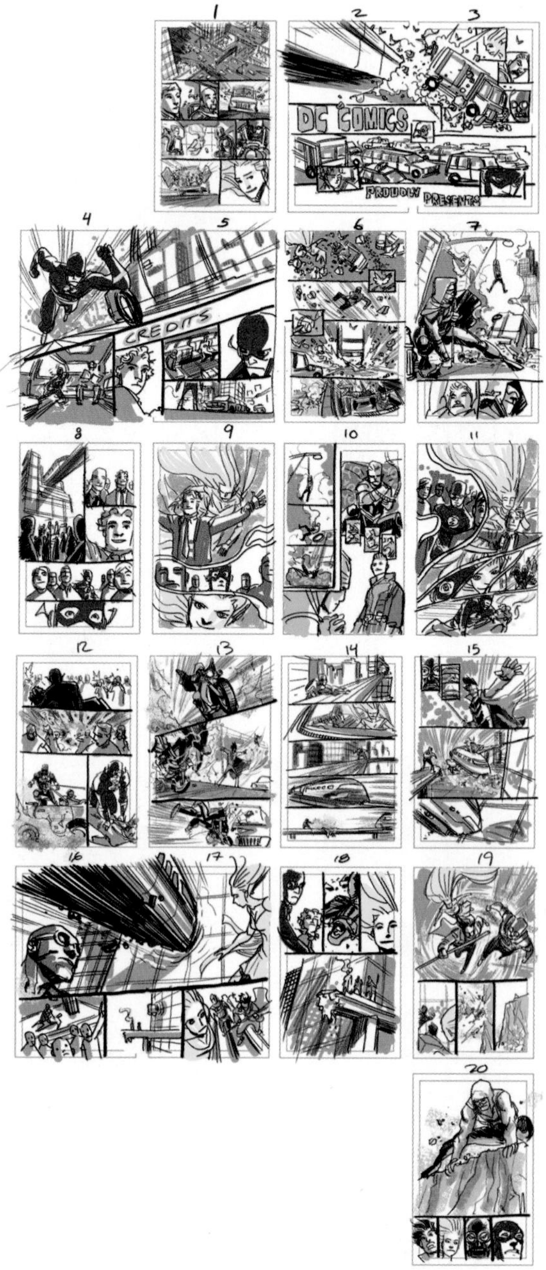
DC COMICS
PROUDLY PRESENTS
FLASH
CREDITS

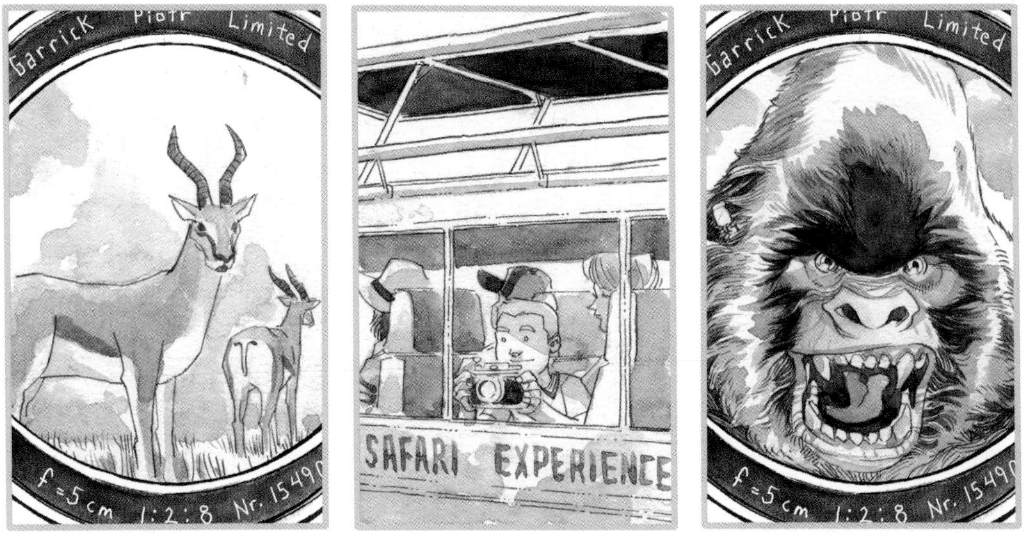
Garrick Piotr Limited
f=5cm 1:2:8
SAFARI EXPERIENCE
Garrick Piotr Limited
f=5cm 1:2:8

THE FLASH #9 page 1 inks

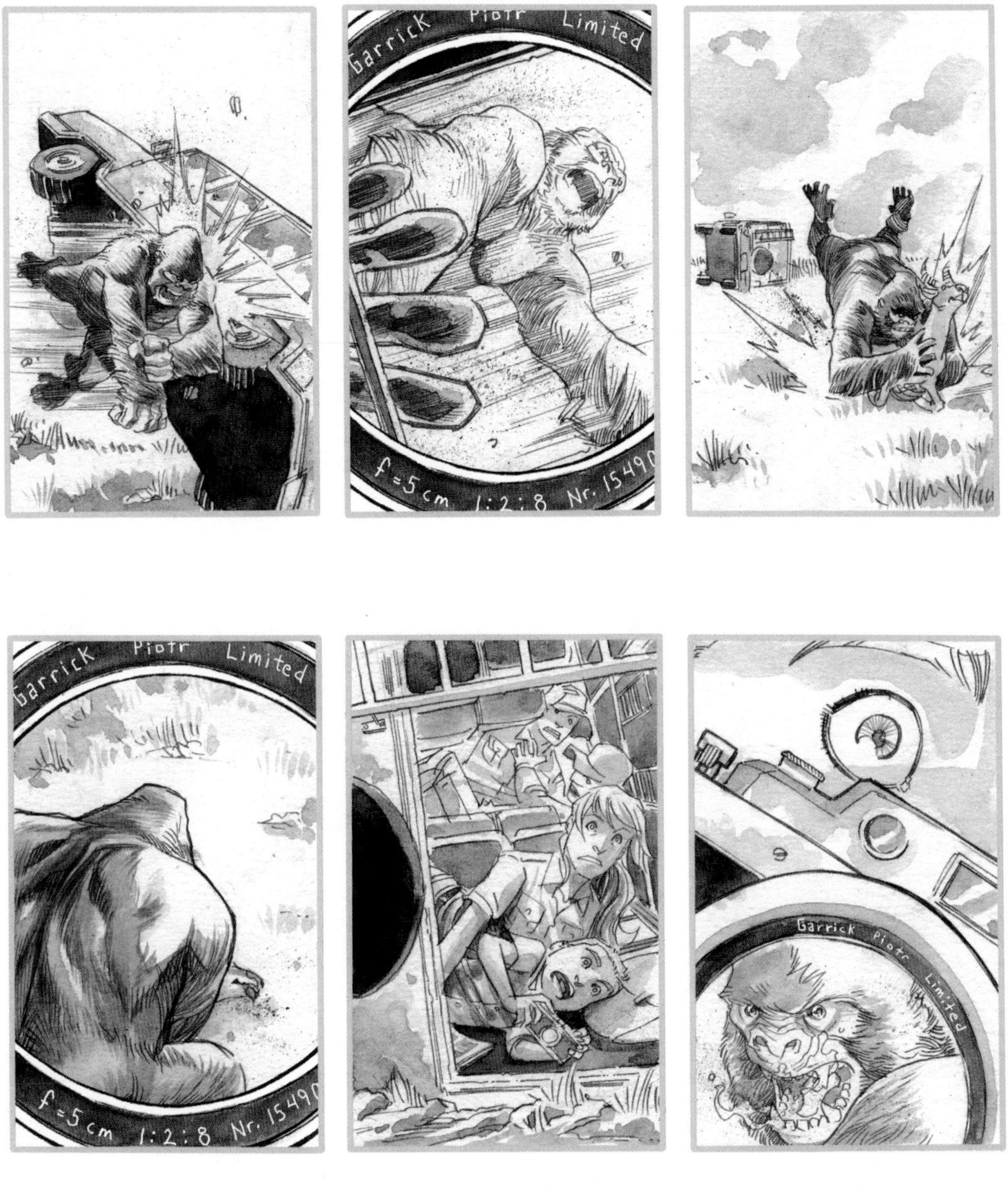
Garrick Piotr Limited
f=5cm 1:2:8
Garrick Piotr Limited
f=5cm 1:2:8
Garrick Piotr Limited

THE FLASH #9 pages 2-3 inks

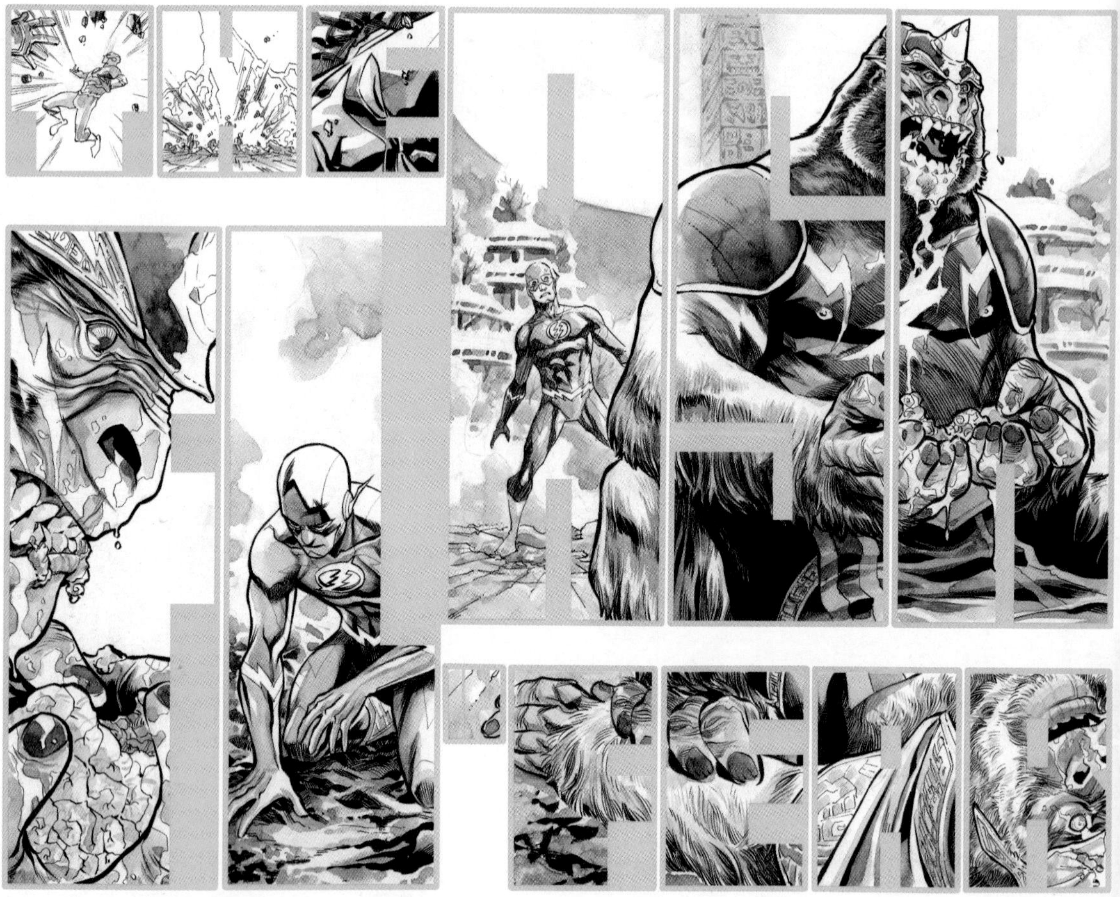

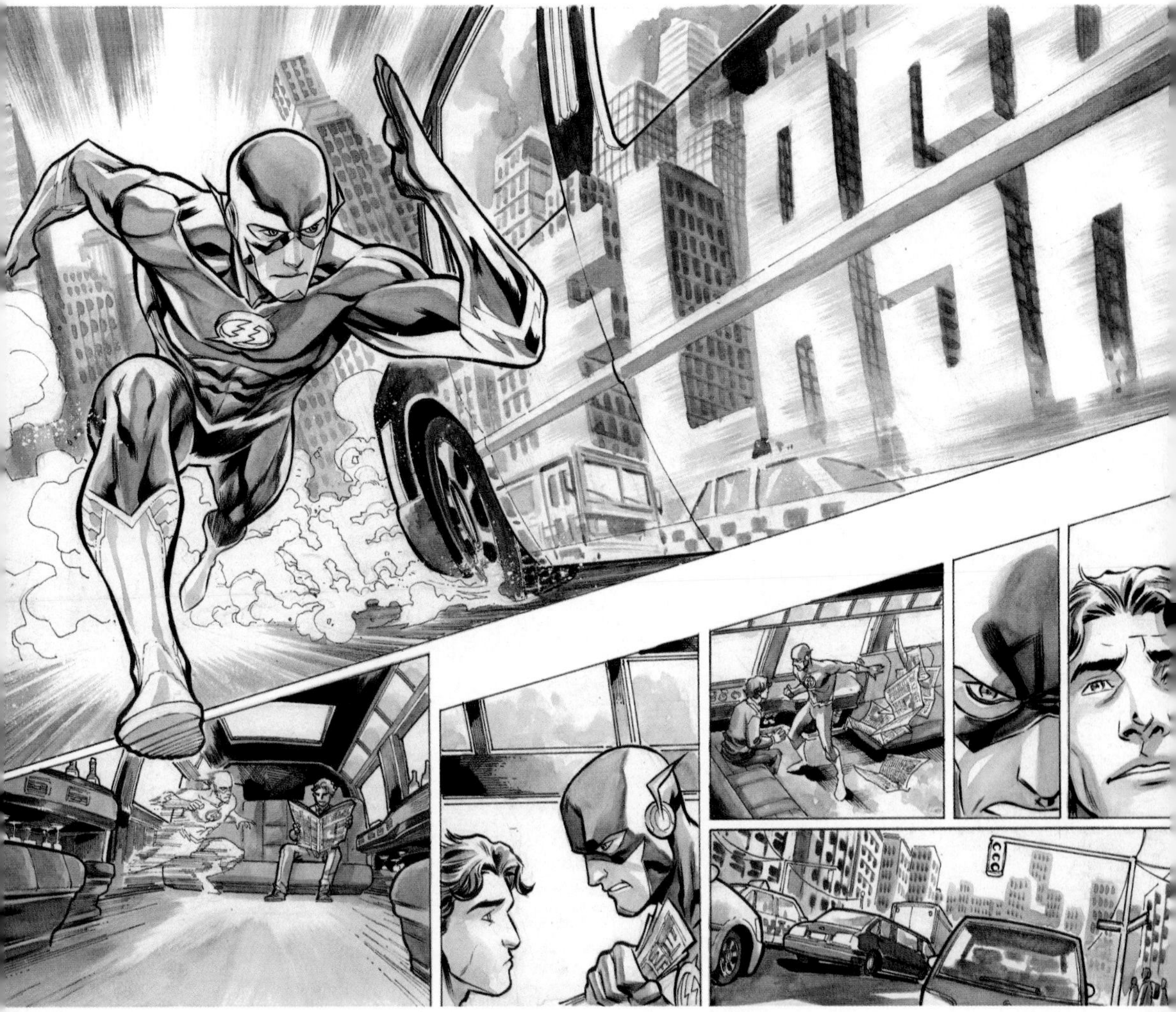

THE FLASH #12 page 9 inks

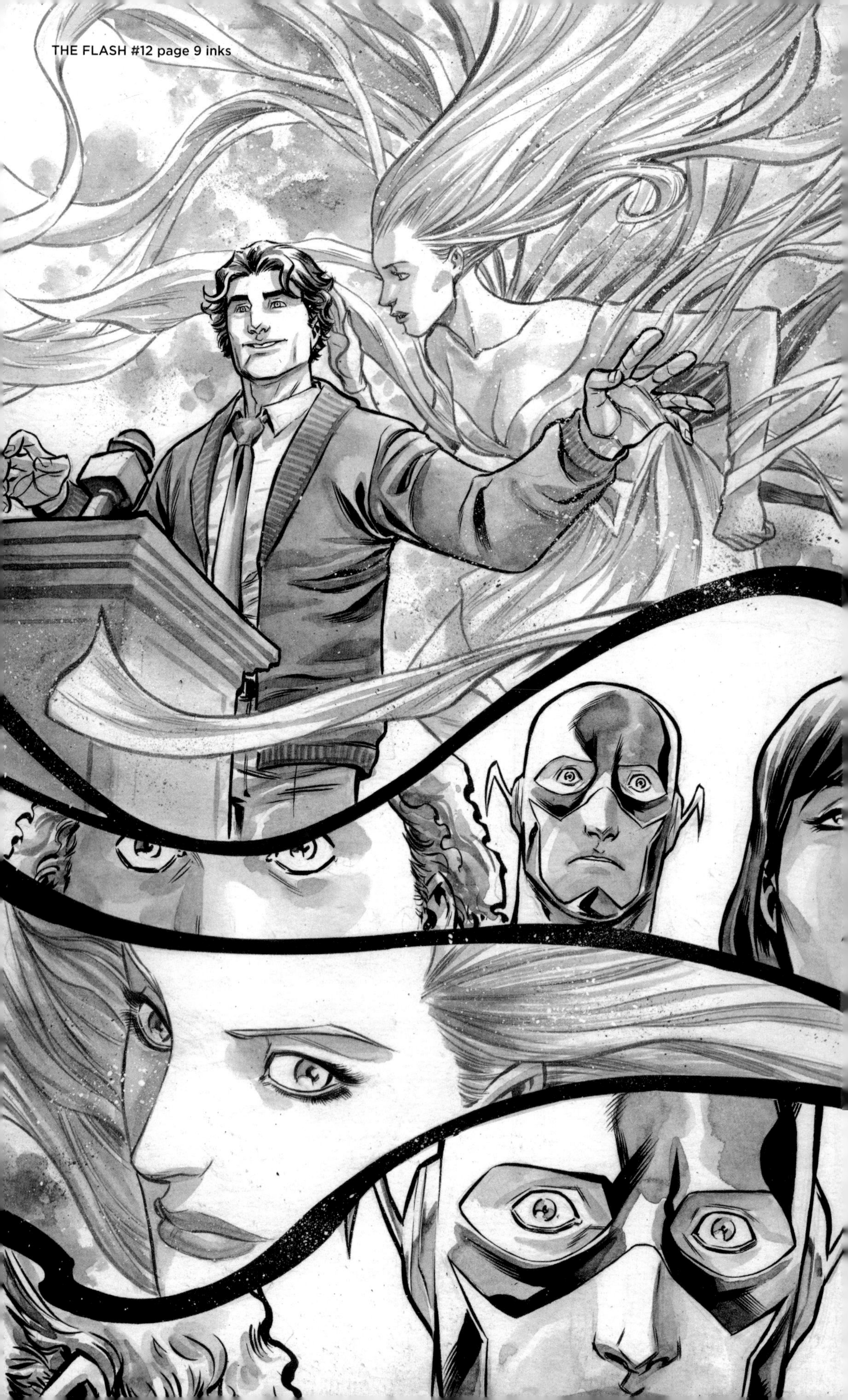

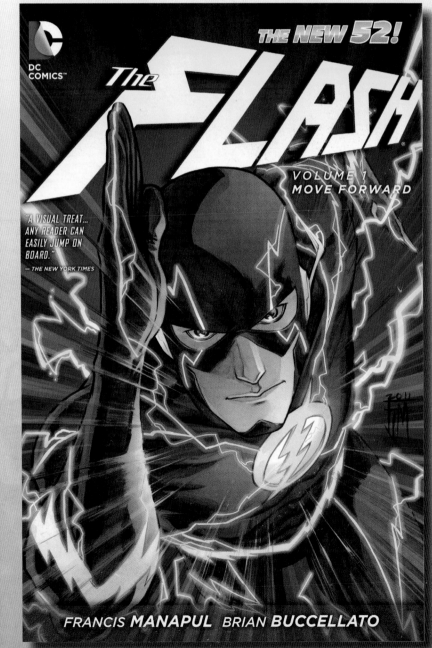

START AT THE BEGINNING!

THE FLASH
VOLUME 1: MOVE FORWARD

JUSTICE LEAGUE INTERNATIONAL VOLUME 1: THE SIGNAL MASTERS

O.M.A.C. VOLUME 1: OMACTIVATE!

CAPTAIN ATOM VOLUME 1: EVOLUTION

"Impressive."
—MTV SPLASH PAGE

"The Flash couldn't be in better hands."
—NEWSARAMA

"Geoff Johns on THE FLASH has been a true boon for the Scarlet Speedster, putting him right up there in popularity with the likes of Batman, Superman and Green Lantern."
—USA TODAY

FROM THE WRITER OF *JUSTICE LEAGUE* AND *GREEN LANTERN*

GEOFF JOHNS

THE FLASH: REBIRTH
with ETHAN VAN SCIVER

THE FLASH:
DASTARDLY DEATH
OF THE ROGUES

with FRANCIS MANAPUL

THE FLASH: ROAD
TO FLASHPOINT

with FRANCIS MANAPUL
and SCOTT KOLINS

FLASHPOINT

with ANDY KUBERT